CULTIVATED ABUNDANCE

Thank you for your support as a Beta Reader! This book would not have been possible without you. I am deeply grateful for your support and contributions that made this book into what it is today.

Change happens one crazy idea at a time.

I hope *Cultivated Abundance* inspires you to join the Greater Fools fighting to build a better future for us all.

Mihir Pershad

CULTIVATED ABUNDANCE

HOW WE CAN BUILD
A BETTER FUTURE THROUGH
TRANSFORMATIVE TECHNOLOGY
ENTREPRENEURSHIP

MIHIR PERSHAD

NEW DEGREE PRESS

CULTIVATED ABUNDANCE

*How We Can Build a Better Future through
Transformative Technology Entrepreneurship*

ISBN   978-1-64137-964-9 *Paperback*

          978-1-64137-791-1 *Kindle Ebook*

          978-1-64137-883-3 *Ebook*

This book is dedicated to the entrepreneurs who aspire to build a better future for humanity.

The world needs your ambition and ingenuity.

Let's start building.

CONTENTS

TABLE OF FIGURES

———

"The reasonable man adapts himself to the world: the unreasonable one persists in trying to adapt the world to himself. Therefore all progress depends on the unreasonable man."

GEORGE BERNARD SHAW

PREFACE

"The greatest threat to our planet is the belief that someone else will save it."

ROBERT SWAN

BUILDING A BETTER FUTURE FOR HUMANITY

What does it take to build companies that fundamentally change the world? And of the companies that attempt to create this transformative change, what separates those who succeed from those who fall short?

This is a book about how we can solve humanity's most challenging problems with Transformative Technology entrepreneurship. This book explores the nature of these Intractable Problems and their shared characteristics. It delves into the characteristics of the kinds of Transformative Technologies that will likely form the basis of the best solutions to these problems. And it illuminates a set of principles, drawn from the successes of prior transformative solutions, that can maximize the chances of success for entrepreneurs who incorporate them into their strategy for building and scaling their solutions.

Though the book explores these problems, technologies, and principles for success in the context of several critical industries, the primary lens is of the agricultural system. This is due in part to the importance of our current moment in the history of our food system: we appear poised to undergo the biggest revolution in agricultural production since the domestication of plants and animals over ten thousand years ago. It is also because food is something anyone can understand. Whether through our fond memories of childhood foods or our experiences buying food at the grocery store each week and cooking for loved ones, we all experience our food at a deeply personal level.

In this way, the personal and emotional connections we have to food are unique, given its place as one of our oldest technologies. We don't feel that same connection to electricity or the Internet. This makes food a unique vehicle for discussing global challenges that would otherwise be impersonal and technology solutions that would appear disconcerting.

My journey into learning about the power of Transformative Technologies began in college, born from my deep interest in human health. When my exploration began, I was primarily interested in learning about the technologies and avenues through which I could have an impact on improving healthcare for people around the world. At the time, I was narrowly focused on the healthcare system itself—on the treatments, pharmaceuticals, and medical devices doctors could apply to treat people who were sick or injured. The more I learned, the more I began to realize my myopic view of human health was blinding me to the potential for Transformative Technologies to improve the human condition more broadly.

For me, the key moment of understanding came in the form of a scientific review article. It detailed the ways in which changing a cancer patient's diet could improve their strength during chemotherapy, reduce their symptoms, and even treat conditions that could not be targeted with medications.[1] After I read this article, my eyes were opened to the vast opportunity we have to solve our most pressing problems if we can understand them in their broader contexts. In this case, food could be medicine and could outperform our most advanced medical treatments in addressing burdensome ailments. What other problems could we solve if we understood them more deeply and applied the right Transformative Technologies to them in the right ways?

Using the agricultural sector as a primary example, this book demonstrates how the very technologies and systems that helped us build our modern society are now creating intractable problems that we must overcome to build a sustainable future. Through the emergence of cellular agriculture, the book describes the ways in which technologies can both produce transformative solutions and fizzle out without leaving a lasting impact. And through an assessment of animal agriculture, the book posits a vision for an abundant future for humanity and what it will take to achieve that vision.

---

1   Laura Soldati et. al, "The influence of diet on anti-cancer immune responsiveness," *Journal of Translational Medicine* 16, no. 1 (2018): 75.

These ideas and principles transcend the field of agriculture. Anyone who aspires to build a better future for humanity and solve the greatest challenges that stand between our present and that future can use these principles to do so. Overcoming intractable problems requires leverage, and the principles and frameworks presented in this book can help to increase the leverage of those who implement them. I hope this book captures the imagination of others who see the opportunity to positively impact billions of people by tackling these problems, in agriculture or other sectors, and inspires them to build the solutions that we need.

AN UNEXPECTED DISCOVERY

In writing this book, I interviewed many of the thought leaders and pioneers in the cellular agriculture industry, including nonprofit advocacy groups, researchers, startup entrepreneurs, investors, and science communicators. I also had conversations with agriculture industry experts, scientists who study climate change, and scientists who investigate the environmental and social impacts of our food system. With their knowledge, I intend to provide a more comprehensive context around the broader impacts of the cellular agriculture movement and its importance to building a sustainable and resilient agricultural system. In addition to these interviews, I sought out the best available research on industrial agriculture—covering everything from costs to externalities and important process innovations to key challenges. My goal is to provide you with sufficient data from independent sources to draw your own conclusions about the future of food beyond the hypotheses I present in this book.

As I conducted research for this book, however, I began to recognize there was a larger story to be told. Much of my exposure to these global, pressing challenges, and transformative technologies came through working with professors to commercialize their biotechnology and medical technology research and from my experience as a serial entrepreneur in the healthcare and agri-food sectors. As a result, my initial research was limited by the scope of my own personal experience. Only during the process of writing this book did I begin to appreciate that many of the questions I was asking of these industries were also applicable more broadly.

In defining a set of principles for succeeding in food and agriculture innovation, I noticed that our agricultural industry is not unique in the challenges it faces or in its importance to our collective human future. Indeed, a number of industries are essential for our individual survival and the continued existence of our civilization. Most of these essential industries face large-scale intractable problems that will require transformative solutions in the coming years.

Could the same principles that have enabled entrepreneurs to solve challenging agricultural problems also pave the way for successful solutions to emerge in energy, transportation, and other critical sectors? If these principles *could* be applied more broadly to facilitate solutions to our most pressing, intransigent problems, how could I attract more entrepreneurs to work on these problems? These were key questions that stuck with me as I began writing this book and shaped my thinking in it.

HISTORY IS DEFINED BY MOMENTS

The birth or death of a great leader. The rise and fall of a civilization. The invention of a Transformative Technology. History is defined by pivotal moments.

By my reckoning, we are currently witnessing the beginning of the greatest change in agricultural technology in ten thousand years. We are also facing a number of challenges unprecedented in the history of our species. In this moment, at the confluence of a rising global population, a changing climate, and dwindling resource availability, the decisions we make will determine the future of our species. Under this perfect storm of conditions that conspire to make our current systems and practices obsolete, we must develop technologies that will enable our civilization to endure sustainably if our civilization is to thrive in the twenty-first century and beyond.

A more abundant future for mankind is in our grasp. Will we seize it or let it go by?

PART I

POWER WITHOUT WISDOM: THE HUMAN STORY OF ABUNDANCE AND SCARCITY

CHAPTER 1

HOW WE GOT HERE

——

"In the end, for the long term to prevail over the short term, we must want what the long term promises. Where there is no vision, there you find short-termism, for there is, then, no reason for compromise today for an unknown tomorrow."

CHARLES B. HANDY

Modern humans have walked the Earth for around two hundred thousand years. In that time, humanity has undoubtedly solved some big problems that may have seemed intractable at the time. To survive that long, we would have had to use our unique brand of intelligence to outcompete other animals, developing better solutions to our common problems. Achieving the scale that our species has on Earth has required overcoming incredible obstacles to finding sufficient food, creating suitable shelter from the elements, and improving our health to dramatically increase our average longevity. All our technological, economic, and social innovations were built on this base of stable access to our basic needs.

As useful as our intelligence and ingenuity have been for our survival, it may be failing us at one of the most critical times in our history.

How can this be? How could the single feature that most differentiates us from other animals—the very sapience after which our species is named—now become a hindrance to solving the most important problems we face as a species?

The issue is two-fold: 1) the greatest problems we face are evolving more rapidly than ever before and at an accelerating pace, and 2) the scale of our ability to impact the world has grown by orders of magnitude, but our ability to conceptualize larger scales of time and impact has not.

One of the biggest challenges humanity has faced throughout our history has been securing a stable supply of sustenance for our population. Given that it is one of our basic needs, it makes sense that food would be a driving influence on our history. But few would probably recognize just how profound an effect on our nutrition has had in shaping our development path and our modern society. Indeed, our early civilizations were formed around agricultural production; social structures developed in which some people specialized in farming, others diversified to provide supporting services and necessities, and a governance structure emerged to manage the infrastructure for irrigation and grain storage.

As Tom Standage, author of *An Edible History of Humanity*, notes, "Food's influence on history can similarly be likened to an invisible fork that has, at several crucial points in history, prodded humanity and altered its destiny, even though people were generally unaware of its influence at the time."[2] Understanding how we navigated the ever-present and evolving challenge of feeding humanity throughout our history can provide a useful lens through which we can more clearly understand the advantages and shortcomings of our evolved mental toolkit for facing the challenges in our present and near future.

FROM APE TO MAN

Modern humans, *homo sapiens*, are descended from a long line of ancestor species going back millions of years. Before we became who we are today, our ancestors were once foragers. In this discussion, we will venture back as far as *homo habilis* which walked the Earth about 2.5 million years ago.[3] They ate berries, leaves, fruits, and other plant matter—much like most monkey species—to get the nutrition they needed to survive. These plants were not very nutritionally dense, particularly in critical minerals and calories, so our ancestors spent quite a lot of their day foraging.[4] Much of this plant matter was quite fibrous, requiring a longer digestive tract and more energy to digest it and extract its nutritional value.[5] This wasn't anything new to the *homo* genus, and our

---

2   Tom Standage, *An Edible History of Humanity* (London: Atlantic Books Ltd, 2012), Introduction.

3   Phillip V. Tobias, "Homo Habilis and Homo Erectus: From the Oldowan Men to the Acheulian Practitioners" *Anthropologie (1962-)* 18, no. 2/3 (1980): 115-19.

4   Ibid.

5   Leslie C. Aiello and Peter Wheeler, "The Expensive-Tissue Hypothesis: The Brain and the Digestive System in Human and Primate Evolution," *Current Anthropology* 36, no. 2 (1995): 199-221.

ancestors were quite adept at feeding themselves by these foraging methods.

But around two million years ago, something shifted quite dramatically, and a new species emerged: *homo erectus.* *Homo erectus* had a brain that was 50 percent larger than *homo habilis.* Our modern brains consume 25 percent of our daily energy needs and 20 percent of the oxygen we breathe while composing only 2 percent of our body weight. With their larger, more complex brains, *homo erectus* would have needed significantly more calories than *homo habilis.*[6] But where would this extra energy come from? It would have been nearly impossible to consume enough plant matter to provide the necessary energy surplus for the development of this more complex brain.

The evidence points to one transformation in the diets of our ancestors that made this larger brain possible: they started eating meat.

THE GIFTS OF FIRE

Homo erectus appeared to have led the hunter-gatherer revolution, introducing meat into their diet in an effort to get a greater density of nutrients and increased calories for less effort. The evidence we have supports this theory. Compared to their ancestors, *homo erectus* had smaller teeth, indicating they spent less time chewing bulky and raw plant matter. They also had shorter digestive tracts, suggesting they

---

6   M.E. Raichle and D. A. Gusnard, "Appraising the Brain's Energy Budget," *Proceedings of the National Academy of Sciences* 99, no. 16 (2002): 10237–39.

ate fewer fibrous plants that would require a longer gut for proper digestion.[7] Together, these changes suggest that *homo erectus* began eating meat, which would have provided a dense source of nutrients that would otherwise be scarce in their foraging diet. But eating meat, especially when raw, created a whole separate set of potential risks related to food-borne illnesses.

Interestingly, *homo erectus* also appear to have lost their climbing adaptations, which would have been incredibly dangerous without a way to see at night and tools to keep predators at bay. According to Richard Wrangham, primatologist and author of *Catching Fire: How Cooking Made Us Human*, this evidence suggests that *homo erectus* also learned to use fire as a tool for protection and for making their meat safer to eat. Now armed with a source of dense nutrients in meat and a way to make those nutrients safer to consume and easier to digest through cooking, *homo erectus* suddenly had an energy surplus. It is this energy surplus that likely enabled the great leap forward in brain development.

Up to this point, a more complex brain could easily have been evolutionarily disadvantageous. The extra energy required to support such a brain would have made it more difficult for those individuals to find enough nutrients to survive, creating a selective pressure against larger brains. But with the energy surplus provided by meat consumption, a larger brain suddenly became an evolutionary advantage. Why? It enabled *homo erectus* to solve hard problems more

---

7   Tobias, "Homo Habilis and Homo Erectus: From the Oldowan Men to the Acheulian Practitioners."

inventively and quickly than others with smaller brain capacity. This hypothesis, first proposed by paleoanthropologists Leslie Aiello and Peter Wheeler, provides an explanation for how some of our oldest ancestors were able to overcome a major hurdle in their development.[8]

So, this one accident of evolution—consuming meat and learning to cook it to make it safer and more nutritious—enabled humans to develop the large, energy-hogging brains that provide the basis for our sapience. This one, unplanned event helped early humans make an evolutionary leap that, as far as we know, had not occurred before in our planet's history and has not been repeated on Earth since.

FOOD SHAPED OUR CIVILIZATION

With this stroke of evolutionary luck, humanity took the first steps toward modern civilization. Our ancestors, now *homo sapiens*, began farming rather than hunting around 13,000 BCE. The first farmed crop, likely rice, was followed by an explosion of crop domestication over the next fourteen thousand years, encompassing grains, nuts, beans, and fruits. As early as 7,000 BCE, our ancestors also realized that they could farm their meat and began domesticating sheep, followed by cows, pigs, goats, and poultry. We now had a consistent source of both calories and nutrition without having to travel as the seasons changed to get it.

---

8   Aiello and Wheeler, "The Expensive-Tissue Hypothesis: The Brain and the Digestive System in Human and Primate Evolution."

But this reliable supply of food did not only come from wild-growing plants and animals that we discovered and grew exactly as they existed in nature. No, these crops and domesticated animals emerged through a process of coevolution with humans, deliberately cultivated and propagated solely due to human farming.

Our ancestors cultivated these plants and animals, and through continuous selection refined the genetic composition of the population to reflect those traits they valued most. For plants, this included larger grains and fruiting bodies, smaller inedible parts, and faster growth rates. For animals, we selected for more docile individuals, those that grew faster, and those that produced more offspring. In many ways, these cultivated plants and animals were some of our first technological inventions, after stone tools and fire. Agriculture became an incredible instrument that made civilization possible, and even as we transformed plants, the plants transformed us.

Throughout our history, food has done far more than provide the energy we needed to live. As Tom Standage said, "[Food] has acted as a catalyst of social transformation, societal organization, geopolitical competition, industrial development, military conflict and economic expansion."[9]

Initially, settling in one place and developing a reliable source of nutrition through farmed plants and domesticated animals enabled our ancestors to think beyond food production. It enabled different groups of people to specialize, completing

9   Standage, *An Edible History of Humanity*, Introduction.

different tasks that benefitted the collective whole of their group while others did the same for them. This lifestyle laid the foundation for civilizations to emerge, particularly as centralized social structures formed around food production, distribution, and storage. These centralized structures eventually led to the development of the first governments, where food was used as a currency for payments and taxation—long before the concept of central, state-backed currency, food was wealth and control of food was power.

Again, we see that some of the most important turning points in human history were driven by innovations in our food system. In this case, cultivation and refinement of crops for desired traits enabled us to produce enough to sustain a growing fixed population, something that would not have been possible if we had only farmed the wild varieties of grains and animals. These innovations were not deliberate or methodically implemented, but they altered the trajectory of our history nonetheless.

But as with most technologies, where they alleviated scarcity in one area, they created it in another.

THE POPULATION BOMB

Our agricultural prowess created a calorie glut. Perhaps inevitably, the availability of food caused the average time between pregnancies to fall and our population to boom. In just a few centuries, the human population on Earth blew past one billion and kept growing. By the seventeenth century, the rapid growth of our population nearly made us victims of our own success. We were nearing a point at which we would not be able to feed the global population with the then-current methods. Just as it happens to other animals that outgrow the resources available in their ecosystems, our population would have collapsed back below the carrying capacity.

The Second Agricultural Revolution provided the solution. By applying newly developed tools and methods—like crop rotation, selective breeding, and a better plow—to agriculture, we were able to make our current land far more productive and to expand the number of hectares that an individual could farm. These new farming methods helped us to overcome the challenge of food scarcity yet again, staving off this recurring challenge for a while longer.

Increased agricultural efficiency meant that fewer farmers were needed. Suddenly, a large portion of society had time available to apply their labor to making other goods and providing services to others. This created the urban labor force required to enable the Industrial Revolution and a shift to a far more diverse economy in which individuals specialized further than ever before.

Inevitably, the growing population caused the challenge of food production to rise to prominence once again in the twentieth century. Though the Second Agricultural Revolution introduced mechanized tools to farms and further increased their productivity, exponential population growth had put these systems under enormous pressure.

Prior agricultural solutions had bought humanity thousands of years before food production became a major hurdle again.

The fruits of the Second Agricultural Revolution only lasted about two hundred years.

After World War II, the world was facing what began to be known as *The Population Bomb*. In an eponymous book published in 1968, Stanford University Professor Paul R. Ehrlich noted that the rate of population growth would outpace agricultural production and lead to widespread famine and subsequent suffering in the 1970s and 1980s.[10]

A global famine that would have threatened the lives of more than one billion people was prevented in large part by the work of one man who never intended to take up that work in the first place. In spite of his monumental impact on the lives of billions of people, few enough know his name even today. That man was Norman Borlaug.

WORLD PEACE WILL NOT BE BUILT ON EMPTY STOMACHS

Norm, as Borlaug was known to all who worked with him, grew up on a farm in Northeastern Iowa. Growing up in the midst of the Great Depression, Norm experienced firsthand the effects of the existing agricultural practices and how the resulting Dust Bowl devastated crop yields, soil quality, and the lives of farmers. These experiences impressed upon him that there had to be better ways to farm while preserving the land.

---

10   Paul R. Ehrlich, *The Population Bomb* (New York, NY: Ballantine Books, 1971).

While in college, Norm attended a lecture that would shape the rest of his life. Dr. Elvin Stakman, the head of the plant pathology department, gave the lecture on the topic of rust, a fungal disease that significantly reduces yields of wheat and a number of other cereal crops. At the end of that lecture, Dr. Stakman made a statement that would have strained credulity at the time, but which Borlaug's work proved to be true. The science of rust resistance, Dr. Stakman said, would "go further than has ever been possible to eradicate the miseries of hunger and starvation from this earth."[11]

After that lecture, Borlaug's life took a different path. Norm went on to work for DuPont Corporation, where he was approached by the Rockefeller Foundation to join a new project to develop a rust-resistant wheat that would alleviate the food insecurity that plagued many Mexican communities. "In 1944, when Borlaug arrived in Mexico, its farmers raised less than half of the wheat necessary to meet the demands of the population. Rust perennially ruined or diminished the harvest," Professor R. Douglas Hurt, of the Department of History at Purdue University, observed.[12]

Initially, things were tough for Borlaug. The local farmers had little reason to trust a young American who did not speak their language and were hesitant to adopt new farming

---

11 Kenneth M. Quinn, "Chapter 1: Dr. Norman E. Borlaug: Twentieth Century Lessons for the Twenty-First Century World," in *ADVANCES IN AGRONOMY*, ed. Donald L. Sparks (San Diego: Academic Press, 2008), 100:13–27.

12 Kenneth M. Quinn, "Norman Borlaug—Extended Biography," The World Food Prize Foundation, 2009.

techniques they thought may leave them in an even more precarious situation.

But Norm, famous now for his work ethic, persevered, learning the local Spanish dialect and working long days in the fields breeding new strains of wheat. "Borlaug labored for thirteen years before he and his team of agricultural scientists developed a disease resistant wheat," Professor Hurt states, "[But] still problems remained."[13] The primary problem was that the new rust-resistant wheat did not have stems strong enough to hold the now heavy heads of grain. As a result, the plants would blow over under heavy wind and rain, a process known as "lodging."

To solve this new problem that stood between Borlaug and his goal of a self-sufficient Mexico, he looked to a dwarf strain of wheat from Japan. He sought to breed this dwarf strain with his rust-resistant strain, producing a wheat variety that could tolerate the hot, dry climate of Northern Mexico without lodging during storms. But time was short. Without this new semi-dwarf wheat strain, Borlaug's rust-resistant wheat was of limited use due to its vulnerability to storms.

To accelerate his breeding efforts, Borlaug developed a new method known as "shuttle breeding." He grew two separate crops of wheat, one in the semi-arid, irrigated plains of Ciudad Obregón in Sonora and the other in the high-altitude, wetter region of Toluca.[14] He would harvest the crop from

---

13   Rolf H. J. Schlegel, *History of Plant Breeding* (Boca Raton, FL: CRC Press, 2018).

14   Quinn, "Norman Borlaug—Extended Biography."

one region and shuttle the seeds to the other for planting, enabling Borlaug to double his output per year compared to his peers.

This method effectively bred a rust-resistant strain of wheat that could grow in most warm climates. The result, a rust-resistant, semi-dwarf wheat, was broadly considered an agricultural miracle. Further, Norm's unconventional shuttle breeding also led his wheat to be photoperiod insensitive, meaning that two crops could be cultivated per year, massively increasing the calories that could be produced per acre. Aided by irrigation and fertilizers, Borlaug's wheat enabled Mexico to achieve self-sufficiency in wheat in 1956, something many others thought would be impossible for many more years.

But Norm did not consider this a victory. Rather, he considered it "a temporary success in man's war against hunger and deprivation."[15] He recognized that the "population bomb" was still looming large in Asia, Africa, and the Middle East, and further work was needed to ensure food security and stability in those regions. Norm was known to say that "world peace will not be built on empty stomachs."[16] Indeed, that statement would describe his lifelong mission.

---

15 Don Paarlberg, "Norman Borlaug: Hunger Fighter," Foreign Economic Development Service, US Department of Agriculture, cooperating with the US Agency for International Development (PA 969), (Washington, D. C.: US Government Printing Office, 1970).

16 Sanjaya Rajaram, "Norman Borlaug: The Man I Worked With and Knew," *Annual Review of Phytopathology* 49, no. 1 (2011): 17–30.

His project in Mexico well in hand, Norm and the Rockefeller Foundation turned their attention to India and Pakistan. These two countries, having just recently won independence from Great Britain and split in the 1947 Partition, were in a precarious food situation. Subsistence agricultural practices were still quite common, but the rapid population growth meant the specter of famine loomed large if conditions reduced agricultural output in a given year. Indeed, 2.5 million people are thought to have starved to death in Bengal in the 1943 famine alone.[17]

Borlaug's initial work involved the introduction of his "miracle" rust-resistant, semi-dwarf wheat to India and Pakistan. But what followed may have had an even greater impact. M.S. Swaminathan in India and Robert Chandler, Henry Beachell, and Gurdev Khush in the Philippines replicated Borlaug's work in rice. Their work yielded IR8, a new high-yield, semi-dwarf strain of rice that was dubbed "Miracle Rice."[18] This rice was introduced in 1966 and, along with Borlaug's wheat, saved India, Pakistan, and the Philippines from massive famine. Miracle Rice spread rapidly across Asia, as it increased individual crop yields and enabled farmers to cultivate two crops per year.

The impact of this work cannot be overstated. The World Food Prize website notes, "This in turn led to tangible improvements in the quality of life: child mortality dropped; malnutrition abated; and children, especially girls, stayed in

---

17   Debora Mackenzie, "Norm Borlaug: the Man Who Fed the World," *New Scientist*, September 14, 2009.

18   Quinn, "Norman Borlaug—Extended Biography."

school longer." Further, tensions were high between India and Pakistan in the 1960s. Both countries fought regular skirmishes and had heated disputes over land and water resources. If persistent famine had raised the stakes even higher, it is not hard to believe that full-scale war may have broken out, killing millions even as millions more starved.[19]

Beyond the India-Pakistan region, the Green Revolution that Borlaug championed and realized led to "a corresponding decrease in the level of armed conflict and military hostilities. It was as though the combination of new roads and new rice seed caused the roots of violent extremism to wither and disappear in a way that military action alone could not."[20]

On October 20, 1970, Norm received a phone call to inform him that he was being awarded the Nobel Peace Prize that year. Well, he would have received the call, but he was out working in a wheat field in rural Mexico. His wife, Margaret, took the call in his stead and then drove an hour out to the farm where Norm was working to give him the news. When she asked him to come back to the house to respond to the many dignitaries and press who wanted to speak with him, he simply stated that he had far too much work to do to leave the fields early. A few hours later, the reporters would arrive at the field to find Norm tending to his wheat.

Norman Borlaug remains the only agricultural scientist to have ever been honored with the Nobel Peace Prize. He is

---

19   David Gale Johnson, *The Struggle against World Hunger,* (New York, NY: Foreign Policy Association, 1967).

20   Quinn, "Norman Borlaug—Extended Biography."

also one of its least known recipients. His work is perhaps the single most important reason that calorie production expanded faster than the human population everywhere in the world outside sub-Saharan Africa. His miracle wheat and rice ended cycles of famine in many countries and prevented mass starvations that would have numbered in the hundreds of millions in the following years. Ironically, his name is largely unrecognized compared to his peer Nobel Laureates, given that he had "probably saved more lives than all of them put together."[21] Indeed, Borlaug is today frequently dubbed "the man who saved a billion lives."

FOOD *IS* TECHNOLOGY

In the years after Borlaug became a Nobel Laureate, a backlash against his methods and the Green Revolution he championed around the world has grown. To many modern environmentalists, these methods are "unnatural" and "extractive" compared to their preferred agricultural practices. Even groups like the World Bank and the Rockefeller and Ford Foundations, who were funders of Borlaug's work, are now separating themselves from it. The mounting pressure from activists who consider themselves environmentalists has largely driven this shift. Notably, these voices rarely offer an alternative solution that would have avoided the cost in human lives had these technologies not been implemented.

Borlaug himself has presented data suggesting that 40 percent of the world's more than six billion people (as of 2003) were alive because of the Haber-Bosch process that enables

---

21   Ibid.

industrial production of eighty million tons of Nitrogen each year.[22] And though the overuse of fertilizers in the wake of the Green Revolution has rightly drawn criticism, claims that organic production methods could feed the world have been broadly exaggerated. The evidence demonstrates that organic fertilization alone could only support a fraction of the current global population.[23]

Though many of Borlaug's supporters bowed to pressure from activists, Borlaug continued to be a strong advocate for Green Revolution-style farming, particularly in areas still plagued by food insecurity and famines. In Borlaug's view, the population was growing exponentially, and the options available were to feed them with the best available tools or to leave them to starve. Ethically, that was no choice at all. As an article about Norm in *The Atlantic* noted, "In this debate the moral imperative of food for the world's malnourished— whether they 'should' have been born or not, they must eat— stands in danger of being forgotten."[24]

From Norman Borlaug's perspective, the choice we face is obvious: either we significantly increase the yields of existing farmland or we destroy the last remaining rainforests and condemn untold species to death to give ourselves the necessary land to farm. Using biotechnology to increase farm yields and productivity would help to preserve wild

---

22 Norman E Borlaug, "Feeding a world of 10 billion people," (The TVA/ IFDC Legacy Travis P. Hignett Memorial Lecture, International Fertilizer Development Center, Muscle Shoals, AL, 2003).

23 Rajaram, "Norman Borlaug: The Man I Worked With and Knew," 17–30.

24 Gregg Easterbrook, "Forgotten Benefactor of Humanity," *The Atlantic*, March 26, 2019.

ecosystems that are being destroyed by slash-and-burn agriculture while also reducing malnutrition and hunger.

Despite what his advocacy for biotechnology and intensive farming practices may imply, Borlaug did not think the fight to eradicate hunger would be won so easily. He recognized that intensive farming had its challenges and that it would only buy humanity a reprieve, perhaps thirty to fifty years, to develop more sustainable, improved methods. One of Borlaug's greatest laments was that his work appeared to encourage governments to reduce their investment in agriculture innovation, thinking that the problem had been solved.

For this reason, and because he was unable to affect the creation of a Nobel Prize for Agriculture, Borlaug established the World Food Prize to recognize outstanding contributions to improving agriculture and to efforts to counter poverty and hunger. He hoped the spotlight the World Food Prize created would draw attention to the important work that still needed to be done in agriculture. As Borlaug foresaw and many others would not recognize until much later, "the Green Revolution wasn't the final answer to our problems, but it was the start of the answer."[25]

Many people will look at this story and state that it demonstrates that we have always been able to develop the technology we needed to save us from an emerging threat just in time. They will point to it as evidence that we should not worry about seemingly intractable problems because things have worked out in the past without a coordinated effort

---

25   Mackenzie, "Norm Borlaug: the Man Who Fed the World."

to develop a solution. This view can be best described as **techno-optimism**, the belief that technology can provide solutions to all of our problems and that such technology will emerge when it is needed because necessity is the mother of invention. Such claims can appear harmless enough. Why does it matter if people think technology will save us from the problems we face? The answer is that this line of thinking obscures a more insidious underlying thought process.

PROGRESS IS NOT INEVITABLE

Putting our full faith in the timely emergence of technology to save us from our problems is essentially betting many hundreds of millions of lives on the emergence of a hero who will solve the problem just as it begins to turn severe, saving us from those effects. Is it rational for us to bet one billion or more lives on the hope that a problem will be solved without a coordinated effort and allocation of resources? Can we rationally wait for another Borlaug to emerge to solve a problem like a global famine just a few years before hundreds of millions of lives would have been lost? What happens if these heroes arrive even two years too late? What if they never arrive at all?

To state that our problems will resolve themselves when this new technology emerges seems flippant. Doubly so given that most of our problems have not resolved themselves without the intervention of a few individuals with the foresight to see what was coming and develop solutions in advance.

This line of reasoning also assumes the past will be a good predictor of the future because the future will mirror the past. But we already have significant evidence that this is not the case. Humans took over one hundred thousand years to transition from hunting and gathering to agriculture as a primary source of calories. We took only two hundred years to develop intensive farming techniques. And in just thirty years, we moved from traditional agricultural methods to intensive agriculture spurred on by the Green Revolution. We now have the ability to genetically engineer crops to tune traits much more rapidly than could ever be achieved through breeding. This last leap occurred in only ten years.

EXPONENTIALS CHANGE EVERYTHING

The rate of change is not linear, but exponential. The exponential rate of change means the past will not be a good predictor of the future, at least not for direct comparison. The slower rate of change in our past provided us far more time to adjust to changing circumstances and develop solutions than we will have today. And if the exponential trends continue, the time frame between the onset of a problem and the need for a solution will continue to shrink. Thus, our past ability to develop technological solutions to emerging problems before they became catastrophic may not tell us very much about our ability to address these problems as they emerge today and in the future.

Further, the scope of these obstacles and the scale of their impact is also growing exponentially. As the human population has grown exponentially, so too has the impact of our activities on the planet. Anthropologists have even classified the current era as a new geologic age, the Anthropocene, to reflect the fact that humans are now the single, most important driver of planetary change. That is why this era is somewhat different from the circumstances under which we dealt with prior grand challenges.

In prior instances, our resource constraints that drove change occurred at the micro-level. We did not have enough wild-caught meat, so we started to farm it. A country's population was growing faster than its agricultural system, so they invented better tools and fertilizers to increase yield. We have historically existed at a small enough scale that we could ignore planetary-level effects and constraints without causing catastrophic fallout. Only once before, with the emergence of the hole in the ozone layer, did we begin to recognize that we humans had begun to operate on a planetary scale.

With ten billion people expected to inhabit Earth by 2050, almost every decision we make now has planetary-scale repercussions. Our choice to ignore planetary-scale impacts of our past activities has created a number of pressing challenges—from climate change to biodiversity loss—that we must contend with when developing our next set of solutions and plans for the future. Now that we are consistently operating on a planetary scale, we must recognize that our constraints exist on a planetary scale as well.

Barring asteroid mining and other futuristic technologies, we will have to develop solutions to feed ourselves and survive that do not exhaust our resources on Earth. At a minimum, we must ensure that we keep the biosphere sufficiently in balance so it does not bring about our downfall. As the pace of change has continued to accelerate since humans' first technological inventions, we must also be able to address these problems in less time, while impacting a greater number of people than ever before.

One thing of which we can be sure is that this question of how we will feed the global population with existing resources will arise again. Several data points would indicate we are actually facing this challenge again now. We now know our current agricultural practices are a substantial contributor to anthropogenic climate change and the degradation of our environment. Now, we are faced with developing new technologies that will enable us to feed over two billion more people while dramatically reducing these effects. We need to develop and implement these solutions by 2050 if we are to deploy them in time to meet the demand.

Even with our prior history of overcoming this recurring problem of food production, that is a daunting challenge. What solutions will we develop? Will we do as some suggest and not worry about the problem because a solution will inevitably arise just in time to avoid a crisis as it has in the past? Or can we take a structured, forward-looking approach to develop and fund the most promising solutions?

Those solutions could come from emerging technologies like vertical farming, regenerative agriculture, cultured meat, and genetic modification technology. Or they could be something entirely new that we have not yet invented. One thing is for certain: solving these challenges will require us to develop the tools to understand exponentials and to think on longer time horizons than our evolutionary path has prepared us for.

CHAPTER 2

CREATING LEVERAGE

"Give me a lever long enough and a fulcrum on which to place it, and I shall move the world. "

ARCHIMEDES

In the twenty-first century and beyond, humanity will have to overcome a number of incredible problems to sustain our modern civilization and ensure the long-term survival of our species. As the pace of change of our world accelerates, we will have to find ways to overcome our evolutionary bias toward short-term thinking and our difficulty understanding exponentials. If we can develop tools and systems for overcoming these evolutionary challenges, we greatly increase our chances of triumphing over our current intractable problems and mitigating the severity of those that may arise in the future.

In general, solving large-scale, intractable problems requires identifying an initial entry point through which we can demonstrate impact and create a foothold. From that foothold, we can then refine and scale those solutions to reach a greater portion of the affected population. But identifying initial footholds and scalable solutions to these problems can be daunting and can often seem hopeless. How can a small group of resource-constrained individuals develop and deploy solutions to such difficult problems that exist on an incredibly large scale?

They need to find a way to create leverage.

HUMANITY THROUGH THE LENS OF FOOD

In this book, we will use the lens of food innovation as a framework for how we can overcome our evolutionary shortcomings to solve the biggest problems we face.

As we will discuss, leverage can come in several forms. Picking the most pressing, intractable problems to solve is one way of creating leverage. Harnessing the power of emerging Transformative Technologies to produce a solution is another way to create leverage. Indeed, Transformative Technologies present a uniquely powerful form of leverage when they are directed at solving Big Intractable Problems.

Food may seem like a strange lens through which to view the world, particularly when discussing innovation and solutions to difficult, large-scale problems facing humanity. But as Tom Standage, author of *An Edible History of Humanity*, affirms, "That food has been such an important ingredient in human affairs might seem strange, but it would be far more surprising if it had not: after all, everything that every person has ever done, throughout history, has literally been fueled by food." As one of our most enduring and recurring challenges throughout human history, food provides a long record of problems emerging and being solved by transformative solutions. From within this uniquely deep historical context, we can identify a core set of principles that enabled our ancestors to successfully solve problems with Transformative Technologies and project how entrepreneurs can use those principles to solve current and future problems.

Food will be the lens through which we explore the principles that will enable us to develop a future of abundance for humanity. However, these principles can be applied to problems far beyond food. Whether the Big Intractable Problem is related to energy, environmental degradation, human health, climate change, or infrastructure, these same principles can be applied to successfully develop and implement solutions at scale. At their core, these principles are about enabling entrepreneurs to increase their leverage to solve our biggest, most pressing problems. In doing so, these principles increase the entrepreneurs' chances of success in creating a massive, positive impact on humanity.

BUILDING EARLY WARNING SYSTEMS

To those who are not actively seeking them out or studying exponential trends, the most significant problems impacting humanity often appear to emerge suddenly and require that solutions be developed imminently. In fact, to be more accurate, we could say that most of our biggest problems lie ignored for many years before suddenly rising to prominence in the public consciousness. Usually, a small number of individuals correctly identify these problems in their early stages and attempt to draw attention to them. But these voices are often decried as alarmists, if not ignored entirely.

Historically, the suppression of these voices has been due to existing systems of power. Entrenched interests have a significant stake in the current status quo and the resources and ability to suppress a new narrative before it can threaten their business. Because of these suppression tactics, even existential problems—like climate change—do not rise to prominence in the public forum until the evidence that these problems are significant and urgent is almost literally staring us in the face. In the context of ensuring the survival of humanity and creating the best possible outcome for our future, silencing these voices is clearly irrational.

A more rational course of action would be to:

1. Develop a system for identifying these problems as early as we can.
2. Study them to prioritize the ones that are most likely to develop into Big Intractable Problems.
3. Allocate collective resources to developing solutions that can be implemented before the problems reach a critical state.

As alluded to earlier in this chapter, however, we humans are incredibly poor as a species at forethought and long-term thinking. In our defense, our ancestors never really faced an evolutionary pressure to evolve such skills. They had pressing problems to solve in the short-term, and life was far too uncertain to plan for what their grandchildren or great-grandchildren might experience.

Unfortunately for modern humans, our natural disinclination to long-term thinking is now a major barrier to effectively managing the types of long-term problems we must navigate to continue our success as a species. We can no longer afford to solve a problem in the short-term and ignore the potential consequences the new solution may have in the near future.

One reason having this foresight is important is that identifying problems early provides more time to develop a solution or set of solutions. The longer our time horizon is to develop new solutions, the greater the solution set available to us and the lower the cost of solving the problem will be. As the time horizon for solving the problem decreases, the available solution set shrinks and the cost to implement the available solutions in time increases significantly. Further, the margin for error shrinks with the shortened time horizon. If the solutions proposed do not work as well as intended, there is not much time to implement improvements before these problems cause significant harm or damage.

In the case of Big Intractable Problems, the consequences of not solving the problems in time range from the deaths of hundreds of millions of people to the collapse of our civilization, if not our species. Facing challenges of this magnitude, we cannot afford to fail. We must develop systems that help us identify these problems early and we must improve our ability to implement solutions to these problems before they cause significant harm.

In many ways, our situation with regard to Big Intractable Problems is similar to that of a person who develops cancer.

Almost every type of cancer, even the most tenacious ones, can be successfully treated if found at an early stage. In fact, many of the deadliest cancers are those that do not manifest symptoms until a very late stage. But once the cancer reaches a late stage, it metastasizes and multiple types of cancer cells form. At this stage, the treatment becomes much more intensive, complex, and expensive. These solutions are often far more difficult and painful for patients because of their intensity and disruption of the body's natural functions. The side effects also tend to be more severe with late-stage cancer treatments because much more rigorous interventions are required to combat a cancer that has taken a stronger hold on the patient's body.

For humanity, choosing not to tackle our biggest problems until they are late stage is electing to suffer much greater collective pain. By waiting so long, we eliminate the possibility of using less painful solutions, leaving us with only the most disruptive, expensive solutions. With a longer time over which to act, we could mitigate the severity of these impacts, ensuring a smoother transition that achieves the same outcome at a lower cost. But to provide ourselves this longer time horizon over which to act, we must better understand what causes our biggest problems to develop and remain alert to those underlying factors.

POWER WITHOUT WISDOM

Out of the many things humans do, developing technology to increase our individual leverage is one of the most important. One of the challenges of creating this leverage through technology is that it can amplify our intentions and our actions, both good and bad. The amplification of our effort can also create unintended consequences on a large scale. And while our brains have the capacity to model out potential scenarios and predict potential consequences, our evolutionary drive to progress in the short-term often leads us to act before fully considering these consequences.

Carl Sagan, the renowned American "astronomer of the people" who made astrophysics and astrobiology approachable to the average person, noted in his book *Pale Blue Dot* that humanity has grown powerful before we have grown wise. He recognized that this imbalance between our power and wisdom posed an existential threat to the long-term survival of our species. As Sagan put it, "If we continue to accumulate only power and not wisdom, we will surely destroy ourselves. Our very existence in that distant time requires that we will have changed our institutions and ourselves."[26] It seems as though humanity is in the teenage phase of its development, where we humans discovered we had some power we could exert upon the world and sought to make use of that power without allowing ourselves time to develop the wisdom to wield that power well.

Indeed, a lot of the Big Intractable Problems we face today are the result of unintentionally geoengineering the planet for short-term gain without the wisdom to recognize the inevitable long-term effects of our actions. It now appears we will need to deploy existing and novel technologies to intentionally geoengineer our planet and biosphere to solve

---

26 Carl Sagan and Ann Druyan, *Pale Blue Dot: A Vision of the Human Future in Space* (New York, NY: Random House Publishing Group, 1994).

the problems we have created. We must also build more sustainable systems that are less likely to create significant problems for future generations. If we only focus on solving our current problems without considering the long-term viability of the proposed solutions, we will perpetuate this cycle of abundance and scarcity endlessly and leave problems for our successors that we could have addressed today.

One of the most compelling cases for a shift to a long-term mindset in developing solutions to our Big Intractable Problems can be found in our food system. The previous chapter provided a much-too-short overview of humanity's progress in our quest to create a reliable and sustainable system for producing the calories and nutrition we need to live. But in that larger story, another narrative exists—one of humanity solving a problem, only to find that the solution had negative consequences we must urgently overcome to solve the same problem once more, albeit at a larger scale. In effect, the very tools that enabled our ancestors to ensure they could feed themselves and live better lives have significantly contributed to the challenges future generations have to overcome to achieve the same goal.

Our population grew from under one billion people—where it had been for 99 percent of human history—to nearly eight billion people in just over two hundred years. But in that time, we almost never faced a global famine because of our technological innovations that spanned intensive farming practices, plant and animal breeding, and animal husbandry methods. As we are now beginning to see, the very animal agriculture methods that provided the nutrition to develop our civilization to this point have created a number of Big

Intractable Problems that threaten our future ability to survive on this planet. Many of these problems are having impacts on the planet that are orders of magnitude greater than what most people think humans are capable of.

ANIMAL AGRICULTURE'S IMPACT ON WORLD HEALTH

With the recent rise in public discourse about anthropogenic (man-made) climate change, the environmental effects of animal agriculture have come to the forefront. The significant carbon footprint of animals raised for meat is chief among these environmental concerns. As *TIME Magazine* puts it, "There may be no other single human activity that has a bigger impact on the planet than the raising of livestock."[27] According to the UN Food and Agriculture Organization's assessments, global agriculture contributes 14.5 percent of all human greenhouse gas (GHG) emissions annually, making it the second highest GHG emitter after energy production.[28] Astonishingly, this estimate is likely an *underestimate* because it does not fully account for the carbon dioxide that these livestock emit when breathing.

CONSUMPTION OF NATURAL RESOURCES

The harm caused to the biosphere (i.e., the environment) has been among the most significant negative impacts of animal agriculture. To feed nearly eight billion people, we have razed

---

27 Bryan Walsh, "The Triple Whopper Environmental Impact of Global Meat Production," *TIME*, December 16, 2013.

28 P. J. Gerber et al., *Tackling climate change through livestock—A global assessment of emissions and mitigation opportunities* (Rome: Food and Agriculture Organization of the United Nations (FAO), 2013).

millions of hectares of old growth forests and grasslands—nearly eighteen million acres per year,[29] including some of the most biodiverse ecosystems on our planet. And we are still doing so today, destroying the last remaining rainforests and mangrove glades to create the farmland we need to feed ten billion people with current methods. In fact, the relationship between agriculture and deforestation is quite well documented. Wageningen University, one of the premier agricultural research institutions in the world, reports that "agriculture is estimated to be the direct driver for around 80 percent of deforestation worldwide."[30]

Animal agriculture now consumes over 50 percent of all habitable land on Earth, while providing just 18 percent of the calories we consume.[31] More than 33 percent of our arable land goes to just producing feed for these animals. Combined, this means livestock agriculture is the world's largest user of land resources, with pasture and arable land dedicated to the production of feed representing 83 percent of the total agricultural land.[32] Animal agriculture requires an outsized land area to produce a relatively small portion of our calories; its expansion is leaving us with less land for us to live on, less

29   Sarah Derouin, "Deforestation: Facts, Causes & Effects," LiveScience, November 6, 2019.

30   G. Kissinger, M. Herold, and V. De Sy, "Drivers of Deforestation and Forest Degradation: A Synthesis Report for REDD+ Policymakers" (Vancouver, Canada: Lexeme Consulting, 2012).

31   FAO, *World Livestock: Transforming the livestock sector through the Sustainable Development Goals* (Rome: Food and Agriculture Organization of the United Nations (FAO), 2018).

32   FAO, "Animal Production," Food and Agriculture Organization of the United Nations, 2019.

land to preserve the amazing biodiversity of our planet, and fewer wild places than ever before.

ENVIRONMENTAL DEGRADATION

Beyond the direct impact of land used for animal agriculture and its inputs, our rearing of livestock has resulted in substantial degradation of the surrounding land and waters. Water runoff and discharge from cattle feedlots, dairy farms, and industrial poultry and hog farms are major contributors to the pollution of waterways. In the US, "agriculture is the main source of pollution in rivers and streams, the second main source in wetlands and the third main source in lakes."[33] One study found that factory farms contribute to 70 percent of all river and stream water quality issues.[34] To think that more than two-thirds of all water pollution in the US comes not from industrial factories or manufacturing facilities but from agriculture almost strains credulity.

This water pollution has a number of knock-on effects including eutrophication, a process in which an excess of nutrients (like nitrogen and phosphorus from fertilizers and animal waste) causes an overgrowth of plant life that depletes the oxygen in a given area of a waterway, killing the animal life. Further, animal waste from factory farms poses a massive environmental challenge. Animals on factory farms produce

---

33 Javier Mateo-Sagasta, Sara Marjani Zadeh, and Hugh Terral, "Water Pollution from Agriculture: a Global Review" (Rome: Food and Agriculture Organization of the United Nations (FAO), 2017).

34 Jennifer Horsman and Jaime Flowers, *Please Don't Eat the Animals: All the Reasons You Need to Be a Vegetarian,* (Sanger, CA: Quill Driver Books/Word Dancer Press, 2007).

130 times as much excrement as humans do, but without the benefit of waste treatment plants.[35] Much of that waste contributes to polluted water runoff from these farms. A lot of it decomposes, releasing untold tons of methane per year—a greenhouse gas that produces a warming effect twenty-eight times as strong as carbon dioxide over its lifetime in the atmosphere.

FOOD SAFETY

One of the most significant concerns of this waste runoff is the potential risks it poses for contaminating our produce. In the United States, *E. coli* outbreaks are the most common effect of foods being contaminated by agricultural runoff. Many types of *E. coli* exist and most are harmless to humans. But a few strains of *E. coli*, some of which live in the intestines of ruminant animals, can make us very sick when we eat foods contaminated by them. How does this *E. coli* get from the intestine of an animal to our produce and food? According to the US Centers for Disease Control (CDC), the major source for human illnesses is cattle.[36] Either from runoff contaminated by animal excrement or punctured intestines during animal processing, these harmful bacteria get into our food supply, contributing to over 265,000 cases and 3,600 hospitalizations per year in the US

---

35 Minority Staff of the United States Senate Committee on Agriculture, Nutrition, and Forestry, *Animal Waste Pollution in America: An Emerging National Problem* (Washington, D.C.: United States Government Publishing Office, 1997).

36 Centers for Disease Control and Prevention, "E. Coli (Escherichia Coli): Questions and Answers," December 1, 2014.

alone.[37] This is an unnecessary, and often unaccounted for, harm that animal agriculture causes even for those who do not consume its products.

ANTIMICROBIAL RESISTANCE

Animal agriculture is also a significant contributor to the growing problem of antimicrobial resistance. Antimicrobial resistance effectively means antibiotics that used to work to treat bacterial infections are no longer reliable because the bacteria are an evolving resistance to those antibiotics. Some causes of antimicrobial resistance include lack of restraint in prescribing antibiotics and improper use by patients. But the greatest contributor by far is the rampant use of antibiotics on livestock, particularly when they are used preventatively to promote faster growth and weight gain.

A study conducted by ETH Zurich, the Princeton Environmental Institute, and the Free University of Brussels found that the rate of antimicrobial resistance in animals had *tripled* in less than twenty years.[38] For chickens, 40 percent of antibiotics used had a rate of resistance higher than 50 percent, meaning those antibiotics would fail to treat an infection in more than half of all cases. Director of the United Nations' Interagency Coordination Group on Antimicrobial Resistance Haileyesus Getahun has called antimicrobial

---

37   Centers for Disease Control and Prevention, "Escherichia Coli (E. Coli)," September 2016.

38   Thomas P. Van Boeckel et al., "Global Trends in Antimicrobial Resistance in Animals in Low- and Middle-Income Countries," *Science* 365, no. 6459 (2019).

resistance the silent tsunami heading for humanity.[39] His sentiment is echoed by Dame Sally Davies, former Chief Medical Officer for England, who identified antimicrobial resistance as a threat as great as climate change but receiving almost no attention.

Why is antimicrobial resistance such a threat to humanity? It goes far beyond having antibiotics to treat bacterial infections like pneumonia and routine illnesses. Our entire system of modern interventional medicine is wholly reliant on antibiotics. Without antibiotics, the risk of infection killing a patient after surgery makes performing complex surgeries and other invasive procedures essentially impossible. It makes cancer treatments like chemotherapy and radiotherapy, that can suppress the immune system, far more dangerous and more likely to fail. Without the capability to use antibiotics effectively, our healthcare system would regress by over one hundred years. Current animal agriculture practices are making this challenge far more pressing than ever before.

BIODIVERSITY LOSS

Perhaps most devastating of all is the impact of animal agriculture on the biodiversity of our planet. The conversion of forests and grasslands into farmland is one of the primary acts driving many species toward extinction. The loss of biodiversity has been accelerating, and a recent study found that animals are going extinct on Earth one thousand times as

---

39 Andrew Jacobs, "U.N. Issues Urgent Warning on the Growing Peril of Drug-Resistant Infections," *New York Times*, April 29, 2019.

rapidly as they would without human intervention.[40] One very visible example is highlighted in the paper "Defaunation in the Anthropocene," which concluded that 40 percent of all insect species are facing extinction as a direct result of human activity, and more specifically our agriculture.[41]

The widespread use of neonicotinoid pesticides has made America's agricultural landscape forty-eight times more toxic to honeybees, and likely other insects, than it was in the 1990s.[42] Though these pesticides are used on over 140 agricultural species, they are primarily used on two crops that are largely grown for animal agriculture: soy and corn.[43] More than 40 percent of *all* grain produced globally is fed to livestock, but corn and soy are on another level entirely. Over 75 percent of all soy grown globally, and over 60 percent of all corn grown in the United States for foods, goes into animal feed.[44] Our need to produce sufficient feed to support industrial livestock agriculture is therefore directly driving the mass extinction of numerous species, including many on which our survival depends.

---

40 David Biello, "Fact or Fiction?: The Sixth Mass Extinction Can Be Stopped," *Scientific American*, July 25, 2014.

41 R. Dirzo et al., "Defaunation in the Anthropocene," *Science* 345, no. 6195 (2014): 401–6.

42 Michael Dibartolomeis et al., "An Assessment of Acute Insecticide Toxicity Loading (AITL) of Chemical Pesticides Used on Agricultural Land in the United States," *Plos One* 14, no. 8 (2019).

43 Stephen Leahy, "Insect 'Apocalypse' in US Driven by 50x Increase in Toxic Pesticides," *National Geographic*, August 6, 2019.

44 Jonathan Foley, "It's Time to Rethink America's Corn System," *Scientific American*, March 5, 2013.

"Why focus on insects?" you may ask. What makes insects so important? Insects form the base of the food web for many ecosystems, and the loss of insects can have catastrophic impacts on the rest of an ecosystem. The declining number of insects has led to a corresponding collapse in the numbers of birds as well, as most birds rely upon insects at some part of their life cycle. Bees, butterflies, and other insects are also responsible for pollinating 35 percent of all food crops, and we're doing our level best to drive them to extinction.[45] Prominent Harvard entomologist E. O. Wilson has said that without insects, the rest of life, including humanity, "would mostly disappear from the land. And within a few months."[46]

The unfortunate reality is that many of these negative impacts of industrial animal agriculture were predictable and could have been foreseen if we had assessed them in the context of our exponentially growing population and projected likely outcomes. Instead, we pursued the short-term gain while ignoring the long-term impacts until they became so dire, we could no longer disregard them. In the case of animal agriculture, we now have a thirty-year window in which we must address these issues to prevent the worst of the long-term effects. Beyond the narrow case of animal agriculture, many of the technologies that have brought us such abundance in the last one hundred years have consequences we must overcome to prevent them from leading to future scarcity.

---

45 Alexandra-Maria Klein, et al., "Importance of Pollinators in Changing Landscapes for World Crops," *Proceedings Biological Sciences* 274, no. 1608 (2007): 303–13.

46 E. O. Wilson, "My Wish: Build the Encyclopedia of Life," March 2007, TED Conference, Monterey, California, MPEG-4, 22:21.

As Norman Borlaug knew when he led the Green Revolution, these technologies have been about buying us time to develop long-term sustainable solutions rather than being long-term sustainable solutions themselves.

BUILDING A NEW MINDSET FOR THE FUTURE

We are now living in a time of very swift change. This type of rapid change is an incredible anomaly in history. Both on vast geologic time scales and on the scale of human history, this pace of change is beyond anything any species on Earth has survived. The lack of historical precedent for this pace of change means we did not evolve a toolkit of adaptations for the situation we now face. In the scale of these problems and the short timescales in which we must solve them, we are now in uncharted territory as far as our evolution is concerned.

And by all indications, the pace of change will continue to accelerate as we develop new technologies that create greater and greater leverage for our species to change our surroundings and ourselves. So, we are faced with a challenge: develop new tools that enable us to overcome the problems our prior technological innovations created or accept that we cannot overcome those problems and write off our potential future.

The challenges that stand before us in the next century will either lead us to a future of prosperity or will cause our civilization to come undone. Solving these problems in time to avoid experiencing the worst of the consequences is going to be one of the hardest things humanity has ever had to do. It will require us to cultivate foresight and develop sustainable solutions, to collaborate when our base instincts tell us to fall back into tribes and turn on one another, and to plan for the long-term in a way we have never done before. Though we lack the evolutionary drive to do these things, we do have the intellectual capacity and the skill to execute upon them. We simply have to find the will and build the toolkit to succeed.

Having to develop new tools and systems to overcome novel challenges is not a death knell for our species and it's not even close. But we cannot afford to ignore the problems facing us until they grow beyond our ability to overcome them. If we are to succeed in becoming a species that can endure for many more generations, we *must* take this opportunity to act.

If we are to successfully overcome the existential challenges we now face, we will need to start by identifying potential Big Intractable Problems earlier. Doing so will provide us a greater set of available solutions and enable us to act with time to spare rather than under the shadow of an urgent crisis. To identify these problems as early as possible, we must learn to listen to the scientists and experts studying these areas when they tell us about potential problems. We cannot afford to blindly believe what we hope to be true or what an entity with a financial conflict of interest tells us is true.

Further, we must appreciate that the very same technologies that are boons today can become burdens tomorrow. No technology is a panacea forever, regardless of how it may appear at the time. The natural cycle of technology is to create abundance followed by scarcity as we outgrow its capacity. Recognizing this is a necessary first step to overcoming these challenges and better managing those that may arise in the future.

The second stage, solving these problems, is far more nebulous. Creating a general framework for developing and implementing solutions to these problems is quite difficult, as they are varied. One key takeaway is that the best solutions to large-scale problems create leverage that enables them to affect the greatest change with the lowest possible application of resources and effort.

A few variables can significantly influence how much leverage we can create. Selecting the biggest, most urgent existential problems can greatly increase leverage compared to choosing to work on a tamer, less impactful problem. Likewise, focusing our efforts on high-potential technologies can create tremendous leverage compared to using existing technologies whose potential is well characterized.

THE LEVER FOR CHANGE

The concept of creating leverage is crucial to understanding how we can overcome apparently insurmountable challenges and tackle Big Intractable Problems in established industries with small groups of people and limited resources. So, describing exactly what creating leverage means in this context is valuable.

In physics, a lever is one of six simple machines that use mechanical advantage (i.e., leverage) to amplify force. Essentially, they enable us to do more work with the same energy input. A physical lever consists of a lever arm (a beam or plank) that pivots over a fulcrum (or hinge) to lift a load. In this case, we are replacing a physical lever with a metaphorical one to describe how we can maximize our positive impact on a significant problem for a given amount of effort.

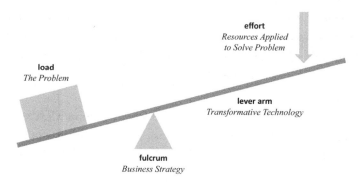

Figure 1. The Lever of Transformative Technology Entrepreneurship

In this metaphorical lever, the lever arm is the technology that underpins our solution. Transformative Technologies can make this lever arm far longer, increasing our potential leverage to lift the load. The metaphorical load being lifted is the problem we are trying to solve. While Big Intractable Problems are certainly heavier loads, achieving maximum leverage requires lifting the heaviest loads with the smallest possible application of force. Without a sufficiently impactful problem or sufficiently heavy load, the lever will not maximize our potential to create leverage.

The fulcrum in our lever is the business strategy we adopt to solve the problem and scale our technical solution. A sound strategy that learns from past successes moves the fulcrum closer to the load, where it enables us to create greater leverage. A strategy based on misunderstanding the problem will move the fulcrum closer to us than the load, dramatically reducing our leverage and ability to solve that problem.

The goal for every entrepreneur looking to maximize their positive impact on the world should be to think about how the problem they choose to work on, the technology solutions they select, and the business models they develop can maximize their leverage—and their corresponding impact on the problem.

So far, this discussion has been about how individuals can maximize their personal leverage to solve important problems and have a significant positive impact on society. But to overcome the myriad challenges we face as a species; we need to scale this thinking to macro strategies that create the most leverage for humanity. How can we create the greatest possible leverage at a macro level that will give us the best chance to overcome the challenges facing us today?

Creating leverage at scale involves encouraging more people to pursue high-leverage career paths and to tackle our biggest problems through their work. But what are these high-leverage career paths and opportunities?

One way to think about high-leverage opportunities is to look at what the most ambitious people are choosing to do with their lives. By its very nature, ambition is a trait that makes people seek out opportunities to create outsized progress toward a goal for a given amount of effort. This means that the most ambitious people typically follow one of two paths depending on their motivations: they choose "prestigious" paths that create outsized outcomes for themselves and their careers, or they pursue opportunities that have the potential to create an enormous impact on the world. Of the two paths, which do you think creates the leverage we as a society need more of to overcome the challenges we face?

Throughout history, following the paths that the most ambitious people took was likely to lead you to opportunities to create significant leverage. With the advent of the printing press in the fifteenth century, literacy became the highest leverage path for ambitious people. At the time, most adults could not even spell their own names. Literacy enabled even the child of a peasant farmer to explore the collective written knowledge of humanity and to contribute their own ideas through writing.

By the 1700s, scientific discovery and exploration had surpassed mere literacy as a desired path for ambitious people. In highly structured societies, scientific discovery drew those who aspired to do work beyond what was allowed for those of their station. This avenue opened the door for women—frequently excluded from formal employment—to make incredible contributions, as Marie Curie went on to do with discoveries that won her two Nobel Prizes.

Nearly simultaneously, the path of physical discovery drew ambitious individuals who sought to build legacies upon their contributions to society. Explorers like Meriwether Lewis and William Clark, Sir Edmund Hillary and Tenzing Norgay, and Sir Ernest Shackleton set out to map uncharted areas of the world, climb unconquered mountain peaks, and reach the Earth's Poles.

CURATING AMBITION

In essence, what the most ambitious people do with their lives, matters. We need the most ambitious people to work on developing solutions to the Big Intractable Problems facing our society because the average person considers such work too risky. Building Transformative Technology-based solutions to our biggest, most challenging problems is probably the highest-leverage career that a person can pursue today, but it is also a risky path where failure is not an unlikely outcome. If solving these problems were easy, they would already be solved. It will take those with ambition to change the world for the better to pursue this path in spite of its risks and create the future that we want to live in.

Today, the clearest path for the most ambitious people to build leverage and create an outsized impact is through entrepreneurship. Many domains in which entrepreneurs can build enterprises exist, however, and not all of them create the same amount of leverage on a macro level. To solve our Big Intractable Problems, we need conscious entrepreneurs who want to work on the tough, complex problems *because* the positive impact in the case of success will be so high. Many opportunities have been found for entrepreneurs to work on more narrow problems where the path to a faster exit and financial payout is clearer. But their long-term impact on humanity will not likely be as great or as needed.

So, what does it take to convince ambitious people to work on Big Intractable Problems that *could* have a lower risk-adjusted financial return for them but a much greater positive impact on the world in the case of success?

THE "GREATER FOOL"

An economic term that describes this archetype is the "Greater Fool."[47] Typically, this term is used derisively to identify the people who are always willing to buy an asset at a higher price. Greater Fools enable the average investor to make money in the stock market by selling assets to them, regardless of whether those assets are overpriced or not. Greater Fool Theory assumes that other people who make apparently irrational decisions are *suckers* because those bets are apparently unlikely to pan out. This is an uncharitable definition that works within the narrow context of economics when only accounting for direct economic value. Consider a larger context.

Choosing to work on Big Intractable Problems is higher risk than developing solutions to less challenging problems. The timelines to success can often be longer, the capital requirements are usually higher, and the technical risk can be quite significant. Those evaluating opportunities purely based on risk-adjusted financial reward would determine that only Greater Fools would pursue such opportunities given the available alternatives.

Indeed, the current implementation of capitalism heavily incentivizes doing whatever possible to continue short-term growth, even at the expense of the long-term. In such a system, it takes Greater Fools to choose to invest their resources into long-term upside for humanity and the planet while

---

47   Vicki Bogan, "The Greater Fool Theory: What Is It?," Cornell SC Johnson College of Business, Accessed December 27, 2019.

"shorting" things that may be profitable in the short-term but are net negative for humanity and Earth in the long run.

American screenwriter Aaron Sorkin frames this mentality brilliantly in HBO's *The Newsroom*,[48] stating,

*"The greater fool is actually an economic term. It's a patsy. For the rest of us to profit, we need a greater fool— someone who will buy long and sell short. Most people spend their life trying not to be the greater fool; we toss him the hot potato, we dive for his seat when the music stops. **The greater fool is someone with the perfect blend of self-delusion and ego to think that he can succeed where others have failed.** This whole country was made by greater fools."*

Personally, I believe we will need all the help we can get from Greater Fools if we are going to successfully overcome the existential challenges that our species will face in the coming years.

WHAT WE CAN DO

One of my primary goals with this book is to identify the things we can do to increase the number of people who work on solving our Big Intractable Problems. By distilling a set of principles based on past successes, I will provide a framework for Transformative Technology startup success.

---

48   *The Newsroom*, season 1, episode 10, "The Greater Fool," directed by Greg Mottola, written by Aaron Sorkin, featuring Jeff Daniels, Emily Mortimer, and John Gallagher Jr, aired August 26, 2012, in broadcast syndication, HBO Entertainment.

Just as *The Lean Startup* provided a framework for systematizing the early stages of building a tech startup, we can learn from prior Transformative Technology successes to develop a framework for similar startups seeking to tackle Big Intractable Problems. Such a framework will enable these entrepreneurs to stress-test their business strategies for developing, deploying, and scaling their solutions to increase their success rate and the impact they can create for the effort and resources expended.

The following chapters of this book outline such a framework and insight into how impact-driven entrepreneurs can implement it as they build their companies.

PART II

AN INTRODUCTION TO THE WORLD OF TRANSFORMATIVE CHANGE

CHAPTER 3

BIG INTRACTABLE
PROBLEMS

———

"There is an art to flying, or rather a knack. Its knack lies in learning to throw yourself at the ground and miss...Clearly, it is this second part, the missing, that presents the difficulties."

DOUGLAS ADAMS

One of the fundamental doctrines instilled into entrepreneurs and innovators is to focus on the problem rather than the solution. Prioritize identifying a problem someone is willing to pay you to solve rather than chasing a solution that has enamored you, states the common startup wisdom. If you address a specific problem a small group of users feel strongly about, you can build upon that initial success to create a successful company. Not enough is said about how to find problems worth working on.

Some prominent voices in Silicon Valley have provided some insight, however. Ash Maurya, creator of Leanstack and an active purveyor of startup wisdom, has said that many founders fall victim to what he calls **innovator's bias**. In effect, Maurya says founders think succeeding as an entrepreneur is about having "big ideas" when they most often fail because they don't select a big enough problem to tackle.[49]

Paul Graham, the fabled father of startup accelerator Y Combinator, offers slightly different advice. Graham tells founders to build products a small group of users love. How should founders figure out what product to build? "The best way to come up with startup ideas is to ask yourself the question: what do you wish someone would make for you?" Graham suggests. He goes on to say, "Just fix things that seem broken, regardless of whether it seems like the problem is important enough to build a company on. If you keep pursuing such threads it would be hard not to end up making something of value to a lot of people, and when you do, surprise, you've got a company."[50]

This advice comes from startup titans. It is considered very nearly gospel by those seeking to start companies. And yet, when I hear this advice, it seems like something important is missing. This advice entirely eschews the macro environment and global context of entrepreneurship in favor of providing aspiring entrepreneurs with tangible advice for taking a first step. And in that context, perhaps it does enough.

---

49   "The Top 20 Reasons Startups Fail," CB Insights, November 6, 2019.

50   Paul Graham, "Organic Startup Ideas," Paulgraham.com, April 2010.

THE MACRO VIEW OF STARTUPS

I cannot help but feel it is an act of hubris to focus only on the microcosm of a startup and defining "good" problems based solely on whether some group of people is willing to pay for a product. What of the macro effects if the startup is successful? Should the founders and investors not understand the externalities and seek to avoid products or businesses whose negative externalities outweigh their benefits? To do otherwise is to fall victim to the myth of the omniscient free market, expecting the market to determine what is or isn't a good idea or an important problem.

That seems to be largely what has driven new startup creation for the last twenty-five years or more. Among other things, this framework has led to the founding and mega-funding of a half-dozen electric scooter companies that seek to "improve mobility." It has driven the development of *everything*-as-a-service, whether or not turning something into a subscription actually improves it in any meaningful way.

All the while, these companies clamor about "changing the world" with their work.

With what we have discovered about our ability to unintentionally alter our planet's suitability for habitation, justifying such a cavalier approach to startups and implementation of new technologies becomes difficult. We are at a time in history where we know that these decisions can matter a great deal. They may well impact how we live in the near-term future, whether we struggle to survive or whether we thrive. While trying to establish a framework for this type of thinking, I was reminded of a concept from astrophysics I came across several years ago.

THE GREAT FILTER HYPOTHESIS

In 1950, physicist Enrico Fermi posed a question: "Where is everybody?"[51] If we are not alone in the universe, why are we not able to detect any signs of other sapient life forms on Earth or elsewhere in our galaxy, especially given the number of these species that should exist based on the scale of the universe and probability? While he was surely not the first to ask this question, it has come to be known as Fermi's Paradox because his thought process provided an unexpected insight. That insight was codified when economist Robin Hanson published the Great Filter Hypothesis in 1998.[52]

The Great Filter Hypothesis goes as follows: since there is no evidence of sapient, or even intelligent, life other than ourselves, the evolutionary process from abiogenesis to a sapient civilization capable of interstellar travel must be unlikely. This implies that at least one step in this "evolutionary path" must be improbable, if not highly so. This improbable step is the Great Filter.

The improbable step could be early on in the path, something like the evolution of multicellular life from single-cell organisms or the first abiogenesis, the initial creation of life from inorganic matter. The improbable step could be in front of

51 James Schombert, "Fermi's Paradox (I.e. Where Are They?)" (Lecture, University of Oregon, December 3, 2008).

52 Robin Hanson, "The Great Filter—Are We Almost Past It?" George Mason University, September 15, 1998.

us. Surviving our ability to unintentionally geoengineer our planet, building a spacefaring civilization, or enduring as a civilization long enough for us to grow beyond our planet could each be highly improbable events.

Depending on where the Great Filter lies in this evolutionary path, the implication for humanity is significant. If the steps to reach our current level of civilization are likely, then the probability that many other civilizations would have developed to the current level of the human species is high. If the Great Filter is found in a later step, the implication is that the improbable step lies in our future. That certainly has bleak implications for our long-term survival as a civilization on Earth and our potential to expand across our galaxy.

While there are a couple of other alternative reasons that could explain Fermi's Paradox—life is far more rare than we thought, the lifetime of civilizations is short for one reason or another, or other sapient civilizations exist but we can't detect them—the idea of the existence of Great Filters seems to be the most probable cause. Even if one of these other explanations is correct, it only reinforces the notion that we should strive to preserve our species for its rarity and be cautious of Great Filters that may be the reasons for the relative brevity of such species' existence.

So, how did Fermi's Paradox and the Great Filter hypothesis help me to develop a framework for assessing which problems are most worth our time and resources?

In essence, any sufficiently challenging problem with broad enough effects has the potential to be a Filter to humanity's long-term survival and thriving. Most of us have come across at least one of these types of problems in our lives. Ironically, these problems tend to receive a significant amount of press, even as we devote far fewer resources devoted to solving them, is wise, given their importance to our continued growth as a species.

If we accept the premise of Fermi's Paradox, intelligent life that achieves sapience and builds a sustainable civilization on its planet or in its galaxy is incredibly rare and precious. Thus, we should rationally assess the challenges we face based on their threat to our future survival and advancement as a species and should treat large-scale, highly challenging problems as though they could be Great Filters for humanity. In my framework, I have named these Great Filter problems: Big Intractable Problems.

As for how this Great Filter framework applies to the traditional micro-view about selecting problems to solve, the traditional Silicon Valley thinking is wrong. Rather, the micro, startup-centric mindset is fundamentally insufficient for the world we now live in. Now that we are aware of the impact we can have on our planet, considering the macro-level effects of our chosen business ideas is just as crucial. In fact, the best way to develop businesses with positive, macro-level effects is to develop a solution to a Big Intractable Problem.

EFFECTIVE ALTRUISM FOR BUSINESS

At this point, I was sure I could not be the only person thinking this way. Other individuals or organizations had to be encouraging people to prioritize working on difficult and impactful problems. I sought out these organizations, hoping to learn more about their way of thinking and how they communicated that thinking to others.

The most prominent of the organizations I discovered is named Effective Altruism. The organization has developed an extensive series of accessible articles that explain the fundamentals and nuances of the movement. Essentially, Effective Altruism views its mission as "using evidence and reason to figure out how to benefit others as much as possible, and taking action on that basis."[53]

Around this concept, it has developed an entire set of frameworks to help us understand which problems are important and how to determine which we should work on. After digesting these resources, I was left firm in my conviction that any framework that sought to identify high-impact problems to solve would seek to answer one question: How can we use our resources to do the most good?

There is another concept from the school of Effective Altruism that has deeply influenced my thinking about why prioritizing the macro-view when choosing problems to solve is so important. In essence, the concept is that we each have limited time, approximately eighty thousand hours, to achieve something in our life through our work. To do the most good with our lives, we must find ways to solve important problems during those eighty thousand hours, rather than leaving such important tasks for our limited time spent outside work.

---

53 "CEA's Guiding Principles," Centre for Effective Altruism, accessed October 27, 2019.

Indeed, if we take the view that small groups of dedicated people *can* create a significant positive impact on the world if they focus on the right problems, then the goal becomes finding the right problems to work on and identifying the highest-impact solutions.

As it turns out, a nonprofit organization named 80,000 Hours was founded by William MacAskill and Benjamin Todd under the Centre for Effective Altruism in the United Kingdom specifically to focus on this work. This organization affiliated with the Future of Humanity Institute at Oxford to develop a set of characteristics that define important problems. These problems must be great in scale, highly neglected, and highly solvable.[54]

In this context:

- *Great in scale* means that the problem must both affect the lives of many people and impact their lives significantly.
- *Highly neglected* means that the problems should not be ones that are "popular" or have drawn the most attention.
- *Highly solvable* means that the application of additional resources will make a great deal of tangible progress toward addressing the problem.

While the Effective Altruism framework for important problems was a useful starting point for conceptualizing which problems are worth expending our resources to solve, I found it lacked the specificity needed to be used in an instructive

---

54 Benjamin Todd, "A Guide to Using Your Career to Help Solve the World's Most Pressing Problems," 80,000 Hours, October 2019.

manner. Of the important characteristics that were insufficiently comprehensive, prioritizing problems by "solvability" struck me as somewhat circular logic.

For one thing, those problems that *appear* most solvable are likely to draw the most attention and resources explicitly for that reason. For another, many problems do not appear truly solvable until, suddenly, they do. As Malcolm Gladwell expounds upon in his best-selling book *The Tipping Point*, tipping points are notoriously difficult to predict.[55] Indeed, many of the most important problems we currently face as a civilization, from climate change to freshwater scarcity to the collapse of our oceans, likely appear far from solvable today.

So how do we classify problems in a way that can help us identify those worth working on?

A NEW FRAMEWORK FOR CLASSIFYING PROBLEMS

For clarity, we can start with the broad characteristics of such problems. By definition, these problems are Big and Intractable. As Effective Altruism noted, Big can imply both large in scale and high in intensity. For our purposes, a Big Problem is both. To be considered a Big Problem, it must affect a sufficiently large population of people and be a non-trivial problem for those people.

As for the Intractable nature of important problems, those problems that are easily remedied with a judicious application

---

55 Malcolm Gladwell, *The Tipping Point: How Little Things Can Make a Big Difference* (Boston, MA: Little, Brown, 2006).

of resources have known solutions that we lack the political will to enact. That does not make such problems unworthy of pursuit, but in those cases, solving the problem simply requires implementing known solutions at scale. In contrast, Intractable Problems are quite difficult to solve, whether due to path dependence, some physical or chemical basis, or a larger trend that we cannot overcome. These problems require the development of new, innovative solutions and an application of technology beyond what has been done to date.

Discussing the nature of problems in such abstract terms is not really illuminating. An example of a Big (in scale) but trivial problem might be that most people sneeze when looking directly into the sun. Yes, it may cause some inconvenience, but it is also readily solved by not looking directly at the sun. Since people rarely, if ever, need to look directly at the sun to accomplish anything of importance in their lives, this problem can be easily overcome.

A case of an Intractable but small problem is a genetic disorder that affects five thousand people around the world. For those five thousand people, the problem has a significant impact on their ability to live their life and is quite difficult to address. Dedicating resources to addressing this problem would improve the lives of these people, certainly, but it would not be a good target for someone seeking to do the *most* good with their efforts.

CHARACTERISTICS OF BIG INTRACTABLE PROBLEMS
Within this context, I identified five characteristics of Big Intractable Problems that can be used to compare problems

and prioritize those for which a solution would generate the greatest impact.

Big Intractable Problems:

1. Impact more than one billion people
2. Are encountered frequently by those affected
3. Are necessary for individual survival or the continuation of civilization
4. Are in industries that are based on physical infrastructure
5. Are made more urgent by an approaching inflection point

Though these characteristics are not absolute, they can serve as a useful guide for examining various problems we encounter to determine how Big and Intractable those problems are. In a way, they can provide a common language that we can use to discuss such problems. With this common language in place, discussions are more likely to move us toward a shared understanding of how we should direct our energies and resources to solve the most important problems we collectively face. As useful as this high-level discussion of the qualities of Big Intractable Problems is, a true common language requires us to have a shared grasp of the thinking that defines these qualities.

1. **Impact more than one billion people**
The first, and perhaps most obvious, quality of a Big Intractable Problem is that it must be large in scale. That is, the problem must impact many people. But how many people must be affected to constitute a Big Problem? By its very nature, this sort of assessment can appear to be entirely arbitrary. How can we decide that a problem that

impacts five hundred million people is not significant enough, but one that affects two billion people is? A logical method by which we can make these assessments, however, would be to start by putting these numbers in context.

Roughly 7.8 billion people live on Earth today. By mid-century, that number is expected to approach ten billion.[56] While many important problems afflict some number of these people, the Big Problems must affect at least a significant minority of the global population, if not an outright majority.

Further, to be useful in identifying the *most* impactful problems to work on, the filter we choose must be stringent enough to whittle down the total number of problems to a small subset of all available problems. To me, any problem that impacts at least 10 percent of the human population seems sufficiently large to merit classification as a Big Problem. If some problems impact two or three or even five billion people, then they would stand out as the most prominent Big Problems on our list.

2. **Are encountered frequently by those affected**
In addition to impacting a large number of people, Big Intractable Problems also tend to be the types of problems that the affected people experience on a frequent and consistent basis. Though the frequency at which people face a problem and the intensity of that problem are

56 United Nations, "World Population Projected to Reach 9.8 Billion in 2050, and 11.2 Billion in 2100," UN Department of Economic and Social Affairs, June 21, 2017.

not directly linked, the frequency with which a problem appears can serve as a useful proxy for the intensity of a problem. Unless a problem creates an obvious life-or-death situation, the intensity of a problem can often be difficult to assess for those who are not directly affected.

While not always the case, problems people encounter on a daily or weekly basis are generally likely to be felt more intensely than problems they only experience a few times in their lives, barring natural disasters. These more frequently emerging problems are also more likely to have a greater negative impact on the quality of life of those who are impacted than problems that only arise rarely. Both of these make these types of problems good targets for Big Intractable Problems.

One clear example of such a problem is a lack of potable drinking water for a community. Drinkable fresh water is something we cannot live more than a few days without, yet some communities lack access to a source of clean water. Some villages do have a source, but it can be miles away and require villagers to walk several hours each day to transport the necessary water to their homes. These communities feel the problem of lacking clean water every day in the labor required to fetch water, the diseases the non-potable water carries, and the time it takes away from their other endeavors. If this problem were solved and these communities had easy access to the clean water they needed to live, the quality of life of these people would be dramatically improved.

3. **Are necessary for individual survival or the continuation of civilization**

As I alluded to in the prior paragraph, the vast majority of Big Intractable Problems fall under the umbrella of "things necessary for our individual survival or the continuation of our civilizations." This may seem readily apparent once it has been stated so plainly, but we would see far more of our resources dedicated to addressing these problems if it were, in fact, so obvious. These problems tied to our survival as individuals and as a civilization are also some of the largest in terms of their intensity. Indeed, few challenges could be considered more severe than those that threaten our very existence.

For individuals, these problems are most often inhibiting our ability to obtain food, water, shelter, and our other most basic necessities. These problems appear in similar sectors at the societal level, tied into the systems that are required to provide these necessities to entire cities and countries. Big Intractable problems can often be found in the systems that provide food, water, and housing to our society.

These problems stretch beyond these most basic categories into the systems that support civilization as we know it: transportation, energy, communications, and more. Without these systems, our civilization would cease to exist as we understand it today, causing a great deal of suffering to a large segment of humanity in the process. While Big Intractable Problems can be found outside of these areas, the problems that will most acutely impact the greatest number of people are most often going to be tied to our ability to survive.

4. **Are in industries that are based on physical infrastructure**

In the context of the third characteristic of Big Intractable Problems, the industries in which these problems are most likely to be found will probably rely upon physical infrastructure to exist. As much economic value as software solutions have created in the past half-century, many of our most difficult problems cannot be solved by software alone. For obvious reasons, sectors like food, water, housing, energy, and transportation are all based on physical goods made through chemical, biological, or physical processes.

Many of the challenges these industries face come from scarcity of inputs, unwanted by-products, or inefficiencies that become unsustainable at a large enough scale. Thus, the solutions to these problems will require innovations in the underlying infrastructure and production processes that minimize the input scarcity, production inefficiencies, and harmful by-products. This basis in the physical world is one of the reasons these problems are Intractable. While software solutions may reduce inefficiencies in these industries, translating the physical world into the digital world will not directly help us create more sustainable sources of food and fresh water Software alone cannot eliminate the harmful by-products of our energy sector.

The physical infrastructure required for these industries to function creates further complications that make solving these problems difficult. Solutions that require upgrading this infrastructure are inherently costly to implement, while those that seek to disrupt an industry may find they do unintended harm during the transition as they also disrupt access to critical resources.

Further, these industries are very often heavily regulated. Why? Industries that provide critical services to the vast majority of the population and are essential to the maintenance of civilization are correctly considered too important to leave entirely to the whims of the free market. While that regulation often means it is more difficult to introduce a new solution in these industries, it also tends to make adoption of solutions more rapid and the solutions themselves more "sticky." Working within the additional constraints makes these problems far more difficult to manage, but the solutions are much more impactful because of the importance of these problems.

5. **Are made more urgent by an approaching inflection point**

The final characteristic of Big Intractable Problems, and one that makes many of these problems increasingly Intractable over time, is that the problems are often made more urgent by an approaching inflection point. While these problems are often quite challenging to solve in their own right due to their sheer scale and complexity, larger mega-trends often make finding solutions a matter of urgency.

These mega-trends can be anything from the population growth rate to changing local and global climate patterns to the consumption rate of key resources. All of these trends can make it significantly more urgent to develop new agricultural practices to sustainably feed the population, for example. These mega-trends can also make a problem less critical to solve: a declining population would reduce the need to develop more efficient housing in a small country. Those issues would not be Big Intractable Problems if mega-trends are aiding in their resolution before they become crucially important to address.

While these trends independently, can significantly influence the need to solve a particular problem, they can also create the right conditions for a problem to finally be resolved. For better or worse, we humans tend to be a fairly short-sighted species, only paying attention to those problems that are imminent and only thinking into the short-term future. Problems that emerged two decades ago may only attract the interest of those who can solve them once they become sufficiently critical. As Paul Graham, founder of Y Combinator, said, "There's nothing more valuable than an unmet need that is just becoming fixable."[57]

COMPARING BIG INTRACTABLE PROBLEMS

These characteristics of Big Intractable Problems are meant to be a guide. They are intended to function as a tool to help us discuss the problems we face and to identify the most important challenges on which we should expend our attention, time, and resources in search of a solution. If I am certain of one thing, it is that there will be exceptions. We will

---

57   Graham, "Organic Startup Ideas."

certainly discover Big Intractable Problems that do not fit all of the above criteria. We will also discover problems that fit the above criteria but do not feel as important to address as other problems.

Even with this framework for evaluating problems for the impact potential of solving them, one challenge remains: How do we effectively compare these Big Intractable Problems to determine how best to allocate our resources? Going back to the core idea of Effective Altruism, "How can we do the most good?" How are we to compare a problem that is life-or-death for five hundred million people, to a problem that dramatically shortens the lifespan of one billion people? A direct comparison would be impossible—a weighing of suffering as ineffective as it is macabre.

After much thought, a solution presented itself: a semi-quantitative assessment.

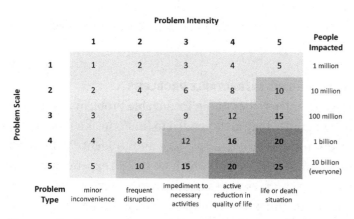

Figure 2. Scale-Intensity Assessment of Problems

Using a semi-quantitative means of assessing how Big and Intractable a problem is can be a useful tool for comparing problems, particularly when they differ significantly in scale and severity. Using a 1-5 scale, we can establish a measure of size of a problem. On this scale, a problem is a "1" if it affects one million people and a "5" if it affects all people on Earth. A similar scale can be established for the intensity of a problem. A "1" would represent a problem of minor inconvenience while a problem that rated a "5" would directly impact survival.

The relative size of a problem—how Big it is—could then be crudely derived by multiplying the scale of the problem by its intensity. Assuming the impact of a solution scales with the size of the problem being solved, the higher a problem ranks on this scale, the more effort should be directed toward resolving it. Using such semi-quantitative methods alongside a qualitative assessment based on the characteristics described above can enable us to prioritize the Big Intractable Problems we should direct our efforts to first.

This approach is not an exact science. Beyond this assessment of its size, we must also consider how Intractable the problems are, how well suited our own skills are to taking on specific problems, and whether we have any unique insights that may help us to solve these problems where others have failed. As we will see in future chapters, considering each of these factors is critical to building a company that will succeed in creating a more abundant future for humanity.

CHAPTER 4

TRANSFORMATIVE TECHNOLOGIES

"Technology is a useful servant but a dangerous master."

CHRISTIAN LOUS LANGE

Throughout our history, we have experienced the power of technology to help us solve our worst problems. When we have been able to apply emerging, exponential technologies to the most pressing problems of our time, we have been able to make tremendous leaps in our capabilities in a very short period of time. These great leaps have historically been dubbed "revolutions" in the sectors in which they occurred. As a species, we have experienced three Agricultural Revolutions, a Computing Revolution, and the Enlightenment just to name a few. In each of these revolutions, a small group of people harnessed sudden advances in technology to rapidly change problems that had sometimes persisted for centuries.

In the case of agriculture, we have seen how Borlaug's rigorous application of selective breeding and intensive farming techniques helped to improve food insecurity in regions that had grappled with inconsistent harvests and resulting food shortages for decades.

In the energy sector, the implementation of coal-fired furnaces allowed us to move from a world in which wood scarcity loomed large to a world in which we had ample energy reserves to power our industry, heat homes, and turn on lights in millions of homes for the first time.

And in healthcare, the discovery of antibiotics enabled the implementation of modern medicine. Everything we do today, from surgeries to chemotherapy to radiation treatments, would be essentially irrelevant without antibiotics.

In each of these cases, the discovery and commercialization of a Transformative Technology enabled a fundamental shift in our ability to solve previously intractable problems and to rapidly create a massive, positive impact on the world.

WHAT GOES UP CAN ALSO COME DOWN

The advance of technology is neither inevitable nor guaranteed. Indeed, many of our greatest technological advances that have created periods of great abundance will be drivers of scarcity and the next generation of intractable problems in time. This is not idle speculation. We have examples of current Big Intractable Problems that have emerged from applying these technologies at scale far beyond the application for which they were initially conceived.

As we discussed in Chapter two, antimicrobial resistance is one problem that is rapidly approaching a critical tipping point. We failed to recognize that bacteria, fungi, and parasites could fight back despite their lack of brains. Without a new solution, we stand to lose a century of medical advancement to the resurgence of untreatable infections that would make it unsafe to perform most modern interventional medical procedures. We are in an arms race with these microbes, and right now, the microbes are winning.

Great periods of socioeconomic and political upheaval can also threaten the continuous advance of technology. The Roman Empire presided over the development of several significant technologies, including sewers, aqueducts, concrete, and a number of surgical tools and techniques. When Rome was sacked in the fifth century and the Roman Empire fully collapsed, Western civilization stagnated in many ways.

While the following Middle Ages were not a period of total regression, a substantial amount of knowledge from Ancient Rome was lost and the rate of technological progress slowed noticeably. For several hundred years, Europe was far more tribal than under Roman rule, factions were constantly at war, and technological advancement slowed. Under the Holy Roman Empire, Europe began to unify and stabilize once again, ending the "Dark Ages" and starting the path toward technological advancement once more. It would take nearly nine hundred years from the fall of Rome for Europe to achieve the conditions required for discovery and progress to once again flourish and kick off the Renaissance Period.

A similar story unfolded in the Islamic world. From the eighth century until the middle of the thirteenth century, the Islamic world was in its own Golden Age.[58] The stable society valued knowledge and technology and ushered in a period of rapid progress and advancement. This society developed a system of pharmacy, consolidated existing knowledge into encyclopedias and textbooks, and made tremendous advancements in architecture and the arts. They even had a form of universal health care in which physicians could not turn away anyone who was sick and came to them seeking treatment.

But this Islamic Golden Age did not last. When the Mongols sacked Baghdad in 1258, they pillaged the civilization and destroyed the House of Wisdom, one of the greatest libraries in the history of the world.[59] The Mongolian conquest caused centuries of knowledge to be lost—at least to their contemporaries—and caused a regression back to more tribal societies, just as had occurred in Europe after the fall of Rome.

If we are to overcome the most pressing problems facing our society today, and in the future, we must recognize that our systems are far more fragile than we may believe at first glance. Solving these Big Intractable Problems will be critical to the continued survival of our civilization and our species. The window for rapid technological progress and societal

---

58 Matthew E. Falagas, Effie A. Zarkadoulia, and George Samonis, "Arab Science in the Golden Age (750–1258 C.E.) and Today," *The FASEB Journal* 20, no. 10 (2006): 1581–86.

59 Kate Raphael, "Mongol Siege Warfare on the Banks of the Euphrates and the Question of Gunpowder (1260-1312)," *Journal of the Royal Asiatic Society*, Third Series, 19, no. 3 (2009): 355-70.

improvement may well be fleeting. We should recognize the opportunity we have in front of us to solve massive problems and build a better future for our civilization while that window is open to us.

If we fail to overcome these challenges, our civilization may go the way of Ancient Rome. The most powerful tools that we have to overcome these challenges are Transformative Technologies. These technologies provide us a path toward a better, brighter future, but only if we harness them correctly and prioritize solutions to the largest, most intractable problems we face.

DEFINING TRANSFORMATIVE TECHNOLOGIES

If Transformative Technologies are our most powerful tools for solving Big Intractable Problems, we should start by identifying what these technologies are and how we can recognize them.

Transformative Technologies are essentially any technologies that can enable us to create a major impact on a problem by opening new avenues of attack that were not previously viable. These technologies make it possible to solve problems that have historically appeared beyond our capability to solve. They also significantly reduce the cost—in terms of human, capital, and time resources—required to solve problems.

In the vast majority of cases, these technologies were recently developed or are classified as emerging technologies. Why? If a technology with such significant potential was already being used commercially for another purpose, attempts likely would have been made to apply it to the problem of interest.

This is not necessarily true for startups in general, as existing technologies and business models from one sector are routinely applied to solve problems in other sectors. But for Transformative Technologies, the potential for impact is frequently so apparent and so significant that it is very unlikely some of that potential would not have been realized if the technology has been commercially viable for years.

CHARACTERISTICS OF TRANSFORMATIVE TECHNOLOGIES

Unlike Big Intractable Problems, Transformative Technologies are somewhat more nebulous. For this reason, providing a set of characteristics that you can use to easily identify them is more difficult. This is due in part to the need to assess how the technology is being applied to determine its potential to be Transformative. As a result, I will focus more on examples of Transformative Technologies that present each of the following characteristics. These examples can serve as a point of comparison when evaluating potential Transformative Technologies, particularly when the characteristics themselves may not be precise enough to provide clarity.

The five characteristics of Transformative Technologies are:

1. Classified as an exponential or a deep technology
2. An order of magnitude (10x) improvement over existing solutions
3. Platforms with many powerful applications

4. Catalysts that reduce the activation energy for affecting change
5. Orthogonal to the existing solution set

1. Classified as an exponential or a deep technology

Transformative Technologies almost always fall under the broad categories of either exponential or deep technology. Exponential technology includes any technology that doubles in performance or capability in a given period of time. Exponential technologies exhibit exponential growth in performance. Put another way, the cost for a given level of performance is halved in each period. Deep technologies, on the other hand, are cutting-edge technologies based on scientific discoveries. These breakthroughs are most frequently seen in engineering, mathematics, physics, chemistry, and biology, but they can occur in any field in which research efforts can result in the discovery or invention of new technology.

The term "deep technology" was coined by Swati Chaturvedi, founder of deep tech investment firm Propel(x). She notes that "most technology companies these days are built on business model innovation or offline to online business model transition using existing technology."[60] Thus, deep technology startups are distinguishable from traditional "tech" startups because they are built upon new, emerging technologies.

What about these types of technologies makes them more likely to be highly impactful, Transformative Technologies? For one thing, technology that is improving at an exponential

---

60 Swati Chaturvedi, "So What Exactly Is 'Deep Technology'?," LinkedIn, July 28, 2015.

rate has massive potential upside based on that exponential rate. Further, technologies that have only recently been developed or discovered open new avenues for tackling intransigent problems that have historically been considered unassailable.

The exponential nature of these technologies implies that the price for a given performance will fall exponentially over time as well. While these technologies are often very expensive at first, the exponential price decrease means these solutions can very quickly move from small volume and high price to the larger volumes and lower prices needed to drive their broad adoption. In the case of deep technologies, the novel technical insight developed at the frontier of a field of study can illuminate non-obvious solutions to significant problems. Often, these solutions have the potential to scale rapidly upon demonstration of the technology.

The Invention of the Computer
The computer is a prime example of a Transformative Technology that also falls under the classifications of exponential and deep technology. The computer was first developed as a tool for solving a problem that impacted over fifty million people: counting the United States decennial census so resources could be appropriately distributed around the country.

By 1880, the US population was large enough that tabulating US census results took nearly seven years![61] This essentially meant the US government was making decisions about representation and resource allocation almost a decade after gathering the data.

Knowing that this problem would continue to worsen as the population grew, the US Census Bureau contracted Herman Hollerith to devise a solution. Hollerith's solution, which he developed in less than three years, was a punch card system that could automatically register which holes had been punched. His technology, which he later used to launch IBM, enabled the US government to finish the 1890 census count months ahead of schedule and under budget.[62]

This large research effort and the reliance on fundamental science and engineering discoveries to progress the field are hallmarks of deep tech. The increase in speed and capability of computers classifies them as an exponential technology. In contrast to the hand counting and tabulating methods they replaced, computers demonstrated a capacity for continued exponential improvement in capability and decrease in cost that human activity could never match.

---

61   Joseph Stromberg, "Herman Hollerith's Tabulating Machine," *Smithsonian Magazine*, December 9, 2011.

62   Jason Gauthier, "Tabulation and Processing," History—US Census Bureau, December 17, 2019.

2. An order of magnitude (10x) improvement over existing solutions

A second trait of Transformative Technologies is that they offer an order of magnitude improvement over existing solutions to a given challenge. This potential to create a 10x improvement is vital to their ability to overcome the status quo and to accrue the resources needed to create impact on an important problem at scale. While it may appear arbitrary, this threshold of creating a solution that is an order of magnitude improvement is anything but.

An order of magnitude improvement is often necessary because implementing new solutions requires facing several hurdles, even when the problems are strongly felt and the solutions clearly work. One of those challenges is that people resist change.

Overcoming the status quo is often one of the most significant barriers to adoption for new technologies and solutions. To get people to change, the new solution must be so much better that switching is the obvious choice and they feel an urgency to adopt the new solution. Though lacking scientific backing, it appears that solutions that are ten times better than what they replace meet this threshold for rapid adoption.[63,64,65]

---

63   Mark Suster, "Your Product Needs to be 10x Better than the Competition to Win. Here's Why," Both Sides of the Table, March 12, 2011.

64   Peter Thiel and Blake Masters, *Zero to One: Notes on Startups, or How to Build the Future* (New York, NY: Random House, 2014).

65   John T. Gourville, "Eager Sellers and Stony Buyers: Understanding the Psychology of New-Product Adoption," *Harvard Business Review,* June 1, 2016.

Solutions that offer less of an improvement often fail to address the problem well enough to drive adoption.

Further, a solution that offers an order of magnitude improvement also provides the company commercializing that solution time to establish itself and begin to scale up before competitors arise. If we assume the technology is improving exponentially, existing solutions will catch up to the $10x$ improvement in 3.2 doubling periods. In the case of computers, where Moore's Law states that a doubling will occur every eighteen months,[66] the startup has almost five years to establish its advantage and scale its solution before the market catches up to it.

Given that Transformative Technologies often require an investment of money and time to develop from the prototype phase to commercial readiness, this period of 3.2 doublings is often critical to their success. Without this period of built-in advantage, these startups would have a difficult time recruiting the people, funding, and resources they need to commercialize the solution. That period of advantage also provides companies with the opportunity to continue to improve their initial solution, maintaining a potential advantage for longer than the initial period.

In practice, a $10x$ improvement over existing solutions means the effort, capital, or resources required to achieve a given outcome are an order of magnitude cheaper than they were. That means that a given problem can be resolved with just

---

66 *Encyclopedia Britannica Online*, s.v. "Moore's law," accessed November 7, 2019.

10 percent of the prior resources required. The result is a dramatic increase in the number of people for whom that solution is accessible and a vast expansion of the market for the solution. In essence, a 10*x* improvement can turn potential solutions from research projects only accessible to those with significant resources into commercially viable products that can scale to reach the majority of people who face the targeted problem.

Nuclear Power

Nuclear energy is one example of a Transformative Technology that's offered a 10*x* improvement over existing solutions. When nuclear energy first became feasible, the primary source of energy at power plants was coal. Compared to coal, nuclear energy provided a 10*x* improvement in energy density, pollution output, toxic waste generated, and more. Regulations imposed to ensure safety made nuclear plants more expensive to build than coal plants, but they are still cheaper to operate over their lifetime.[67] The energy density of uranium (the primary fuel for nuclear reactors) is about twenty thousand times higher than coal per unit weight, far beyond the 10*x* threshold.[68]

Further, though nuclear waste is often portrayed as being uniquely harmful, coal power plants generate multiple orders of magnitude more waste—including coal ash, boiler slag, and desulphurization products from the scrubbers that

---

67   IER, "Electric Generating Costs: A Primer," Institute for Energy Research, August 22, 2012.

68   "Economics of Nuclear Power," World Nuclear Association, March 2020.

remove pollutants from the flue gas. These coal waste products contain numerous heavy metals including radioactive uranium and thorium and toxic metals like arsenic, mercury, and chromium.[69]

Where nuclear waste is primarily solid, coal plant waste is emitted into the atmosphere or captured and stored in water, making it more difficult to contain without leaks. In fact, coal power is 330 times more deadly than nuclear power,[70] and pollution caused by coal and other fossil fuels is directly linked to more than 4.5 million deaths per year.[71]

Nuclear power's outperformance of coal across nearly every performance metric led to its rapid adoption as a power source in the 1960s, demonstrating how an order of magnitude improvement can even spur governments to move quickly. Unfortunately, many environmentalists have come to vilify nuclear energy, in large part due to the meltdown of the Chernobyl reactor in 1986 and vocal opposition that claims nuclear energy is unsafe. The politics of nuclear energy aside, it clearly demonstrated a 10*x* improvement over the status quo solution and was rapidly adopted as a result.

---

69 Olli Dahl, Risto Pöykiö, and Hannu Nurmesniemi, "Concentrations of Heavy Metals in Fly Ash from a Coal-Fired Power Plant with Respect to the New Finnish Limit Values," *Journal of Material Cycles and Waste Management* 10 (2008): 87–92.

70 Anil Markandya and Paul Wilkinson, "Electricity Generation and Health," *The Lancet* 370, no. 9591 (2007): 979–90.

71 Lauri Myllyvirta, "Quantifying the Economic Costs of Air Pollution from Fossil Fuels," Centre for Research on Energy and Clean Air, February 2020.

3. Platforms with many powerful applications

Transformative Technologies share another characteristic that makes them far more impactful than other technologies: they are platforms. "Platform" is a word commonly thrown about today by startups that want to prove they have the potential to scale beyond their initial product. But are they really platforms?

Let's explore the difference between a product and a platform. A product is a specific solution to a specific problem or set of problems. **Platforms** are solutions that enable others to solve problems, often acting as a connector. Transformative Technologies act like platforms in that they amplify the ability of others to solve problems by employing the technology. In doing so, they compound the efforts of those who use them, enabling them to create scalable impact far faster than if they had been building individual products from scratch.

As platforms, Transformative Technologies also have a number of other positive benefits. The platform solutions that typically emerge from Transformative Technologies are powerful tools that enable a much broader range of entrepreneurs to develop solutions to Big Intractable Problems. Before the introduction of these technologies, the number of people who had the requisite skill set to tackle many Big Intractable Problems would be quite low.

Any such innovator would need to be able to solve several base problems, problems that the Transformative Technology helps them overcome, before they could take on the primary Intractable Problem they are trying to solve. Anyone who wanted to create a novel solution for energy generation would also have to create the means of transmission and devices that could use that new type of energy if electricity had not already laid the common groundwork as a platform solution.

In addition to increasing the number of people who are able to work on solving significant problems, Transformative Technologies also amplify their efforts by reducing barriers to entry. A number of aspiring entrepreneurs may have contemplated solutions to Big Intractable Problems but found themselves unable to implement those solutions until a new technology emerged creating a platform on which they could launch their technology. This effect compounds. While a single entrepreneur could develop a solution to a single Big Intractable Problem with significant effort, commercializing a Transformative Technology creates a platform upon which other entrepreneurs can develop additional solutions to problems that were once out of reach.

Transformative Technology platforms can also open new solution space, enabling new solutions to emerge that those who developed the technology could never have conceived of. In effect, these technologies are tools that can increase human leverage across many dimensions by decreasing replicative work, creating common standards upon which new solutions can be developed, and expanding the solution space. When implemented as platforms, Transformative Technologies increase the leverage of many rather than just a few, exponentially increasing the total leverage they create.

The Power of Electricity

Perhaps the best example of a Transformative Technology that became a platform is electricity.

Prior to electricity, we had begun to develop tools that could amplify our ability to do work beyond what could be done through the labor of a person or horse. The first significant milestone was the use of steam to power machinery. The common application of steam as a power source led to an explosion of inventions to amplify human work. But steam had a serious flaw: it could not be centrally generated and easily transported; you had to co-locate the boiler and machinery to convert steam into mechanical work. This flaw meant you had to have the money to buy a steam engine if you wanted to power anything with it—an expensive proposition at the time.

Enter: electricity.

Electricity could be generated at a central power station and transported to the location where work needed to be done. The invention of electricity as a tool led to a rapid proliferation in devices and machines that could be powered by electricity to amplify human potential for work. Electricity became the platform on which these tools were built.

Because it solved the intractable problem of how to power machines that amplify human effort, electricity enabled thousands of people to develop inventions to solve specific problems that had been waylaid for lack of a viable power source. This gave humanity far greater leverage to solve these numerous problems than we would have had if electricity had been deployed as part of a product rather than as a platform. The establishment of electricity as a platform for powering machines enabled innovation on both the supply and consumption side because there was an understanding that the technology in the middle (120V or 220V alternating current electricity) would remain constant.

Electricity is so ubiquitous that we hardly consider it to be technology today. But electricity was one of the most Transformative Technologies ever developed. It is the silent platform that underlies a vast majority of modern technological advancements—particularly among machines and computing—and the advancement of humanity. Even the Internet, lauded as the transformative platform technology that has driven most innovation in Silicon Valley since the 1990s, is entirely dependent on the underlying platform of electricity. Electricity enabled computing as a platform to develop, which in turn led to the Internet.

The power of Transformative Technologies as platforms is tremendous. Which technology will emerge as our next platform? Will it be biotechnology, cellular agriculture, or something completely new and unexpected?

4. Catalysts that reduce the activation energy for affecting change

As our initial discussion of Transformative Technologies alluded to, one of the powers of these technologies is their ability to reduce the barriers to creating change. Effectively, Transformative Technologies reduce the activation energy for affecting change on a Big Intractable Problem.

What is activation energy? **Activation energy** is a concept from the field of chemistry that defines the amount of energy that must be put into a system to cause a reaction to proceed to completion. It is, put simply, the energy needed to get over the "hump" and move unimpeded toward the desired end result. In these types of chemical reactions where this activation energy is very high, a catalyst is added. The catalyst helps to lower the activation energy, making it easier for the reaction to proceed.

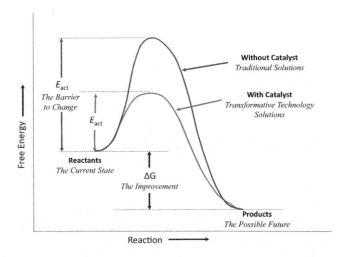

Figure 3. Activation Energy for Chemical Reactions and Big Intractable Problems

This concept also has a parallel in physics that most of us have learned from experience. The concept, drawn from Isaac Newton's First Law of Motion, states that it is easier to keep something moving than it is to get it moving in the first place. In this case, we are referring to an industry that is at rest and requires additional energy to get it to move (i.e., to change) toward adopting a better solution. Even in cases in which the chemical reaction results in a lower energy (more favorable) end state, some initial energy input is required to start the reaction.

Big Intractable Problems often share these characteristics, particularly in the critical industries in which they are most often present. The new Transformative Technology solutions could save the industry money and solve momentous problems, but overcoming the industry's inertia and kickstarting the transition require an input of energy or resources. This is where Transformative Technologies acting as catalysts can help to accelerate the adoption of these solutions.

The application of Transformative Technologies to an intractable problem generally reduces the activation energy by turning a problem that would require a Nobel Prize-level discovery to solve into one that is just a very difficult engineering challenge. This should not be surprising. Many of the most challenging problems we face today have been intractable in one form or another for decades or even centuries. It is unlikely that our ancestors failed to *conceive* of a workable solution or at least part of one. It is far more likely that the solutions were out of reach without scientific and technological breakthroughs on par with those that are awarded Nobel Prizes.

Cellular Agriculture

Cellular agriculture is one such technology that has already begun reducing the activation energy for developing solutions to some of the most pressing problems in our agriculture system, both in animal and intensive crop agriculture. Many of these problems are directly tied to the fact that we use animals in agriculture at scale. That is quite a difficult problem to solve without technology that can reproduce animal products without needing animals.

Before cellular agriculture, reducing the climate and environmental impact of our food system meant going vegan—something a small minority of people were willing to do. In fact, meat consumption is expected to nearly double over the next thirty years.[72] Traditional technologies provided no workable solution to this problem.

With cellular agriculture, opportunities have emerged to still serve people the meat and animal products they want while reducing our reliance on animals to provide these products. Cellular agriculture reduces the barrier to changing this industry because it does not require making consumers change their behavior—one of the most difficult things to do successfully in short periods of time. Rather than hoping to change consumer behavior worldwide, cellular agriculture opens the door for entrepreneurs to develop a number of different solutions that directly replace animal agriculture products or produce viable imitation products that are close enough to the original to satisfy consumers.

---

72 Nikos Alexandratos and Jelle Bruinsma, *World Agriculture Towards 2030/2050: The 2012 Revision—ESA Working Paper No. 12-03* (Rome: Food and Agriculture Organization of the United Nations, 2012).

5. Orthogonal to the existing solution set

Transformative Technologies are also defined by their orthogonality to the existing state of the industry and the current solution set for problems of interest. In fact, one of the reasons these technologies have such potential to create large-scale impact is that they enable new solution spaces to emerge, some of which are orthogonal to the existing solutions.

Orthogonality is a fairly esoteric concept, so discussing what it means in a traditional context and how it applies to solving Big Intractable Problems is worthwhile.

Orthogonality is a concept from geometry that is the most general description of objects that intersect at a ninety-degree angle. Lines that are orthogonal are often said to be perpendicular to one another. The concept of orthogonality can be thought of as a description of the alignment of ideas as well. Later in this book, we will explore the path dependence of industries and how it shapes the future path an industry is most likely to take. That path dependence can be thought of as a line within the solution space for a given problem. Lines that are parallel to this line of path dependence, and those that branch off from it, represent the solutions that could emerge by following the assumptions of prior solutions and building in alignment with previous decisions that were made.

Lines that are orthogonal to this line of path dependence, on the other hand, represent fundamental shifts in assumptions and patterns of thought. These orthogonal lines travel through regions of the solution space that the line of path dependence would never enter. The areas of the solution space that these Transformative Technologies open are entirely unexplored and offer non-traditional opportunities to solve these problems. When people describe bending the future by introducing new revolutionary technologies, this is one way to visualize that idea. Those revolutionary technologies can alter our future by shifting us from the line of path dependence toward these orthogonal solution spaces made possible by new Transformative Technologies.

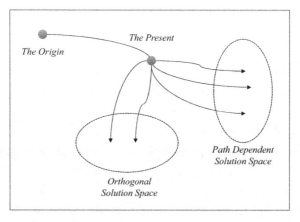

Figure 4. The Solution Space

In less abstract terms, Transformative Technologies open entirely new, non-obvious applications and business models that entrepreneurs can leverage to develop solutions that are fundamentally different from those that currently exist. These new solutions will often be extraordinarily difficult for existing industry giants to replicate because they require looking at the problem in an entirely new light and changing the way they operate. Within the industry giants, shifting their paradigm in such a way will come as a shock to existing leadership whose worldview is built upon their past experience (i.e., path dependence) rather than a future view of what is possible with the emerging technologies.

Industry incumbents often struggle to understand and react to orthogonal competition for several reasons. The primary reason is that orthogonal solutions often don't appear to be directly competing or at all threatening in the early stages. The new solution looks crazy to the incumbent who thinks their approach to solving the problem is the most likely to succeed—they have grown to a market-dominant position with their current strategy after all. However, they fail to recognize that the world has changed due to the intensification of the problem or emergence of a Transformative Technology. But even when they do recognize that new solutions based on these technologies can seriously threaten their business, they are often unable to react.

To achieve efficiency at scale, these established businesses have built well-oiled machines that are efficient at achieving the desired goal by moving in one particular direction and producing a specific solution to their target problem. These companies have sacrificed their versatility and optionality for efficiency. When they do recognize that an orthogonal solution is far better than their product at overcoming a Big Intractable Problem, they are unable to marshal the resources they need to compete head to head. The new solution is so different from their current approach that they cannot directly leverage their infrastructure and institutional resources to compete directly.

The structural difference in thinking enabled by Transformative Technologies provides entrepreneurs who use them tremendous leverage to establish their new solution even in complex industries in which getting a foothold otherwise appears almost impossible. This leverage arises because changing our underlying assumptions about how the world operates shifts the lens through which we view the world and our resulting decisions. With this leverage, entrepreneurs can solve problems that have plagued humanity for years and bend the future toward abundance.

Solar Energy

Solar energy was a solution based on a Transformative Technology that was able to establish itself in the market because it was orthogonal to traditional power producers. Before solar panels ushered in the era of distributed energy generation, nearly every commercial power plant was centralized. Hydroelectric, nuclear, geothermal, coal, or natural gas—it didn't matter what specific fuel a power plant used. They all produced power at central locations and transmitted it to users. Solar panels flipped that model on its head.

Solar panels could be placed directly on users' homes, generating power where it would be consumed and pushing extra unused electricity back to the main electrical grid. This distributed model of electricity generation was orthogonal to the traditional, centralized model and left utility companies without a logical avenue to directly compete. Path dependence with regard to regulations, electricity pricing, and distribution has altered the deployment trajectory of distributed solar. But this Transformative Technology clearly demonstrated how startups with orthogonal solutions could

overcome many structural disadvantages to establish themselves and demonstrate impacts with their solutions.

WHAT TRANSFORMATIVE TECHNOLOGIES AREN'T

In a discussion of what characteristics define a Transformative Technology, it can be helpful to examine some counter-
factuals that can clarify what is *not* transformative technology.

Most commonly, we will want to distinguish between Transformative Technologies and similar terms, like exponential
and deep technologies. The best way to think about this is to
understand Transformative Technologies as a subset of exponential technology and deep tech. While the vast majority
of Transformative Technologies would also be considered an
exponential technology, deep tech, or both, all of the technologies in these categories are not necessarily Transformative.

In the case of exponential technologies, the definition only
requires the performance to double per time period. It says
nothing of the capability of a technology to have a large-scale
impact on a Big Intractable Problem. Many of these exponential technologies, like artificial intelligence or biotechnology,
have a clear, inherent ability to create massive improvements
when applied as part of solutions to significant problems.

On the other hand, exponential technologies like virtual
reality and blockchain could be deployed in solutions for
noteworthy challenges, but they don't necessarily create
a transformative impact on that problem. This could be
because some exponential technologies have a lower potential for creating impact, but it could also be that the "killer

application" for that technology—the application that will create massive, transformative impact—has not yet been conceived or developed.

Either way, Transformative Technology is exponential, but not all exponential technology is Transformative.

We can think of deep tech in the same way. Deep tech refers to those technologies that emerged from a significant investment of time and effort and often from a technological breakthrough. These deep technologies are at the frontier of current knowledge. These properties make deep technologies compelling as Transformative Technologies because the breakthroughs that created them can open new paths to tackling Big Intractable Problems.

Just because a technology emerged from a scientific or engineering breakthrough, does not mean it automatically has a high potential for impact.

Many technologies are developed by research institutes, universities, and other development institutions that, while potentially impactful in their own way, are not inherently high-potential in the way that Transformative Technologies are. Some medical devices and niche pharmaceuticals provide a clear example of the distinction. While both the devices and drugs may cost tens or hundreds of millions of dollars and years of effort to develop, they can frequently have only a small impact on the problem they are solving.

A new version of insulin that can be produced by novel means may be 5 percent better for diabetes patients but come with a one billion-dollar development price tag. The newest heart valve replacement, considered deep tech due to the one hundred million-dollar cost to develop and commercialize it, may improve patient survival rates by 3 percent compared to the prior device. Both of these technological improvements are examples of deep tech innovations that would not be considered Transformative Technologies. That is not to say that these types of inventions and technologies are not valuable, but their lack of inherent scalability and relatively lower potential for impact means they are not Transformative Technologies.

TRANSFORMATIVE TECHNOLOGIES CREATE LEVERAGE

What is it that makes Transformative Technologies special enough to justify focusing our attention on them?

Transformative Technologies are unique tools for enacting scalable change because they enable entrepreneurs to create massive leverage. The defining characteristics of this type of technology create some structural advantages that entrepreneurs can use to take on Big Intractable Problems that would be nearly impossible to overcome with solutions built upon more traditional technologies.

The fact that these technologies enable solutions in order of magnitude better than existing ones provides the entrepreneurs who leverage these technologies a few years to demonstrate impact at scale before copy-cat companies emerge. By reducing the activation energy required to effectively solve a problem, Transformative Technologies also give entrepreneurs leverage to solve problems that others may ignore due to their apparent Intractability. Their orthogonality to the existing solutions makes it difficult for market-dominant incumbents to easily and immediately begin competing with the startup that has found a novel, far better solution.

The structural advantages of Transformative Technologies do not guarantee that any solution developed with them will be successful. However, they do provide entrepreneurs something of a head start in developing impactful solutions to Big Intractable Problems. And when the path to success is so challenging, any advantage can be the difference between success and failure.

CHAPTER 5

OVERCOMING OBJECTIONS TO TRANSFORMATIVE TECHNOLOGIES

———

"Technology is usually fairly neutral. It's like a hammer, which can be used to build a house or to destroy someone's home. The hammer doesn't care. It is almost always up to us to determine whether the technology is good or bad."

NOAM CHOMSKY

Opinions toward Transformative Technologies are generally two-fold: people are either enthusiastically supportive of them or they are intensely cautious of the potential risks of such technologies. In fact, the reaction often tends to be even more polarized than this. One group of people believes these technologies will help to solve all of our greatest problems and lead us into utopia—a belief known as technofideism.

The other claims that these advancements pose a dangerous threat to us and will create a dystopia.

Why do these technologies have such a polarizing effect on us? What is it that makes Transformative Technologies elicit these strong, almost visceral reactions among so many?

Transformative Technologies are inherently exponential— and as humans, we really do not understand exponentials. What are exponentials? The term comes from the term exponential function in mathematics. The exponential function is a function in which the rate of change increases over time (for exponential growth) and decreases at a decreasing rate (for exponential decay).

This concept probably does not seem so difficult to understand. In theory, it isn't; we should be able to spot these exponential trends in the world once we have learned about this function. But in practice, time and again, we have shown that we really cannot see exponentials. This failing of the human brain is so notorious that physicist Al Bartlett once quipped, "The greatest shortcoming of the human race is the inability to understand the exponential function."[73]

THINKING IN LINES

The problem is this: humans think linearly. It isn't even our fault really. Comprehending exponential trends in the world goes against our evolution. We often forget that we humans

---

73   Allen Bartlett, "Arithmetic, Population and Energy: Sustainability 101" (Lecture, University of Colorado at Boulder, Boulder, CO, February 26, 2005).

also have path dependence. That is, our bodies, including our brains, evolved in response to the environment and the times we developed in.

THE ACCELERATING SPEED OF CHANGE

For the vast majority of human existence, far beyond even our oldest histories, things changed more slowly than they do today. Local climates shifted over hundreds or thousands of years, causing our ancestors to migrate. Sudden changes, like tsunamis or volcanic eruptions, may have easily doomed the local populations, who had no time to adapt to the rapid changes in habitat and food availability.

But now, changes are happening at a pace our ancestors could scarcely have imagined. In a seventy-year period, we went from the Wright brothers' first demonstration of powered flight to launching a rocket that landed two men on the moon. In a forty-year span, we transitioned from room-sized computers that cost a small fortune to "a computer on every desk and in every home."[74] And in just thirteen years after the commercialization of the modern smartphone, over 45 percent of people on Earth have one in their pockets.[75] The rate of change of technology itself appears to be exponential, making it ever more difficult for us to keep up with the advances happening in our world and plan for our future.

---

74   Claudine Beaumont, "Bill Gates' Dream: a Computer in Every Home," *Telegraph*, June 27, 2008.

75   S. O'Dea, "Smartphone Users Worldwide from 2016 to 2021," Statista, February 28, 2020.

We are now facing another challenge to our brains' evolution. We must deal with numbers on a scale that the human brain does not truly comprehend. Sure, we can write two hundred thousand miles (nearly the distance to the moon), two million miles, or two billion miles. And the numbers those words represent are different. But can any of us actually distinguish between two hundred thousand miles and two million miles, let alone between two million and two billion? They all represent "a lot" of miles, but what context do we have that could truly provide meaning to those numbers?

Our ancestors hardly needed to conceptualize quantities of *anything* on such a scale. If they could count the two mammoths they were tracking, the seven children they had, or the one hundred people in their village, that would have been entirely sufficient. We are floundering in our inability to instinctively understand the sheer scale of what these numbers represent.

This is one of the primary reasons that those who trust their own perception over scientific reasoning are inclined to say, "humans cannot *really* alter the planet in any meaningful way." Without trusting the scientific method and the data it gives us, we are easily led astray by our minds, which are woefully unprepared for the task of processing information on this scale. Now we must deal with 7.8 billion people who annually consume seventy-one million metric tons of beef while burning nearly eight billion tons of coal and are told that the impacts of those activities are changing our planet.[76, 77]

We *see* the numbers, but their sheer scale impedes our ability to *understand* what they are telling us. As Sherlock Holmes is fond of telling Dr. Watson, "You see, but you do not observe."[78]

When faced with the exponential nature of Transformative Technologies, most people who are not looking for an exponential trend will see a pseudo-linear one. Over a short enough period of time, even an exponential trend can appear linear. We see what we expect to see. Since most things in life are either linear or cyclical trends, we see these patterns and take them at face value. We do not look deeper to confirm that what we are seeing is what actually is.

Our brains are built to reason by analogy and to use these frameworks, these archetypes, to help us understand the world around us. When we encounter something new, our brains immediately seek out past analogues to help us quickly place that new experience into the context of what we already know. We take for granted that it must be similar to something we already know, discounting that it may be quite different. That's why alligators, snakes, and many other animals "taste like chicken" to those who grew up eating chicken. Evolution, not mental laziness, is at play here.

---

76 Hannah Ritchie and Max Roser, "Meat and Dairy Production," Our World in Data, November 2019.

77 IEA, "Coal Information 2019," International Energy Agency, August 2019.

78 Arthur Conan Doyle, "A Scandal in Bohemia," In *The Adventures of Sherlock Holmes* (Fairfield, IA: 1st World Library—Literary Society, 2004).

Developing frameworks based on our past experiences and reasoning by analogy to predict the future is fast and efficient. When our ancestors encountered a leopard, they didn't need to stop and contemplate whether it was a new species they had never seen before or to pontificate as to why it had spots instead of stripes. They needed to compare it to a lion and cheetah they had seen before, conclude "it may try to eat me," and recognize they should avoid it.

This construction of mental frameworks is most obvious today in the way parents pass on knowledge to children by way of stories. These stories provide analogies for real life lessons that help children build their frame of reference for understanding the world. This skill has served humans incredibly well for generations, and it is still useful today for linear or cyclical trends. Farmers know autumn follows summer and that shorter days and cooler temperatures mean it is time to harvest before winter arrives because that is how it has always happened in the past.

EXPONENTIALS DON'T FIT OUR MENTAL MODELS

But using the past to predict the future doesn't work so well for exponential trends. It took just under five years for the first one billion people to get touchscreen smartphones. Using traditional thinking, we would assume that it would take that same amount of time, five more years, for two billion people to have smartphones. Instead, those next billion smartphones were acquired in just two more years. When assessing exponential trends, our traditional modes of thinking fail us.

Instinctively, our brains seek out inflection points, or critical indicators that something has changed. In a cyclic trend, like the changing of seasons, we look for the first frost to signal that winter has truly begun or the first rain to indicate the start of the monsoon. But exponential trends don't have inflection points. They don't have "knees in the curve."

When we look at a graph of an exponential trend, the inflection point always seems to be toward the right edge of the curve. Then we zoom out, and the inflection point *still* seems to be near the right edge of the curve.

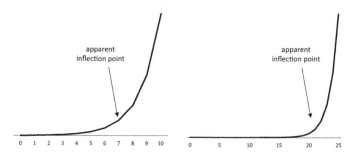

Figure 5. Exponential Curves Have No Inflection Points

This is a mental trap. The early part of the trend *always* appears to be gradual, while the late part of the trend *always* appears to be steep. Even when viewed visually, exponential trends are difficult to grasp.

So, what do we do? If exponential trends represent many of the most important problems and technologies, how are we to truly comprehend the nature of those trends so we can develop impactful solutions? The clear answer is that we have to train ourselves to see exponential trends and actively question whether a trend may be exponential in nature when we come across new information.

We must learn to be skeptical of our "gut" reactions. These primal reactions are initiated in the less evolved parts of our brain. For all the strength of the reactions the primal brain induces, they are very often misguided—produced in anachronistic bits of anatomy ill-suited to our current challenges. By priming our brains, we will be more likely to notice exponential patterns in data and to recognize when we are forcing new experiences into old archetypes when they do not fit. We will explore methods for training our capability to see exponential patterns in Chapter eleven.

Failing to understand exponentials will lead us to make bad decisions about our future. We would make those decisions with a high degree of confidence due to mental models that led us to draw the wrong conclusions from the available data.

The incorrect assumptions that stem from using linear models to assess exponential trends lead to a number of undesirable outcomes. Chief among these are objections to Transformative Technologies that are based on a misunderstanding of the future and the nature of change. Only by abandoning the urge to reason by analogy and instead reasoning from first principles can we understand exponential trends and how they will impact our future.

COMMON OBJECTIONS TO TRANSFORMATIVE TECHNOLOGIES

While many objections to Transformative Technologies are rooted in a misunderstanding of exponentials, there are a number of legitimate concerns around the emergence and adoption of such technologies. One such concern is the equality of access to the new technology and the potential for worsening inequality between groups of people or regions. The impact of emerging technologies on individual rights and liberties is another legitimate concern. Given the recent discourse around the effect of digitization on individual privacy, this is likely to be a persistent concern for new digital technologies going forward.

Another, is the concern about potential "dual use," or the use of a technology for dangerous purposes as well as the intended beneficial purpose. In the case of the development of nuclear weapons, the dual use concern was actually reversed, as the harmful initial application led to the development of nuclear power as a source of clean energy.

But these well-founded concerns are rarely the most prominent concerns in the public discourse about Transformative Technologies. Instead, conversations on these issues are relegated to discussions amongst scientists and ethicists, while mostly speculative concerns based on misunderstanding of exponential trends dominate the conversation on social media and in the mainstream media.

OBJECTION #1: IT'S TOO EXPENSIVE!

One of the most often cited criticisms of Transformative Technologies is that they are too expensive. These criticisms tend to emerge soon after these technologies have been successfully demonstrated for the first time. Often, the concern manifests as a statement along the lines of, "It doesn't matter that the technology was shown to be effective in solving a major problem because it is too expensive to become mainstream."

Sometimes, we may be inclined to agree with these comments because the new technology is in fact quite expensive and has only been demonstrated at small scale. But in agreeing, we would fall into the trap of looking at a data point rather than the overall trend. We would be feeding a common misconception based on a failure to recognize an exponential trend at work.

Throughout history, there are numerous examples of prototypes and products based on new technology being launched at high price points and in small volumes. In nearly every case, those prices dropped quite rapidly as the technology developed further. But why is this the case? As with many trends involving Transformative Technologies, the price of these technologies tends to follow an exponential function.

New technologies, particularly those that involve a major scientific breakthrough, usually require a substantial investment of capital and time in research and development. While the earliest money may have come from governments and other grant agencies, the later development work to turn a scientific discovery into a first product generally relies on private capital. Further, an initial product launch of a Transformative Technology-based product is usually low volume due to technical hurdles to scaling production for the mass market.

These conditions together result in a higher cost for an initial product, but these prices fall exponentially as the new technology matures and achieves scale. If you assume the price will decrease linearly, rather than exponentially as it has for similar technologies in the past, you would assume the technology will remain too expensive to survive in the market.

Sequencing the Human Genome

Perhaps the best example of this exponential decrease in price is in the cost of sequencing a human genome.

In 1990, the biomedical research community set its sights on a lofty goal: sequencing the 3.3 billion bases in a human genome. The effort was conducted by thousands of scientists at twenty research centers and universities across the globe.

It took thirteen years and three billion dollars to sequence that first genome.[79] In 2003, The National Human Genome Research Institute estimated that the cost to sequence a second human genome would be fifty million dollars, or *sixty times less expensive* than the first genome that was completed

---

79   Kris A Wetterstrand, "DNA Sequencing Costs: Data," National Human Genome Research Institute, October 30, 2019.

that same year. By 2007, the cost of sequencing a genome had fallen another 5x to ten million dollars.[80]

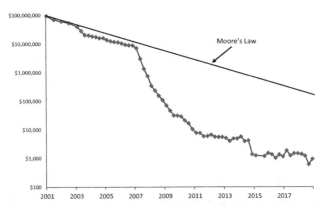

Figure 6. The Cost of Sequencing a Human Genome[81]

Just look at those numbers again. That three hundred-fold drop in price to do the exact same thing—sequence one human genome—demonstrates the power of exponential trends. The trend did not stop there.

In 2007, something unexpected happened: a new Trans-formative Technology called next-generation sequencing emerged. Over the course of the next 3 ½ years, the exponential decrease in the price of sequencing a human genome *accelerated*, falling an unprecedented **1000x** in forty months to just ten thousand dollars.[82]

---

80 Ibid.

81 Wetterstrand, "DNA Sequencing Costs: Data."

82 Wetterstrand, "DNA Sequencing Costs: Data."

Today, the price of sequencing a human genome is about one thousand and expected to fall below one hundred dollars within two to three years, creating an entirely new industry in its wake. When applied to an already exponential trend, this Transformative Technology created an impact very few could have foreseen.

OBJECTION #2: THE TECHNOLOGY ISN'T MATURE ENOUGH!

A second objection to Transformative Technology is that the technology does not appear mature enough to be sold commercially. This objection is actually quite similar in nature to the first objection about price in that it is based on an inherent assumption that the maturation of Transformative Technologies is linear. When framed that way, most people would probably agree that the development of new technologies is rarely a linear path. In spite of that, our brains still look for trends based on archetypes we have developed, even when the data does not fit those trends.

When it comes to the development of technologies, we expect to see an "inflection point" at which the technology changes from "still a research project" to "commercialization-ready." As our exploration of exponentials has shown us, though, an exponential curve does not have an inflection point. At any given time, we can observe the trend and our brains will tell us that the inflection point is coming in the near future but is not here yet.

Some seek to remedy this challenge by using measures of adoption of the new technology as a proxy for its maturity. Unfortunately, such methods are only useful in hindsight.

Not to mention that the logic of using technology adoption as a metric to predict whether a technology is mature enough to be adopted *en masse* is a circular form of reasoning.

One solution is to study the early adopters of the technology. Though this does not truly provide the foresight of learning to see exponential trends, it can enable us to overcome this objection to technology immaturity. If these early adopters are using Transformative Technology to solve a significant, important problem—sometimes referred to as a **killer application**—that can be a good indication that rapid mass adoption of the technology will soon follow. If the early adopters are using the technology for a niche application that does not address a major problem, exponential adoption will not likely occur in the short-term.

The Power of Moore's Law

Truly moving beyond this objection requires training ourselves to see exponential trends as they are unfolding. Luckily, we have past examples of exponential adoption to learn from and use as a guide. Moore's Law is perhaps the most often cited illustration of the speed at which technology can mature.

Moore's Law is named for Intel co-founder Gordon Moore who first predicted that the number of transistors (the basic building blocks of computer chips) on a computer chip of a given price would double every eighteen to twenty-four months. Essentially, he predicted that processing power of a computer chip would double every two years. The underlying principle of Moore's Law is that the technology of computer chips would mature and advance exponentially.

In practice, Moore's Law has essentially held for over forty years, far longer than most "experts" anticipated. The exponential nature of Moore's Law is so powerful that the entire modern revolution in computing has been built upon its back.

The rapid maturity of transistor technology has given rise to the modern electronics that power everything from our smartphones to modern televisions to autonomous vehicles. And while Moore's Law appears to be slowing down as we approach the fundamental physical limits of the silicon hardware; the human genome sequencing case study has demonstrated how a single breakthrough innovation could again accelerate the pace of change beyond even what an exponential trend would predict.

OBJECTION #3: IT ISN'T NATURAL!

When we examine the trends in technology breakthroughs, the twenty-first century increasingly seems like it will be the "Century of Biology." Our twentieth-century achievements were driven by engineering, physical in the beginning and software toward the end. We are entering an era in which biology is transitioning from a research discipline to an engineering one in which the engineering of biology will be a primary driver of innovation and change.

This transition to "biology as engineering" will be a great boon for a number of industries that are working with legacy technology. In particular, important industries with significant Big, Intractable Problems—like healthcare, agriculture, and energy—are likely to be transformed by engineered biology in a way software solutions alone could not achieve. Famous Silicon Valley venture capital firm Andreessen Horowitz has even updated its infamous "Software is Eating the World" manifesto with a document announcing that "Biology is Eating the World."[83]

Not everyone is thrilled by this transition to biological engineering as a Transformative Technology. Even more than prior technology revolutions in industry, manufacturing, and software, biology as technology has attracted a substantial group of detractors and opponents. Because biology is the technology that is the foundation of humans and the living world around us, many people tend to view it through a different lens than computers or advances in manufacturing.

The rallying cry of these opponents to biology as technology is that "it isn't unnatural!" The underlying assumption is that natural products are good while those that are engineered or developed are bad. The reality, of course, is far less binary.

A broad spectrum of products exist, ranging from naturally occurring to largely engineered, and most biological products fall somewhere in the middle of this spectrum. Interestingly, the opposition to these products is not directly tied to the degree of engineering applied. Some plants and animals that are the result of thousands of years of breeding are often

---

83   Jorge Conde, Vijay Pande, and Julie Yoo, "Biology Is Eating the World: A Manifesto," Andreessen Horowitz, October 28, 2019.

considered "natural" while any use of more modern and specific techniques is enough to earn the "unnatural" label.

These objections appear to primarily stem from the idea that humans should respect nature rather than seeking to engineer it to suit our needs. Further, the objectors would argue that we should not "play God" by extending our agency to things that should remain outside the scope of human activities. But considering "natural" to be good is an untenable position when it is readily apparent that not all of what is natural is good for us.

What Does 'Natural' Mean?

In fact, a brief look at human history will tell us that natural goods were often quite efficient at making our ancestors ill or killing them. Eating our meat raw would be the most natural course, but the parasites and diseases from that raw meat would certainly sicken or kill our ancestors far more often than cooked meat. And while raw soybeans are toxic to humans, cooking and fermenting them is the foundation for Chinese cuisine.

Many of the techniques humans have adopted to improve our lives would certainly be considered far from natural. Almost none of the food we consume today is the same natural form that our ancestors discovered thousands of years ago. Over that span, we directed the evolution of these organisms or cross-bred them to create hybrids, cultivars, and breeds that had more of the traits we desired: greater yields, higher caloric density, better flavors, easier harvesting, disease resistance, and adaptations to different climates.

We created synthetic antibiotics, based on Louis Pasteur's discovery of *penicillin,* to help protect us from the bacterial infections that killed our ancestors far too frequently. Indeed, these antibiotics laid the foundation for all modern interventional medicine. In spite of their "un-naturalness," or perhaps because of it, these applications of biology as technology enabled our nomadic ancestors to build the first civilizations and drove the development of modern societies.

OBJECTION #4: IT ISN'T SAFE ENOUGH!

Another objection often raised in discussions about new Transformative Technologies is that we do not have enough data to prove these technologies are safe. In fairness, this objection is actually rooted in a modicum of truth. When new technologies emerge, we usually lack the data to *prove* that something is safe in the long-term. But does that mean we should limit the introduction of any new technology until a set of ten-year studies can be carried out to determine the risks of long-term use and exposure?

The sentiment underlying this objection is that assuming that we can understand the effects and applications of new technology when it is first developed is the height of hubris. While this view is sometimes supported by the actions of a small subset of technologists, it is not reflective of the larger community that seeks to do good in the world through the application of Transformative Technologies.

What those who object to the perceived lack of safety in new technologies fail to recognize is that all discovery has inherent risks.

Risk in the Age of Discovery

In the 1400s, the Age of Discovery, hundreds of expeditions crewed by thousands of men set out across the Atlantic Ocean in search of opportunity, riches, and glory in the "New World." Though the risk of such voyages was quite high, as evidenced by the more than 681 shipwrecks found off the coast of the "New World" by archaeologist Carlos León's team,[84] men continued to sign up for such voyages in the name of discovery and for personal reward.

Even half a millennium later, when Sir Ernest Shackleton set out on his famous Nimrod Expedition to Antarctica, the risk-opportunity trade-off was at the forefront of the discussion. Shackleton's apocryphal advertisement for this expedition captures the ethos of the exploration mindset quite well:

Men wanted for hazardous journey. [S]mall wages, bitter cold, long months of complete darkness, constant danger. Safe return doubtful. Honor and recognition in case of success.[85]

As Shackleton's alleged advertisement so poignantly highlights, the risks are inherent to these high-potential endeavors. Asking whether something is too risky is the wrong question. Instead, the correct question we should ask is: "Is the potential impact of the proposed application worth the possible risks?"

---

84 Sam Jones, "Spain Logs Hundreds of Shipwrecks That Tell Story of Maritime Past," *The Guardian*, March 1, 2019.

85 TIME Staff, "The Greatest Survivor: Ernest Shackleton," *TIME*, September 12, 2003.

Risk is Relative

This question is particularly relevant when considering the initial application of a Transformative Technology. Why? The first application of a new technology is likely to have the highest risks because the technology is unproven. Over time, the technology should get safer as we better understand its strengths and pitfalls. So, the risk/reward trade-off assessment is most important for the first application.

We must then evaluate how much risk we are willing to tolerate. A rational framework would be to accept greater risk for Transformative Technologies that are applied to solve Big Intractable Problems where there is tremendous potential to improve lives than we would for a low-impact application of the same technology.

In the case of the space tourism industry that will likely emerge on the back of new low-cost, reusable rockets, the risks are significant given the application is leisure rather than addressing an important problem. This framework would suggest that such an application would be approached with greater caution and an increased focus on safety before a first launch was allowed.

In contrast, when a new treatment for *ebolavirus* emerged in the midst of a major outbreak, the scientists correctly chose to accelerate its path to market because the potential upside for the patients was high enough to justify the relatively high risk. When the base case is a 90 percent death rate for *ebola*-infected patients, providing them a treatment that may not work or may have side-effects yields little additional danger compared to the opportunity to dramatically increase their odds of survival. While the treatment may not have been tested enough to be "safe" by usual standards, it was certainly "safe enough" to justify its use given the situation.

OBJECTION #5: WHY WORRY ABOUT THESE IMPENDING PROBLEMS? TECHNOLOGY HAS ALWAYS SAVED US BEFORE!

There is a belief that is unfortunately all-too-common amongst technologists and those who are immersed in the Silicon Valley ecosystem. Many people believe technology will advance enough to solve all of our most significant problems by itself. This belief is also known as **technofideism**.

Why people buy into the myth of technofideism and why it holds such appeal is easy to understand. Believing that technology will be able to solve our problems itself is comforting. It allows us to not worry so much about the tremendous and apparently intractable problems that we face in the present. It relieves the pressure that many people would otherwise feel to dedicate their energy and resources to addressing these Big Intractable Problems. Historically, it is also detached from reality.

THE DANGERS OF TECHNOFIDEISM

Buying into technofideism also has impacts far beyond just those who hold these beliefs. It has significant downsides for humanity broadly. When a big enough group of talented people think that technology will address our greatest challenges on its own, those people tend to work on other, less important problems. Over time, we end up in our current situation. While most startups talk about how their technology is "changing the world" or "making a difference," the vast majority are no longer focused on solving the Big Intractable Problems that would actually change the world for the better.

Technofideism in many ways parallels the "common wisdom" that the free market is omniscient and will develop solutions to problems once those problems get big enough. The problem is that technology and the market are not sentient. They have no intrinsic desires and no drive to advance certain interests. Rather, they are tools that we developed to help us build our society and they reflect the thinking of those who develop them.

But Technofideists will point to a number of times in history when humanity faced an ominous situation in which the most catastrophic predicted outcome never materialized because a technology solution was implemented in time to avoid that disaster. In fact, I have had a number of conversations in which this counterargument emerged, and the apparent prevalence of technofideism is one of the things that led me to write this book.

What these editorialized versions of history fail to mention is just how close we came to disaster and the enormity of the effort that was required of a small, dedicated group of people to develop and launch the solutions that saved us.

The Ozone Hole
In May 1985, scientists with the British Antarctic Survey stunned the world when they announced their discovery of a massive hole in the ozone layer—a protective layer of ozone

that shields all life on Earth from harmful radiation—over Antarctica.[86] The scientists also declared that chlorofluorocarbons (CFCs), abundant compounds used in everything from hairsprays to refrigerators,[87] were responsible for creating the ozone hole.

In a nearly miraculous show of global action, the United Nations unanimously approved the Montreal Protocol in 1987 banning CFCs. This was, and still remains, the only unanimous action in the history of the United Nations.[88] The small group of activists who recognized the very real threat posed by the loss of the ozone layer and led the charge were lucky. Replacement technology happened to already exist and the activists were able to convince the CFC-reliant industry to change by dangling new patent rights in front of them.

Otherwise, we would likely have seen an analogous situation to the current lethargy toward climate change action. The companies with vested economic interests in the status quo would have done everything in their power to protect their short-term profits, even at the expense of humanity's future. Had we missed the effects of CFCs on the ozone for just thirty or forty more years, we would likely have damaged the ozone layer enough to trigger an extinction-level event

---

86 "The Ozone Hole," British Antarctic Survey, April 2017.

87 American Chemical Society National Historic Chemical Landmarks, "Chlorofluorocarbons and Ozone Depletion," American Chemical Society, 2017.

88 Mario Molina and Durwood Zaelke, "The Montreal Protocol: Triumph by Treaty," UN Environment, November 20, 2017.

that may well have precipitated the fall of modern human civilization and our species.

The context of the ozone hole discovery is astonishing: in just over sixty years, humanity altered a part of the Earth that we hardly understood, coming perilously close to bringing about our own destruction in the process. Indeed, most of us could scarcely imagine planet-level change on a fifty-year timescale before we learned from the ozone hole. Even with the rapid, drastic global action to eliminate CFCs, scientists do not expect the ozone layer to fully recover until 2080, or 150 percent of the time it took us to create the hole in the first place.[89]

WE MUST ACT

Technology alone will not solve our problems for us. Nor will market forces act to solve the very problems they had a hand in creating, at least not within the timeframe that is often required.

If we desire a more abundant, remarkable future for ourselves and for our children, we must take on the responsibility of solving our Big Intractable Problems ourselves.

Relying upon the chance that others will unravel them or that these challenges will resolve themselves is far too risky. After all, the risk we are talking about is the stability of modern civilization and the ability for humanity to thrive rather

---

89 Brian Handwerk, "Whatever Happened to the Ozone Hole?" *National Geographic*, May 7, 2010.

than simply endure. Solving these problems will require the responsible development of Transformative Technologies, a focus on the highest-impact applications, and the right approach to build successful businesses to launch these solutions into the world.

PART III

CELLULAR AGRICULTURE: A NEW LEVER FOR CHANGE

CHAPTER 6

CELLULAR AGRICULTURE: A POWERFUL TOOL FOR CHANGE

―――

"We shall escape the absurdity of growing a whole chicken in order to eat the breast or wing, by growing these parts separately under a suitable medium."

WINSTON CHURCHILL

A BREAKOUT MOMENT: THE FIRST CULTURED MEAT

August 5, 2013, was a breezy, partly cloudy day in London. Intermittent showers were forecast for the afternoon. It was the picture of a typical summer day for London and its residents. Well, nearly all of its residents. For a small group of journalists, food critics, and scientists at Riverside Studios in West London, August 5th was a remarkable day. On that day, they witnessed the tasting of a lab-grown burger—the first of its kind—that was *five years* and $330,000 in the making. But this event was far from inevitable; in fact, it very nearly never happened.

The original funding to develop a cultured burger came from the Dutch government agency SenterNovem in 2005.[90] To those not familiar with the Netherlands, the fact that this small country would be supporting pioneering research in new food production methods may seem odd. In fact, the Netherlands is quietly one of the world leaders in food and agriculture innovation and the second biggest exporter of food globally—quite the achievement for a country that is one third the size of the state of New York.[91]

The funding supported work on three technologies required to bring the project to fruition: 1) tissue engineering work conducted at Eindhoven Technical University by Dr. Carlijn Bouten, 2) stem cell biology work conducted at Utrecht University by Dr. Henk Haagsman and Dr. Bernard Roelen, and 3) cell culture media engineering work conducted at the University of Amsterdam by Dr. Klaas Hellingwerf.

In 2008, just one year before the grant was to be completed, an illness led Dr. Bouten to pass her portion of the project onto then part-time professor Dr. Mark Post. When the project concluded in 2009 without a completed burger, Dr. Post decided to continue the work because he saw the potential

90   Isha Datar and Daan Luining, "Mark Post's Cultured Beef," New Harvest, November 3, 2015.

91   Frank Viviano, "This Tiny Country Feeds the World," *National Geographic*, September 2017.

for broad impact of cultured meat. But funding was difficult to come by, and by early 2010, there was very little money left to support the project. There was a very real risk that the work would be terminated, and the progress made shelved for a later time—an occurrence that is all too common in academic research.

But then, a private foundation contacted Mark Post inquiring about supporting his work. They had been directed to his lab by Jason Matheny, founder of New Harvest, a nonprofit research institute that supports cellular agriculture.[92] The foundation saved the project, committing the funding to support the continued development of the cultured burger and a media launch event once the burger was ready for demonstration. At the tasting event in London, this foundation was revealed to be the private family foundation of Google co-founder, Sergey Brin.

With renewed funding, the work of producing the first lab-grown burger continued. In Dr. Post's lab at Maastricht University, researchers painstakingly grew tens of thousands of strands of cow muscle fibers that were just 0.02 inches in size.[93] Once they had grown enough muscle fibers, the challenge became determining how to arrange them into a hamburger patty that best mimicked the texture and mouth-feel of a traditional burger. After a year of growing muscle fibers and making test burgers, they found a workable formulation.

---

92 Datar and Luining, "Mark Post's Cultured Beef."

93 Alok Jha, "First Lab-Grown Hamburger Gets Full Marks for 'Mouth Feel'," *The Guardian*, August 6, 2013.

The burger that arrived in London for the tasting was made of more than twenty thousand of these cows' muscle fibers.[94] Though it took five years to produce the burger from the start of the research project, growing the cells for the five-ounce patty at the tasting took just three months. According to Dr. Post, "that's faster than a cow," which takes about thirty months to grow to market weight.[95] That burger arrived at the demonstration event in London by train, carried in a dry-ice filled cardboard box by Dutch food technician Peter Verstrate in an amusing juxtaposition of high tech with very low tech.

The cultured burger was prepared and cooked by Richard McGeown, chef of Couch's Great House Restaurant in Cornwall. He then served the burger to Hanni Rützler, an Austrian nutritional scientist and founder of futurefoodstudio, and Josh Schonwald, American author of *The Taste of Tomorrow*.[96] Dr. Mark Post also got a chance to taste the burger he labored over for five years.

So, after all the work it took to get that demonstration burger to the stage in London, how was it received? As the audience watched with bated breath, Hanni Rützler seemed to appreciate the importance of the moment if her first comment was any indication. "I would have said if it was disgusting," she noted wryly.[97]

---

94 Datar and Luining, "Mark Post's Cultured Beef."

95 "A Quarter-Million Pounder and Fries," *The Economist*, August 10, 2013.

96 Jha, "First Lab-Grown Hamburger Gets Full Marks for 'Mouth Feel'."

97 Ibid.

On texture, Rützler was ambivalent, stating, "I was expecting the texture to be more soft. The surface was surprisingly crunchy." On taste, Rützler had a more positive take. "There is really a bite to it; there is quite some flavor with the browning," she said. "I know there is no fat in it, so I didn't really know how juicy it would be, but there is quite some intense taste; it's close to meat but it's not that juicy. The consistency is perfect."[98]

Josh Schonwald said the cultured burger tasted like "an animal protein cake." He also echoed Rützler's comments about the flavor, indicating that the burger tasted *almost* like a conventional one, but that it was not quite ready for prime time yet.[99] Promisingly, Rützler said she would have thought the product was meat, not a plant-based substitute, in a blind taste test. Rützler's final verdict: "This is meat to me. It's really something to bite on and I think the look is quite similar."

Naturally, there was also sticker shock at the $330,000 price tag. Dr. Post's response was that, "there's no reason why it can't be cheaper."[100] He is right. Much of this initial cost came from paying several experienced lab technicians to do work at research scale using research-grade components. As the process is scaled up and automated, that price is likely to drop dramatically.

98 "A Quarter-Million Pounder and Fries," *The Economist*, August 10, 2013.

99 Jha, "First Lab-Grown Hamburger Gets Full Marks for 'Mouth Feel'."

100 Henry Fountain, "Building a $325,000 Burger," *The New York Times*, May 12, 2013.

LEARNING FROM EXPONENTIALS

Some people might ask, "Why would a private investor agree to finance such an early, incredibly risky effort? What value do they hope to create even if they succeed in producing a burger in a lab at a cost of hundreds of thousands of dollars?" These are valid questions, though they reinforce one of the key challenges to achieving impact: humans fail to understand exponentials.

As we have discussed, training yourself to understand the exponential nature of Transformational Technologies is essential to creating the highest impact. In the case of the first cultured burger, Dr. Post recognized the potential impact cultured meat could have on the world even in the very earliest stages of his research. His ability to see the exponential potential of cultured meat led him to continue pursuing its development even when the funding from the Dutch government dried up.

Similarly, Sergey Brin's experience scaling Google helped him to understand the exponential impact Transformational Technologies have as they scale. He knew that the visible impact of these technologies is often underwhelming right up to the moment when it is suddenly fantastic.

What most people fail to recognize is that initial proof-of-concept efforts are rarely about the prototype. Rather, their purpose is to demonstrate the initial iteration of a bigger idea. The goal of making a prototype is to reduce a complex scientific and technological problem to practice, to demonstrate that the product can be made at all.

For Dr. Post, his research team, and Sergey Brin's foundation, the purpose of making and publicizing a cultured beef hamburger was to demonstrate to the world that making a hamburger from cultured cow cells is scientifically possible. The purpose was not to make a mass-market product, but to prove that their proposal is *technologically feasible* and had potential for significant global impact. To those looking for such signals, the importance of these first-of-their-kind events is clear.

THE POWER OF WATERSHED MOMENTS

Once an initial pioneer demonstrates technical feasibility, it often creates a **watershed moment**. That prototype signals to entrepreneurs and technologists that what once was a problem of scientific discovery is now an engineering problem. Engineering problems are where entrepreneurs seeking to create impact excel.

For those who study the history of Transformational Technologies and how they create impact in the world, engineering innovations and production method improvements will clearly drive down costs and increase scalability given time. They understand that, though new technologies often require significant time and investment to achieve a proof of concept, the potential for impact can rapidly grow once that watershed moment has been reached.

To Julian Savulescu, Uehiro Professor of Practical Ethics at the University of Oxford, the potential for impact was immediately apparent once he learned about the successful launch event of the cultured burger. "Artificial meat stops cruelty to animals, is better for the environment, could be safer and more efficient, and even healthier," he said. "We have a moral obligation to support this kind of research."[101]

Beyond drawing attention to the potential cultured meat has to create significant improvements in the ethical, environmental, and health externalities of our meat industry, the event also had more broad-reaching effects.

First and foremost, the publicity brought much-needed attention to the challenges our food and agriculture industries face over the next thirty years. Despite the importance of sustainably feeding ourselves in the near future, these issues have not received the attention or the funding that is needed if we are to solve them. And while no single event can bring adequate attention to a problem, no matter how loud the fanfare, watershed events like the cultured burger tasting on August 5, 2013, can create large movements that spur action far beyond anything that has existed to date.

Watershed moments are powerful largely because they generate significant wide-reaching publicity for a new technology or idea and enable those behind the event some ability to direct the narrative to best convey their message. Dr. Iain Brassington of the University of Manchester's Centre for Social Ethics and Policy highlights the value of this directed publicity. "While the sight of someone eating a very expensive burger is clearly something of a publicity stunt, the

101 Nathan Gray, "Lab Grown Meat? Surely It's a Matter of Taste..." Food Navigator, William Reed Business Media Ltd., August 8, 2013.

underlying idea behind laboratory-grown meat is sound," he notes.[102]

These "publicity stunts" are incredibly powerful tools for building public awareness and excitement that is needed to drive transformational technologies forward. They can rapidly build momentum that would otherwise take many months or years to accrue. However, they are not without risk. Those pursuing Transformative Technologies must be careful not to build their entire companies around publicity stunts, lest they find themselves with only flash and no substance to show for their time and effort.

Since Dr. Post presented his burger to the world, over thirty companies have been launched to develop cultured meat and other cultured products to replace their traditional equivalents. Among those companies is Mosa Meat, a company born from Dr. Post's research and where he now serves as Chief Science Officer. Dr. Post's work to demonstrate that cultured meat is technically feasible has launched a new industry of scientists and entrepreneurs who seek to realize the promise of cellular agriculture. It also has de-risked the technology enough to help those new cellular agriculture companies raise over $250 million in private capital financing to date.[103]

In addition to that single watershed event, Dr. Post has continued to present at conferences and spread the word about

---

102 University of Manchester, "Why Lab-Grown Meat Is a Good Thing," Phys. org, August 5, 2013.

103 Pitchbook, custom search for *Cellular Agriculture* and *Cultured Meat* in January 2020, Pitchbook.

the transformational potential of cultured meat. He has leveraged the power of that watershed moment to inspire thousands of people to start working on solving Big Intractable Problems in our food and agriculture system and in doing so, helped to launch the field of cellular agriculture.

CHAPTER 7

APPLICATIONS OF CELLULAR AGRICULTURE, PART I: TERRESTRIAL AGRICULTURE

―――

"Next-generation protein isn't about creating more—it's about making meat better. It lets us provide for a growing and wealthier world without contributing to deforestation or emitting methane. It also allows us to enjoy hamburgers without killing any animals...lab-grown meat improves our quality of life."

BILL GATES

Though cellular agriculture has only been established as an industry for a few short years, dozens of companies have launched with the goal of developing a diverse range of products. These companies are largely working on research and development efforts to create these new products and to engineer novel methods for producing them at commercial scale. For many, the technical work has been progressing rapidly. Some of these startups have recently launched initial demonstration products at private tastings and conferences, while others are planning reveal events for their products in the next year.

Based on the current rate of progress, we will likely see the first cellular agriculture products reach the market in 2021 or 2022. Though many hurdles remain to mass production of these goods, the initial work these companies have done provides a glimpse of the future promise of cellular agriculture: a world in which animals are not needed to provide the products we know and love.

Within the field of cellular agriculture, a diverse range of product applications is emerging. Some of these applications are becoming saturated as many new startups work to develop highly similar products, while others remain underexplored and underfunded compared to their high potential to create impact. As we will explore in this chapter, the Transformative Technology of cellular agriculture can have a tremendous positive impact on our future, particularly if it is applied to problems that have not received as much attention.

A NEW WAY TO FEED HUMANITY

CULTURED MEAT

Likely the most well-known application of cellular agriculture is cultured meat. Cultured meat primarily focuses on producing muscle tissues that can serve as replacements for common livestock meats, like beef, pork, poultry, and turkey. Some companies in the cultured meat industry also seek to replace aquatic species, like fish and shrimp, and some want to create replacements for endangered species that are harvested from the wild today.

In many ways, the fact that cellular agriculture has gravitated toward cultured meat as a primary application is entirely understandable. The negative externalities of livestock agriculture, which we have discussed previously, are most visible in the livestock raised for food because of the sheer scale of the industry required to feed 7.8 billion people. Let's look at some of the solutions that startups working in cultured meat have come up with to mitigate the externalities of this industry.

THE IMPACT OF CULTURED MEAT

Based on the criteria we have discussed in the prior chapter, producing alternatives to meat sourced from livestock can qualify as a high-impact application of cellular agriculture. Not all applications of cultured meat have the same potential for impact.

Cultured beef, for instance, will yield the greatest reduction in feed requirements, land use, freshwater use, and carbon dioxide emissions even though it is less than 25 percent of total meat consumption. On the other hand, cultured pork will reduce food contamination risk and impact the greatest number of people globally due to its much higher rate of consumption.

Poultry, in comparison, is the fastest growing source of animal protein globally and essentially at parity with pork production in volume. Given its low cost, accessibility in developing regions, and comparatively low environmental impact, cultured poultry will likely face a greater challenge in communicating its benefits to consumers. Cultured poultry's most compelling argument for impact may be in the sixty-six *billion* chickens per year that can be removed from factory farms in which animal welfare is a serious concern.[104]

Though we have discussed the different ways in which each variety of cultured meat can create a significant impact on a major externality of livestock agriculture, none of these solutions alone will be sufficient. To create the sweeping impact these founders seek, the reality is that a concerted effort to produce cultured alternatives for all major sources of animal protein will be required.

The relative exposure of cultured meat compared to other applications of cellular agriculture belies its relative lack of funding and early stage of development compared to other applications. Its prominence highlights something important about how we as humans view emerging technologies: our

---

104 Food and Agriculture Organization of the United Nations, "FAOSTAT: Global Chicken Production," 2019.

imaginations are often captured by the most tantalizing or fearsome applications of a technology, even as we tend to gloss over other high-impact potential applications that are right in front of us.

CULTURED DAIRY

One of those high-impact applications of cellular agriculture that has received relatively little attention is cultured dairy.

Many prominent voices in the cellular agriculture industry are advocating for cultured meat on the basis of its potential to drastically reduce our reliance on animals for agriculture (and the negative externalities that animal agriculture entails). Interestingly, these same advocates tend to fail to recognize the impact cultured dairy products can have on the same problems.

A few early pioneers are developing alternatives to traditional dairy using both cellular and acellular agriculture approaches. Perfect Day Foods was an early entrant into the field of cultured dairy and has made the most progress toward the launch of a commercial product, including sale of a limited release ice cream in 2019.[105] Perfect Day's approach is considered acellular agriculture, using microbes to produce the main proteins found in dairy and then isolating those proteins to make milk. New Culture and Real Vegan Cheese are two other acellular agriculture companies that are

---

105 Catherine Lamb, "Perfect Day Launches Ice Cream Made from Cow-Free Milk, and We Tried It," The Spoon, July 11, 2019.

taking a similar approach, using microbes to produce casein, one of the main proteins found in milk, to make cheeses.

TurtleTree Labs has recently announced its entrance into the field of cultured milk with the first cellular agriculture approach. TurtleTree Labs is culturing cells from the mammary glands of mammals—the milk-producing glands for which the class of animals are named—including cows and even humans. Of the products described here, only Turtle-Tree Labs' cell cultured milks serve as exact replacements for milk, since they are in fact milk made from the same cells that would produce it in an animal.

THE IMPACT OF CULTURED DAIRY

Why do I suggest that cultured dairy is a high-impact application of cellular agriculture? Let's look at the numbers. Of the one billion cows that are raised worldwide, more than 260 million are reared just for producing milk.[106]

In addition to the sheer number of dairy cows impacted by the industry, serious concerns exist about animal welfare that dwarf those of the beef industry. Just like humans, cows produce milk only when pregnant and nursing. To maximize milk production, this means dairy farms must continually impregnate dairy cows over and over until they are worn down and "retired" (sold for meat) after just five or six years on average.[107]

---

106 "Statistics: Dairy Cows," Compassion in World Farming, July 1, 2012.

107 Karin Alvåsen et al., "Farm Characteristics and Management Routines Related to Cow Longevity: a Survey among Swedish Dairy Farmers," *Acta Veterinaria Scandinavica* 60, no. 38 (2018).

And as you might imagine, impregnating hundreds of millions of cows leads to hundreds of millions of calves being born every year. What happens to these calves? The female calves will grow up to become the next generation of dairy cows. But the male calves are often not worth raising to adulthood and tend to be harvested as calves to produce veal.[108]

As you can see, the dairy and meat industries are intertwined. It will be impossible to successfully migrate the meat industry away from its reliance upon animals without also developing solutions for dairy. Cultured dairy presents a less crowded sector and a corresponding opportunity to create large-scale impact with a relatively smaller investment for entrepreneurs evaluating options within cellular agriculture.

CULTURED EGGS

Remember those sixty-six billion chickens that we just talked about? About seven billion of those chickens (plus or minus a few hundred million at any given time) are raised purely for egg production.[109] These chickens will lay over *1.2 trillion eggs* every year, with individual chickens on industrial farms laying up to three hundred eggs per year.[110]

---

108 Tom Levitt, "Dairy's 'Dirty Secret': It's Still Cheaper to Kill Male Calves than to Rear Them," *The Guardian*, March 26, 2018.

109 Hans-Wilhelm Windhorst, Barbara Grabkowsky, and Anna Wilke, "Atlas of the Global Egg Industry," International Egg Commission, September 2013.

110 Food and Agriculture Organization of the United Nations, "FAOSTAT: Global Egg Production," 2019.

The majority of these eggs are sold for food, but some are kept to raise the next generation of layer hens. Of the eggs that farms keep, about half will produce roosters and half will produce hens. But only hens will lay eggs and provide economic value for the farm. As a result, over six billion male chicks are destroyed annually because the farms have no use for them.[111] The culling of these male chicks is one of the greatest cases of animal abuse found in our modern livestock agriculture system, at least in scope if not degree, and this occurs as a *byproduct* of the industry. The fact that the male chicks are killed while providing no sustenance to people and for no useful purpose is reason enough to advocate for the development of cultured alternatives to eggs.

To date, only two companies are producing cultured egg proteins, Clara Foods and BioscienZ. Both companies are using acellular approaches to use yeast to produce ovalbumin, the primary protein found in egg whites. Their initial products will be egg white replacements, but work is likely underway to produce an alternative for egg yolks as well.

Using cellular agriculture to produce a whole egg replacement or an egg yolk replacement will be a significantly more difficult technical challenge, but one that is well worth pursuing to eliminate the waste and animal cruelty of our current egg industry.

111 Lukas Blazek, "FFAR Offers $6 Million for in-Ovo Sexing Solution," WATTAgNet, October 18, 2018.

THE CARCASS BALANCING PROBLEM

As we have discussed before, carcass balancing is one of the challenges of traditional animal agriculture. Typically, carcass balancing is discussed in the context of high-value and low-value parts of livestock animals and the challenges that stem from having a relative excess of the low-value components. In the case of cellular agriculture, however, the carcass balancing problem is actually the opposite.

Livestock agriculture has existed for so long that entire industries have come to depend on animal by-products as part of their supply chain. Everything from soaps to crayons and cosmetics to cello strings has components derived from livestock. The pervasiveness of animal-derived products is a hurdle to the goal of replacing livestock with cellular agriculture. Without providing a competitive animal-free alternative to these animal carcass components, a number of global industries, including critical industries like healthcare and pharmaceuticals, will continue to rely upon livestock as an input.

Thus, cellular agriculture startups must tackle the long tail of products made from livestock by-products. A couple of startups have recognized the importance of developing products that will help solve the carcass balancing problem. To their benefit, they appear to have significantly less competition than peers who are pursuing more popular applications of cellular agriculture, like cellular meat.

GELATIN

An unexpected, but nonetheless important, by-product of the livestock industry is gelatin. Gelatin is a protein derived from collagen; a major structural protein found in the connective tissues of animals. Collagen is the single most abundant protein in mammals, accounting for 25 to 35 percent of their total protein content.[112] When this collagen is processed and broken down, gelatin can be extracted.

Gelatin is used for a wide variety of applications, but especially for foods, cosmetics, and biomedical products. Animal-derived gelatin is a key component of Jell-O, is used as a thickener in many other food products, and is often found in research labs where it is used to grow cells and for biomedical testing. Even with this broad range of applications, you may be wondering if there really is enough gelatin used globally to make it an important problem for a cellular agriculture company to target. Well, as of 2017, over four hundred thousand metric tons of gelatin were used annually![113]

Currently, Geltor stands alone as the only company actively pursuing an animal-free gelatin product. Geltor is using an acellular agriculture process to manufacture collagen in microbes which they then extract and process. From this collagen, Geltor has developed a line of products, including collagen for the cosmetics industry and gelatin for food applications. In fact, Geltor was the first company to demonstrate

112 Joaquim Miguel Oliveira and Rui Luís Reis, "Natural Polymers," In *Regenerative Strategies for the Treatment of Knee Joint Disabilities*, 21:100–103, Springer, 2016.

113 "Global Gelatin Market Projected To Reach $2.79 Billion In 2018," Nutraceuticals World, Rodman Media, July 15, 2013.

a cultured leather product—which makes sense when you consider that leather is predominantly made from collagen.[114]

LEATHER

One of the primary by-products of livestock agriculture is leather. As you might expect, leather is one of the highest-volume products that comes from livestock agriculture outside of meat. The use of leather for everything from shoes to bags to clothing to housing is a testament to the five thousand-plus years that we have been relying on animal leather to help us meet our most basic needs. Unfortunately, the leather industry is also an incredibly dirty one.

The majority of the environmental impact of leather comes from the livestock whose hides are used in its production. That said, the process of leather tanning, preserving the animal hide and transforming it into leather, also produces large volumes of hazardous waste that contains harsh chemicals and heavy metals. Since a majority of leather tanning occurs in regions with poor regulatory enforcement, much of this waste ends up being improperly disposed of and polluting rivers and agricultural land.

For the people who work in and live near leather tanneries, the impacts can be much worse. Chromium and arsenic, both commonly used in the tanning process, are known irritants and are carcinogens (cancer-causing agents) with

---

114 Mika McKinnon, "This Book Is Bound in Lab-Grown Jellyfish Leather," *Smithsonian Magazine*, Smithsonian Institution, January 30, 2018.

long-term exposure.[115] In fact, the Centers for Disease Control and Prevention discovered that the incidence of leukemia was *five times* the US national average near one tannery in Kentucky.[116]

Short-term exposure to tanneries also poses significant risks. Raw animal hides can be breeding grounds for the bacteria that cause anthrax, especially if they are improperly stored or disinfected.[117] Sean Gallagher was awarded a Pulitzer Prize for his documentary *The Toxic Price of Leather*, which details these impacts.[118]

THE WAY FORWARD

The first cultured leathers are being produced by acellular agriculture methods. Modern Meadow is producing collagen, the structural protein that is the primary component of leather, in yeast and then forming that collagen into leather. Ecovative is taking a fungi-based approach, growing mycelium (the roots of fungi) into mats that can be formed into leather-like products. A relative newcomer to the sector is

---

115 S K Rastogi et al., "Occupational Cancers in Leather Tanning Industries: A Short Review," *Indian Journal of Occupational and Environmental Medicine* 11, no. 1 (2007): 3–5.

116 Richard Sclove et al., "COMMUNITY-BASED RESEARCH IN THE UNITED STATES: An Introductory Reconnaissance, Including Twelve Organizational Case Studies and Comparison with the Dutch Science Shops and the Mainstream American Research System," (1998).

117 Mehmet Doganay, Gokhan Metan, and Emine Alp, "A Review of Cutaneous Anthrax and Its Outcome," *Journal of Infection and Public Health* 3, no. 3 (September 2010): 98–105.

118 Sean Gallagher, "India: The Toxic Price of Leather," Pulitzer Center, Pulitzer Center on Crisis Reporting, May 8, 2014.

Vitro Labs, a company that is growing actual leather using cellular agriculture.

As with other sectors, these acellular and plant-based (or fungi-based, in this case) companies are coming to market earlier than their cellular agriculture alternatives. However, the closest replacements will come from the cellular agriculture products that are not far behind.

BEYOND HUMAN FOODS

PET FOOD

Another cellular agriculture application that is gaining traction is cultured pet food. Why pet food? Because feeding our pets is big business.

Over one quarter of all meat consumed in the United States goes into pet foods. If dogs and cats comprised their own country, they would rank *fifth* in global consumption of meat, trailing only the United States, China, Brazil, and Russia.[119] The trend of increasing meat demand for pet food is showing no signs of slowing down.

Historically, pet food has been produced from the parts of animals that humans don't want to eat but pets would enjoy without consequence. Known as **animal by-products**, these components most often include organs and bones, though not the hair, teeth, or intestines. While these may seem

---

119 Karin Brulliard, "The Hidden Environmental Costs of Dog and Cat Food," *Washington Post*, August 4, 2017.

unappealing to us, they are healthy for animals to consume and provide a valuable use of the 44 percent of a cow or 30 percent of a pig that would otherwise go to waste.[120] As the cultured meat industry works to reduce the total number of animals raised and slaughtered for food, they cannot ignore the tremendous meat demand of the pet food industry if they are to succeed in their mission.

THE IMPACT OF PET FOOD

Given the trends driving the demand for meat in the pet food industry, cellular agriculture holds incredible potential to create outsized impact in this industry relative to the investment required.

With a slightly easier technical development pathway and a shorter regulatory pathway for approval than human food applications, cultured pet food is likely to be one of the first approved cellular agriculture products. For these reasons, cultured pet food has the opportunity to be one of the vanguard applications of cellular agriculture that helps create the market for the next generation of products.

By demonstrating that their products are safe for pets, many of whom are treated like family by their owners, cultured pet food companies can help to build a much larger market of consumers for cultured meat. Those customers will have developed trust in cellular agriculture products and will be

---

120 Daniel Marti, Rachel Johnson, and Kenneth Matthews, "Beef and Pork Byproducts: Enhancing the US Meat Industry's Bottom Line," United States Department of Agriculture Economic Research Service, September 1, 2011.

willing to purchase them for their own consumption. Further, as these companies scale their production, they will likely develop technologies and production methods that will be transferable to cultured meat and many other cellular agriculture products, helping to address the scale-up challenges that many of these companies face today.

Perhaps surprisingly, there are only a handful of companies working on cultured pet food today. Given its technical overlap with cultured meat and significant potential for impact, cultured pet food is a prime opportunity for entrepreneurs. All three companies working on cultured pet food today— Because Animals, Bond Pet Foods, and Wild Earth—are currently using acellular agriculture approaches, mixing microbial products with plant-based ingredients to make their products. However, Because Animals is planning to launch a product that includes cultured meat in a few years.

WHAT CREATES THE GREATEST IMPACT?

At this point, you may be asking, "But aren't companies pursuing any cultured meat still generating a significant positive outcome? Does it really matter that some other application could produce a marginally larger impact?" The answer is: yes, but with some significant caveats.

The cultured meat sector is rapidly approaching a level of saturation at which there are diminishing returns for each additional company that joins the pursuit of cultured beef, pork, or chicken. Essentially, once the number of companies working on a particular solution to a problem reaches a minimum threshold, the impact of each additional company working on that problem is significantly reduced.

A number of reasons explain why we see diminishing impact returns from later players in crowded sectors. First and foremost, having dozens of companies working toward the same goal in the same way is bound to lead to significant duplication of effort and a less-than-optimal allocation of resources. Counterfactually, there is good reason to have more than just one company working on the same problem: diversity of ideas, thought, and approaches may lead one company to succeed where another fails.

Thus, the key to analyzing an opportunity is to ensure that your approach is meaningfully differentiated from existing approaches in a way that minimizes the duplication of effort to achieve the target outcomes. We will discuss this idea, which I have termed **solution concentration**, in greater depth in Chapter thirteen.

For entrepreneurs, time and focus are the most precious and scarce resources available. Many teams spending their money to duplicate their efforts in pursuit of the same goals is certainly wasteful. These startups' time could otherwise be spent pursuing problems with significantly higher potential for impact when adjusted for the resources allocated to solving them. Effective Altruism, a nonprofit organization that uses evidence and reason to identify the most high-impact actions each person can take with their time and resources, provides an excellent framework for assessing these trade-offs, and that can provide some clarity when assessing which problems to focus on.[121]

In future chapters, we will revisit the conversation about optimizing decision-making to maximize potential for impact and will explore a framework for evaluating opportunities that considers many factors, including solution concentration, to help you determine the most impactful path you can take.

---

121 "Introduction to Effective Altruism," Effective Altruism, June 22, 2016.

CHAPTER 8

APPLICATIONS OF CELLULAR AGRICULTURE, PART II: SEAFOOD

———

"If you're overfishing at the top of the food chain, and acidifying the ocean at the bottom, you're creating a squeeze that could conceivably collapse the whole system."

CARL SAFINA

THE STATE OF OUR SEAS

While land-based livestock agriculture has a number of environmental and ethical externalities that have received increased attention recently, it is not the only part of our food system that has significant room for improvement. Whether due to a bias based on Western diets or just the attention drawn to cattle by the cultured burger demonstration, land-based cultured meats have been the primary focus of media attention. Indeed, when you think of the cultured food products with the highest potential for impact, seafood probably doesn't come to mind.

Between wild catch and aquaculture (fish farming), we consume an astounding amount of seafood: over 170 million tons per year.[122] For context, we consume 320 million tons of livestock meat per year.[123] And global demand for seafood continues to rise, particularly in the regions with the largest projected population growth through 2030 and beyond. Between 2018 and 2030, the UN Food and Agriculture Organization projects that Latin America will experience an 18 percent increase in seafood consumption, while Asia-Pacific is expected to experience an 8 percent increase.[124]

But global seafood production is in trouble. Roughly half of all seafood is still caught from wild fish stocks in the open ocean. Today, approximately 33 percent of monitored fish populations are overfished and more than 50 percent are fished up to their sustainable limits.[125] Including the 10 percent of stocks considered "depleted" by the UN, that means more than 90 percent of global fisheries are not being fished sustainably and are in serious decline.[126]

122 FAO, "The State of World Fisheries and Aquaculture," Food and Agriculture Organization of the United Nations, 2018.

123 Hannah Ritchie and Max Roser, "Meat and Dairy Production," Our World in Data, November 2019.

124 FAO, "The State of World Fisheries and Aquaculture 2018."

125 FAO, "The State of World Fisheries and Aquaculture," Food and Agriculture Organization of the United Nations, 2016.

126 Ibid.

In a 2006 study, a Stanford researcher-led team projected that if current conditions continue almost *every single species* of wild-caught seafood will *collapse* by 2050.[127]

For those looking for exponential trends, that study insight is both powerful and frightening. The fact that every species lost *accelerates* the degradation of the overall ecosystem and hastens the collapse of our oceans indicates the exponential nature of this trend. That it was not noticeable until recently is a testament to the two-sided nature of exponentials: they are difficult to spot early on and are often very difficult to affect in the later stages.

When trends like these emerge, they often indicate that significant challenges, and opportunities, lie ahead.

THE IMPACT OF WILD-CAUGHT SEAFOOD
In the context of salvaging the fate of dozens of aquatic species in our oceans, the opportunity presented by cultured seafood appears tremendous. But the apparent likeliness of collapse of these species is far from the only reason that cultured seafood is a very high-impact application of cellular agriculture.

The systems we have developed to harvest fish from the oceans were built with one purpose: to catch enough fish to fill the cargo hold as quickly as possible. In essence, the

---

127 Boris Worm et al., "Impacts of Biodiversity Loss on Ocean Ecosystem Services," *Science* 314, no. 5800 (2006): 787–90.

fishing fleet was built for volume, not efficiency. The results have been disastrous for our oceans.

Over 40 percent of all the aquatic animals we catch every year are considered **bycatch**, or animals we catch unintentionally while fishing for specific species.[128] In general, fishing vessels want to catch moderate-to high-value species that consumers want to eat. Bycatch often includes more abundant, lower-value species but can also include undersized or juvenile individuals of the target species.

Bycatch is not worth enough to occupy space on the boat, so these dead or dying aquatic organisms are dumped overboard to make space for the target species. That means we are needlessly killing and dumping *sixty-three billion pounds* of fish into the ocean every year to catch ninety-five billion pounds of fish that we actually want.[129] For some seafood species, like shrimp, fishing trawlers can catch twenty pounds of bycatch for every pound of shrimp caught.[130] That is like throwing away twenty hamburgers for every hamburger you eat.

Bycatch is also primarily responsible for the worldwide decline of protected aquatic species' populations, killing an estimated one hundred million sharks and three hundred thousand whales, dolphins, and seals every year.[131] Oceana, a leading ocean advocacy organization concluded

128 R. W. D. Davies et al., "Defining and Estimating Global Marine Fisheries Bycatch," *Marine Policy* 33, no. 4 (2009): 661–72.

129 Amanda Keledjian et al., "Wasted Catch: Unsolved Problems in US Fisheries," Oceana, March 2014.

130 Ibid.

131 Ibid.

that "bycatch…is one of the largest threats to maintaining healthy fish populations and marine ecosystems around the world."[132] It is not difficult to understand why they came to this conclusion.

If the massive bycatch problem is not a sufficient reason to seek alternatives to current wild-catch fishing techniques, the fishing industry is also a primary contributor to ocean ecosystem destruction and plastic pollution.

A fishing technique known as **trawling** (or bottom-trawling) involves dragging a net along the seafloor to catch aquatic species that live on or near the ocean bottom. Every year, fishing trawlers drag nets across six million square miles of ocean bottom.[133] That is the equivalent of bulldozing an area almost two times the size of the US every year, destroying coral reefs, plant life, and entire ecosystems in the process.[134] These ecosystems will take hundreds of years to fully repair themselves, further threatening our ability to rely on the oceans as a dependable food source in coming years.

These fishing vessels also contribute to another tremendous problem: plastic pollution of the oceans. According to Dr. George Leonard, Chief Scientist at Ocean Conservancy, half of all plastic found in the ocean comes from fishing vessels.[135]

---

132 Ibid.

133 Les Watling and Elliott A Norse, "Disturbance of the Seabed by Mobile Fishing Gear: A Comparison to Forest Clearcutting," *Conservation Biology* 12, no. 6 (1998): 1180–97.

134 Ibid.

135 Laura Parker, "The Great Pacific Garbage Patch Isn't What You Think It Is," *National Geographic*, March 22, 2018.

Most often this plastic is in the form of discarded nets, fishing lines, and plastic traps. These plastics pollute our food supply, kill oceanic animals, and slowly choke off our oceans. At current rates, the Ellen MacArthur Foundation projects that we will have more plastic than fish in the oceans by 2050.[136]

FARMING FISH PRESENTS SIMILAR PROBLEMS

The good news is that these problems are readily apparent, even to those in the industry. Over the last forty years, the aquaculture industry has been developed to enable us to raise our seafood on controlled farms like we raise land-based livestock. And while aquaculture has progressed rapidly and developed functional production systems for dozens of aquatic species consumed for seafood, the solutions we have produced to date have not been good enough.

Looking at the development of aquaculture, it seems that in many ways, we have not learned from the mistakes of land-based livestock agriculture. While aquaculture certainly eliminates the problem of bycatch and the direct environmental destruction caused by fishing trawlers, it has a similar set of negative externalities that make it unsuitable as a long-term sustainable source of protein.

ANTIMICROBIAL RESISTANCE

One of the primary challenges with aquaculture is the overuse of antibiotics, which can lead to the emergence of

---

136 World Economic Foundation, Ellen MacArthur Foundation, and McKinsey & Company. "The New Plastics Economy—Rethinking the Future of Plastics," Ellen MacArthur Foundation, 2016.

antimicrobial resistant bacteria. According to a 2015 study, the overuse of antibiotics in aquaculture is "contributing to the same resistance issues established by terrestrial agriculture."[137]

In the case of aquaculture, the risk of the antibiotics spreading beyond the farm and creating a large community of antibiotic-resistant bacteria is larger than on land-based livestock farms. Studies have found that approximately 80 percent of antibiotics administered through feed are excreted or otherwise released into the aquatic environment.[138] Given that most fish farms release their partially-treated wastewater into adjacent major waterways or are in the oceans themselves, these antibiotics can spread far beyond their initial source at sub-therapeutic doses that dramatically increase the risk of creating antimicrobial resistance.

ENVIRONMENTAL DEGRADATION

Beyond the threats to human health posed by antibiotic-resistant bacteria, aquaculture is also a major contributor to the degradation of the environment surrounding the farms. Across Asia, shrimp farming has become a lucrative business, but shrimp aquaculture at such a massive scale, comes with a cost. In this case, one major cost is mangrove trees.

---

137 Hansa Y. Done, Arjun K. Venkatesan, and Rolf U. Halden, "Does the Recent Growth of Aquaculture Create Antibiotic Resistance Threats Different from Those Associated with Land Animal Production in Agriculture?" *The AAPS Journal* 17, no. 3 (2015): 513–24.

138 Felipe C. Cabello et al., "Antimicrobial Use in Aquaculture Re-Examined: Its Relevance to Antimicrobial Resistance and to Animal and Human Health," *Environmental Microbiology* 15, no. 7 (2013): 1917–42.

Mangroves grow in the brackish water of estuaries along tropical coastlines around the world. These forests provide a critical ecosystem for young aquatic organisms to grow in safety, create a buffer zone that minimizes coastal erosion and protects coastal communities from storms, and store more than four times as much carbon dioxide as rainforests per pound![139]

Coastal aquaculture is responsible for the loss of over 10 percent of the world's mangrove forests, primarily in Thailand, Indonesia, Ecuador, Vietnam, and Bangladesh, and further degradation of more than a third of remaining mangrove forests in these regions.[140]

These coastal and marine aquaculture farms also introduce large volumes of nutrients into the waterways. Through the accumulation and degradation of unconsumed feed pellets and waste, these nutrients can cause dead zones as algae grow rapidly in the presence of so many nutrients and consume all the oxygen in the water.[141] Recently, these dead zones have been appearing around Tasmanian and Norwegian salmon farms,[142,143] demonstrating that even some of the

---

139 Daniel Donato et al., "Mangroves among the most carbon-rich forests in the tropics," *Nature Geoscience* 4 (2011): 293-297.

140 Nathan Thomas et al., "Distribution and Drivers of Global Mangrove Forest Change, 1996–2010," *PLOS ONE* 12, no. 6 (2017).

141 Monique Mancuso, "Effects of Fish Farming on Marine Environment," *Journal of Fisheries Science* 9, no. 3 (2015): 89–90.

142 Emily Fisher, "Love Salmon? Listen Up," Ocean, Smithsonian Institution, December 2010.

143 Wes Young, "Tassal's Second Dead Zone in Macquarie Harbour," Environment Tasmania, 2019.

best-managed aquaculture systems in the world are creating broad negative impacts on the environment.

CULTURED SEAFOOD IS A UNIQUELY POWERFUL OPPORTUNITY

When faced with the options of optimizing existing systems for limited gain or developing a new source of seafood, we must consider: Which path presents the opportunity to do the most good and has the highest potential impact? Because of the myriad negative externalities of both wild catch and aquaculture, cultured seafood demonstrates tremendous opportunity for a better, more sustainable alternative.

Why does seafood present a more compelling opportunity for creating outsized impact than some of the other applications of cellular agriculture that we have explored so far?

One of the primary factors is that the seafood industry as a whole is facing an intractable crisis. Though many in the industry hoped that the rapid growth of aquaculture could help to meet the growing demand for seafood and allow the ocean fisheries to recover, fisheries around the world continue to be in serious decline. This problem has reached an inflection point—one that will help to drive much-needed change.

PATH DEPENDENCE IN SEAFOOD

That inflection point creates opportunity for the introduction of cultured seafood. Like many old industries, the seafood sector is path dependent. It has developed an incredibly complex supply chain over the last century; millions of producers supply their catch or harvest to processors, who then ship the seafood to exporters and distributors for delivery to markets and restaurants.

In this case, however, that path dependence can work to the advantage of the cultured seafood innovators.

This supply chain complexity has almost entirely separated the suppliers from the businesses that package, transport, and process the seafood. According to industry insiders, these seafood processors, transporters, and packagers are happy to source any product their customers want to buy. As plant-based seafood, cultured seafood, and traditional seafood can all be used as inputs into their existing infrastructure, this creates an opportunity for cultured seafood companies to fit into the existing supply chain.

If cultured seafood companies can develop their own products successfully, companies within the existing supply chain are ready and willing to buy and distribute their products. That is the power of accounting for path dependency when launching a Transformational Technology.

SOLUTION CONCENTRATION IN SEAFOOD

But what will those initial products be? Unlike cultured beef, pork, or poultry, where the decision is which of a few cuts of meat to culture, cultured seafood startups are spoiled for choice. We could eat over twenty-seven thousand known aquatic species, more than a hundred of which are routinely consumed by different cultures around the world.[144] That broad species variety means that cultured seafood has a far lower solution concentration than all other applications of cellular agriculture that have been developed to date.

The low solution concentration in cultured seafood dramatically reduces the likelihood that multiple companies are duplicating their efforts by working to produce similar products in parallel. That means more of their resources can be spent on novel work. The marginal impact of each dollar and hour spent also has a higher potential impact. Even if twenty companies were formed to produce cultured seafood, each one could develop a different species with a global market opportunity greater than one billion dollars. That's how big the market opportunity is in seafood and why the low solution concentration works to the advantage of entrepreneurs who choose to work in this area.

TECHNICAL ADVANTAGES OF CULTURED SEAFOOD

Cultured seafood also benefits from a key technical advantage that most cellular agriculture companies do not have: seafood includes animals of varying structural complexity whose value is not determined by the complexity of their tissues.

Seafood encompasses a broad range of organisms, from lower-order organisms like clams and mussels (bivalves), to crabs and octopuses (mollusks), to high-order organisms like salmon and grouper (cartilaginous fish). These taxa

---

144 "Seafood Handbook," SeafoodSource, Diversified Communications, 2020.

of organisms have tissues of varying complexities, meaning that some seafood will be technically easier to produce, while more complex tissues will require new technologies to successfully achieve. And while not every technique will be transferable between species, it is highly likely that the majority of the knowledge base developed from the first cultured seafood products, will speed the introduction of more complex future products. For cultured seafood startups, the obvious benefit is that they may be able to bring a less complex product to market, and begin generating revenue, faster than their cultured meat colleagues.

Further, many of these low-order, less complex species are high-value seafood products that have large markets, making them viable initial products for cultured seafood companies to bring to market first. For most land-based livestock, the highest value cuts of meat tend to be thick, marbled, texturally complex tissues. In seafood, numerous low-structure organisms and products have high market value and sufficient demand. This lucky happenstance enables cultured seafood startups to follow a principle for success that we will discuss in Chapter eighteen: transformative disruption starts top-down. Thus, while cultured beef companies are making a less structured, low-value burger product and working toward a high-value Wagyu beef steak, a cultured seafood company can start with a high-value but low-structure crab cake, fish maw (swim bladder), or surimi (fish purée).

Peter Diamandis, founder of the XPrize Foundation and Singularity University and noted futurist, frequently discusses the power of convergence of trends. Because of the convergence of trends, Diamandis notes, "the world is getting faster, and the power [we] have to change the world is getting greater."[145] In this case, the convergence of principles for success in cultured seafood is just as powerful as a force for maximizing the potential for impact.

CULTURING SEAFOOD

In spite of this confluence of fortuitous conditions, only a handful of companies pursuing cultured seafood remain today.

Finless Foods was one of the first cultured seafood startups to launch. For its initial product launch, it is pursuing bluefin tuna, a species that is under serious threat of overfishing and which is enjoyed in low-structured forms like surimi.

Wild Type is seeking to bring cultured salmon to market, focusing on a high-value fish and betting that it can develop the technology to produce the structure required for a filet.

Shiok Meats, the first cultured seafood startup in Southeast Asia, is developing cultured shrimp. Shrimp is a relatively high-value for a commodity product and is served in low-structured form in several foods, including the dumplings that the company demonstrated in 2019.

Blue Nalu is developing yellowtail tuna, another moderate-value fish, and demonstrated its ability to produce chunks

145 Vanessa Bates Ramirez, "Why the Future Is Arriving Faster Than You Think," Singularity Hub, August 22, 2018.

of fish, much like you would see in a fish taco, in a variety of foods.

Avant Meats is initially focusing on fish maw, a specialty product with significant demand in Asia. As a number of fish are killed specifically for their swim bladders, this cultured fish maw will offer a viable alternative to harvesting larger fish specimens for a single body part.

Umami Meats, the startup I co-founded, is developing a range of cultured seafood products based upon a novel formulation for low-cost growth factors. The growth factor product will accelerate the development of the field by lowering production costs and enable the cost-effective production of numerous products across a range of aquatic species.

The work of these companies shows incredible promise given their short existence and highlights just how great an impact cultured seafood will have once the products reach the market.

PART IV

PRINCIPLES FOR SUCCESS WITH TRANSFORMATIVE TECHNOLOGIES

CHAPTER 9

INTRODUCTION
TO PRINCIPLES

"Every game has principles that successful players master to achieve winning results. So does life. Principles are ways of successfully dealing with the laws of nature or the laws of life. Those who understand more of them and understand them well know how to interact with the world more effectively than those who know fewer of them or know them less well."

RAY DALIO

We only need to look at what was promised by futuristic advertisements, science fiction, and cartoons like *The Jetsons* to see the gap between what technology could enable and what we have today. On the path from the conception of a transformative solution to the development of the enabling technology to the commercialization of the product, something went wrong that derailed the sci-fi future and yielded our present circumstances and challenges.

And while history does not often repeat itself, it does rhyme. So, we can look to the historical examples of the commercialization of prior Transformative Technologies to identify the common failure modes and the strategies for success.

STACKING THE DECK

The path to scaling a Transformative Technology company and succeeding in achieving durable impact on an intransigent problem is anything but straightforward. Of the entrepreneurs that set off down this path, only a small handful end up succeeding. The impact of their successes is so great that it often results in a massive transformation of our society and creates periods of abundance where there was once scarcity.

Given the impact of these successes, I sought to understand why some companies were successful where others were not. I wondered whether their methods could be distilled to increase the odds of success for future entrepreneurs with similarly audacious aspiration.

Though the path to commercializing and scaling these solutions was somewhat different for each company, it stands to reason that a set of principles can be applied to the problem of how to scale Transformative Technologies. Identifying, defining, and disseminating these principles could encourage many more entrepreneurs to pursue startups that seek to solve our Big Intractable Problems and increase their odds of success.

If entrepreneurship is the avenue of the highest leverage for individuals to create a transformative impact in the world today, then one of the best avenues for increasing that lever-age is to identify a set of principles that can increase these entrepreneurs' chances of success. For entrepreneurs, the lever is the technology they are using to solve the problem while the fulcrum is the strategy they use to tackle that prob-lem. Thus, we can maximize entrepreneurs' leverage by pro-viding them with a roadmap of proven strategies that will enable them to implement and scale their solutions to our biggest, most challenging problems.

Given the multitude of Big Intractable Problems we face over the next twenty to thirty years, developing a framework for identifying Transformative Technologies early and hastening their commercialization to solve these problems is of para-mount importance. By teaching founders the principles and frameworks that have led to past success, we enable them to create maximal leverage of their time and ingenuity.

COMPANIES THAT MAXIMIZE LEVERAGE SHARE SIMILAR TRAITS

In my quest to discover what it is that enables some Trans-formative Technology companies to succeed and others to fail, I have studied dozens of these companies. I read their public statements, watched their presentations, studied their patents and market-entry strategies, and interviewed some of their leaders and employees. This was a difficult task, partic-ularly because most companies and their leadership do not publicly share their deepest insights about their industries, their businesses, and their strategy.

Some were surprisingly open about divulging their points of view about what it takes to succeed. I also discovered that it is possible to elucidate the principles behind a company's success by examining what products they launch, where they choose to develop core competencies, and how they engage with others in their industry.

A number of apparent similarities exist between the strategies and actions of failed Transformative Technology companies that provide a strong indication of what does not work when building a company seeking to create high impact on Big Intractable Problems. The strategies and principles these companies applied are notably different from the methods used by more traditional startups that are solving less complex, entangled problems.

Building a startup into a successful company is difficult. Building a successful Transformative Technology startup that achieves impact at scale is *tremendously difficult.*

A Transformative Technology startup must overcome all the usual startup challenges while also navigating additional technical and regulatory risk that most other startups never encounter. In addition, Transformative Technology startups often face a more difficult path to market than traditional consumer or enterprise startups because of the time and additional capital required to advance the technology, develop a viable first product, and obtain regulatory clearance.

In spite of these additional hurdles these entrepreneurs face, they must continue to pursue these startups because of the impact they can have on Big Intractable Problems if they succeed. I personally believe that the more entrepreneurs that choose to work on solving important problems, the better chance we have of creating a more abundant future for humanity.

I wrote this book to help increase the number of people working to solve Big Intractable Problems *and* to increase their odds of success. To that end, I synthesized what I learned from my exploration and conversations with founders, employees, investors, and researchers and developed a set of principles for success in Transformative Technology.

Companies whose strategy and business models are built upon these principles are more likely to be successful than those that do not. Luck, founder background, and a number of other factors contribute heavily to the success or failure of a startup. But following these principles, can stack the odds in founders' favor and make their Transformative Technology company more resilient to the challenges that lie ahead on the path to realizing large-scale impact.

The following are the ten principles for success that I have distilled from my research. In the following chapters, we will explore each of these principles, how they have been successfully used in the past, and how entrepreneurs can use them to create impact themselves.

THE PRINCIPLES FOR SUCCESS WITH TRANSFORMATIVE TECHNOLOGIES:

1. Choose the Right Problem
2. Learn to See Exponentials
3. Reason from First Principles (Rather Than by Analogy)
4. Consider Solution Concentration
5. Recognize the Value of Ideas
6. Account for Path Dependence
7. Start with Scale in Mind
8. Harness Vertical Integration as The Great Equalizer
9. Enter the Market Top-down
10. Build the Machine That Makes the Machine

The goal is to place each of these principles in a context that makes its implementation clear. Often the discussion of these principles will explore stories that highlight how prior Transformative Technology companies relied upon them to build strategic advantages or to identify opportunities that others missed.

Many Transformative Technology startups are still relatively early in their journey to achieve impact commensurate with their missions. They may fall short of that impact for one reason or another or they may go on to become more successful than any of us can imagine. Either way, their future performance should not be the sole measure of whether these principles worked for them.

Each of the companies included in the upcoming chapters have already achieved significant success in bringing a Transformative Technology to market, building a product that solves important problems, and surviving the long journey that killed many companies that were just like them. For these companies, these principles for success enabled them to overcome the odds, and provided the opportunity to create impact on a planetary scale through their work.

CHAPTER 10

PRINCIPLE I: CHOOSE THE RIGHT PROBLEM

—

"Successful problem solving requires finding the right solution to the right problem. We fail more often because we solve the wrong problem than because we get the wrong solution to the right problem."

RUSSELL L. ACKOFF

Unsurprisingly, the first principle to building a successful Transformative Technology company is choosing the right problem to work on. Though personal traits like perseverance and grit are frequently mentioned as keys to success in entrepreneurship, working hard and overcoming adversity can only take you so far. This is often true for startups that are solving problems that do not actually exist or trying to make a product successful by brute force when it is clear that the product is not solving the problem well.

A KEY IN SEARCH OF A LOCK

Starting with a solution in mind rather than a challenging problem to solve is like holding a key without knowing what door to unlock. You could easily spend years trying your key on every door you can find without finding the right door. Even with the best of intentions, if you find a problem that you can solve with your technology, you are unlikely to have the highest impact you could have had if you had started from the problem. Rather than starting with the key, find the door you want to open, understand what the right key would look like, and then develop that key.

"It sounds obvious to say you should only work on problems that exist," says Paul Graham, founder of renowned startup accelerator Y Combinator. "And yet, by far the most common mistake startups make is to solve problems no one has."[146] Returning to the door analogy, you could plausibly start with a key for which no door exists. You could have a product based on a Transformative Technology that still does not provide a useful solution to any problem. This is a real risk for those who try to build a company by solving a problem that they have personally experienced.

As we saw in the chapter on Big Intractable Problems, the common advice from Silicon Valley is to choose a problem you have and develop a solution you would use. This method of problem-solving is humorously referred to as "dogfooding," a play on the phrase "eating your own dog food" that describes entrepreneurs or companies using their own products personally. Amusing references to dog food aside, there

---

146 Paul Graham, "How to Get Startup Ideas," Paul Graham, November 2012.

are a number of reasons why solving your own problems is not the best way to build a company that has a high impact on Big Intractable Problems.

THE PROBLEM WITH "DOGFOODING"

The first challenge with choosing problems that happen to be personally salient is that it may cause us to overlook some of the most important and challenging problems of our time. As Effective Altruism puts it, "Given that most interventions seem to have low impact, we're likely to focus on something that is not very impactful if we don't pick carefully."[147] And as much as we would like to consider ourselves unique, the problems that are most readily apparent to us are likely also obvious to others like us who may be developing solutions. This situation can lead to very high solution concentration for problems that are low impact but experienced by many people.

Thus, the way to find the important problems we should spend our time on is to carefully consider a number of problems and to evaluate our ability to create an impactful solution to solve them. Using the framework established in the Big Intractable Problems chapter, we can evaluate problems as we discover and research them and build a comparative list of problems rated by their scale, difficulty, and impact of resolution.

---

147 Centre for Effective Altruism, "Introduction to Effective Altruism," Effective Altruism, June 22, 2016.

FOUNDER-PROBLEM FIT

Then, the process comes down to choosing the problem that is most compelling to you personally from that list. The problem may still be compelling because you experienced it personally, but now you have validation that the problem is sufficiently large and impactful rather than pursuing it exclusively for personal reasons. You may also find that a problem is a high priority for you because something in your prior experience, skill set, technical background, or industry knowledge gives you a unique insight into the problem. In startups, this is sometimes referred to as **founder-problem fit.**

Selecting a problem that is a good fit for your background and interests is an important aspect of doing the most good you can with your time and resources. Building a Transformative Technology company that has a real impact is a monumental task. Success will require a deep-rooted intrinsic motivation that can only exist when you are working on something you believe in deeply.

As Richard Hamming, a noted mathematician at Bell Labs, posited, "If what you are doing is not important, and if you don't think it is going to lead to something important, why are you at Bell Labs working on it?"[148]

---

148 Richard Hamming, 'You and Your Research' (Speech, Bell Communications Research Colloquium Seminar, 7 March 1986).

ON THE VALUE OF TIME

When identifying high-priority problems to work on, a question that often arises is one of timeliness. If we take the long view of important problems, that some problems may be important but transient becomes apparent—that is, they will not last for a long period of time, such as a generation—while others are likely to persist until a solution emerges. The question is: Does focusing on the transient problem that is important now create greater impact than prioritizing the long-term problem?

On the one hand, if the problem that only impacts the present is sufficiently intractable, it may set us on a track to a more negative in the future. On the other hand, the future is likely to be much bigger than the present, as there could be far more people in the future than just the current generation. That would imply that ensuring the future goes well in the long-term is the best way to positively impact the greatest number of people. This concept is called **long-termism**. In this context, working on the problem that only impacts the present, but is inherently transient, is only the best choice when that problem is Big or Intractable enough to potentially alter the trajectory of humanity toward a much darker future.

Unfortunately, the dominant global economic theory proposes exactly the opposite approach to long-termism.

Economic theory, as it applies to decision making, values short-term capital and returns over long-term value creation. This principle is captured in the concept of **discounting**. In essence, discounting involves applying a discount rate to future earnings relative to those same earnings realized today.

A business that earned five thousand dollars three years from now would value that sale less than a five thousand-dollar sale today. Why? Because if you earned the money today, you could invest it or otherwise use the money to create additional value. If you earn it three years from now, you have lost the potential gains you would have made had you deployed that money today.

While discounting is logical in a limited capacity in economics, this concept has been misapplied to everything from environmental costs of business to human impacts. Governments, companies, and individuals make decisions in which we value the present output over any future value creation or negative cost. Climate change is a textbook example of this phenomenon. The science is extraordinarily clear about the perils to future generations if we continue down our current path. Yet, we overweigh the potential short-term impacts on economic stability too much to make changes at the scale and pace necessary to mitigate harm in the near future. So, we continue burning fossil fuels at a prodigious rate in spite of our knowledge that we are mortgaging our future to maintain our present.

Economics has taught us to *discount our future.*

If the reason why we cannot discount human lives and environmental impact isn't clear, consider the following. If a person is born thirty years from now, should their life be valued any less than a person born today? Should we value the future person's potential any less than a person alive today? If things go well, many more people will likely live in the future than live in the present or in our past. If each of those lives is not individually worth less than a current life, then the future, taken holistically, is worth more than the present.

BALANCING THE PRESENT AND THE FUTURE

One of the sectors in which we have a number of problems that are both urgent in the short-term and likely to negatively impact our long-term future is the food and agriculture sector. In the short-term, we currently face the challenge of feeding ten billion people within thirty years with diminishing available land and freshwater resources. This would be a challenging problem on its own, as it requires a 70 percent increase in global protein production and a 56 percent increase in total calorie production.[149]

In this case, however, the short-term challenge is compounded by long-term problems like climate change and biodiversity loss. Given the significance of the long-term consequences for humanity of the broader problems like climate change, even people who want to address the short-term problems—like producing enough protein to feed ten billion people—will need to be conscious of how they will impact the long-term problem as well. When viewed through this longer-term lens, the problem of "increasing protein production by 78 percent in thirty years" becomes the more complex problem of "increasing protein production by 78 percent in thirty years while decreasing the total climate impact of that production by 50 percent."

---

149 Tim Searchinger et al., "Creating a Sustainable Food Future," (World Resources Institute, 2018).

Rather than discounting the future, we should be taking it into account and weighing the problems we choose to work on based on how solving them will impact the future. Given the need to solve problems that we actually experience today, this means that the best problems to work on are those for which solving the problem will both improve the current situation and create the best foreseeable future for humanity in the long-term.

CHAPTER 11

PRINCIPLE II: LEARN TO SEE EXPONENTIALS

"The greatest shortcoming of the human race is our inability to understand the exponential function."

ALBERT ALLEN BARTLETT

From identifying a problem to solve to developing a strategic plan for the company, understanding exponentials is a critical skill for each stage of building a Transformative Technology company. The evolution and maturation of Transformative Technologies most often follow an exponential curve. Viewing these technologies through this lens can provide insight into how they can be used to create outsized impact. Without an ability to understand exponential trends, leading a Transformative Technology company through the market changes, challenges, and surprises that will inevitably arise along the journey of building the business will be nearly impossible.

To see the difference between a company under the leadership of a CEO that understands exponential trends compared to one who does not, we only need to look at the way Apple functioned under Steve Jobs versus Tim Cook. Under Jobs' leadership, Apple released two products that fundamentally changed the way we use technology in our daily lives: the iPod and the iPhone. While not every application of those devices was truly Transformative, some of the things these devices allowed us to do helped solve Big Intractable Problems in our lives. Apple seemed to have a sense for exponential trends in technologies and markets, and it leveraged that knowledge to launch products that it felt like met a real need.

Since Tim Cook replaced Steve Jobs at the helm, Apple appears to have lost the foresight that made it so successful at launching new products on the back of Transformative Technology. As a result, its product launches have taken a turn for the pedestrian. Instead of a touchscreen that was 10x better than what it was replacing, we now expect the iPhone n+1 to replace the iPhone n. This is innovation that Peter Thiel, co-founder of PayPal and author of *Zero to One*, would describe as 1-to-n. It is iterating on a known formula to achieve a larger scale rather than the 0-to-1 innovations that are transformative in nature and signal a change in paradigm.

IDENTIFYING EXPONENTIALS

If being able to understand exponentials is so important, then we must first establish how to identify them in the first place. Only once we can see exponential trends can we learn to analyze them to understand what they are telling us about problems and how to solve them.

To explore how we can identify exponentials, let us consider a key trend that has emerged: climate change.

Based on historical data spanning over one million years, we know that global carbon dioxide (CO_2) levels have fluctuated between 180 and 290 parts per million (ppm) in the atmosphere.[150] These fluctuations usually occurred over one-hundred-thousand-year cycles, with changes of just 100 ppm moving the Earth in and out of ice ages.[151]

So, when we detected a continuous increase in atmospheric CO_2 above the 290-ppm level, scientists who were observing these phenomena started to take notice. Over time, atmospheric CO_2 was clearly increasing exponentially, and that increase was closely correlated with human activity and fossil fuel consumption.[152] The shift from the expected cyclic trend is what first alerted us to the potential for humans to change the global climate.

Studying the exponential increase in CO_2 levels has enabled scientists to project the future increase in global temperature. The Earth is a complex system with many feedback loops that can increase or mitigate trends such as global temperature changes. By studying the exponential increase in CO_2 and comparing the observed effects to the expected effects, we

150 "Graphic: The relentless rise of carbon dioxide," NASA Global Climate Change, NASA, accessed 7 January 2020.

151 Nicola Jones, "How the World Passed a Carbon Threshold and Why It Matters," Yale Environment 360, Yale School of Forestry & Environmental Studies, January 26, 2017.

152 Susan Solomon et al., *Climate Change 2007: Working Group I: The Physical Science Basis* (New York, NY: Cambridge University Press, 2007).

can discern some important trends that highlight non-obvious problems and alert us to issues we should work on. For example, the current UN report on climate change shows that 94 percent of the warming effect is being absorbed by the oceans.[153] Effectively, our data tells us the oceans are mitigating the heating effects that we would otherwise feel more robustly.

Water is excellent at absorbing thermal energy, but at some point, the oceans will reach their heat-sink capacity and no longer effectively buffer these warming effects. Indeed, the impacts of absorbing so much heat will also be catastrophic for marine plants and animals. Based on this trend, it is even more urgent to develop technologies to mitigate global warming than we previously thought.

We can also discern that the oceanic effects of climate change will become significant and cause damage more quickly than effects we will see on land due to the more rapid heating and accompanying acidification. The more rapid onset of these effects on the oceans makes work that supports climate resilience and mitigation for the oceans more of a priority than we may initially have thought.

In this way, identifying exponential trends and the potential impacts of these deviations from the "normal" can be powerful tools for those trying to determine which Big Intractable Problems should be prioritized.

---

153 Ibid.

STARTUP TIMING

In effect, these questions about prioritization are also questions of timing. Startups are often told that timing can be a more important factor of success than nearly any other. This can be seen in the graveyard of startups that entered the market too early or that tried to leverage technology that was not developed enough to succeed in the market. In both cases, timing the market and technology development curve is essential to building an impactful company.

Common dialogue around startup timing implies that it is a nebulous subject that is difficult to understand. however, exponential trends shed light on how to identify the moments when the timing is right to solve a particular problem and commercialize a specific Transformative Technology. When examining the exponential trends impacting a given field, look for trends that are making a problem more urgent to solve or trends that are making a Transformative Technology increasingly viable.

While exponential trends do not have true inflection points, minimum thresholds along the exponential curve must be met for companies to be successful when market forces are at play. The problem a company is solving must be pressing enough to draw immediate interest from customers. Similarly, the technologies a company is working with must be sufficiently developed so they can build a viable business before they run out of money.

Venture capital firm Andreessen Horowitz has recently released its take on this concept of timing, which it calls "product-zeitgeist fit."[154] Its assessment is that developing products that "ride the cultural wave of the moment" is one way founders can stack the odds of success in their favor. It is an interesting concept, and it outlines a number of characteristics that may be helpful to a number of founders.

The idea of chasing what is in vogue seems like a poor way to make sure you are solving important problems. While "riding the wave" of cultural and technological phenomena can help good businesses to grow faster, what is in vogue today can easily fall by the wayside tomorrow, taking the public support, investor funding, and customer interest with it. Rather than planning around what is popular at any given moment, instead strive to build a business that solves a Big Intractable Problem by the most efficient path possible.

TIMING THE MARKET OR MAKING THE MARKET?

In fact, many Transformative Technology startups launch *before* the zeitgeist sets in. Looking in from the outside, they appear prescient. What did they see that others missed? What allowed them to come to market before anyone realized the problem they are solving is interesting?

These companies did not time the market, they created it. Often, these companies are the ones that show us that certain stagnant or uninteresting industries are actually home to Big Intractable Problems. They are the first to recognize

---

154 D'Arcy Coolican, "Product Zeitgeist Fit," Andreessen Horowitz, December 9, 2019.

that relevant Transformative Technologies have matured sufficiently to provide potential solutions to those problems.

Before the emergence of Beyond Meat and Impossible Foods, most would have declared alternative proteins an uninteresting and stagnating category. There had been no major innovation since the bean burger, Tofurkey, and Soylent after all. What real problem needed solving, anyway?

These companies emerged with a clear vision: mitigate the impact of meat production on climate change and animal welfare by producing plant-based meat alternatives that appealed to meat-eaters. In stark contrast to those who came before them, their goal was explicitly to produce a product that closely mimicked actual animal meat. In doing so, they would convince meat-eaters to eat their products enough to impact the total amount of meat produced. Now, an alternative protein explosion is underway because these companies demonstrated that they could help solve a Big Intractable Problem (animal agriculture driving climate change) with new technology that didn't exist a few years earlier.

Seeing the exponential trends hit a tipping point that created an opportunity helped Beyond Meat and Impossible Foods to recognize the opportunity that was developing before anyone else.

Identifying exponential trends and building impactful businesses on them is not unique to the food industry. This technique has helped a number of Transformative Technology companies to form with the goal of solving a Big Intractable Problem when many others thought they were crazy, that there would not be a market for their products, or that the technology was not advanced enough.

THE FIRST SUCCESSFUL AMERICAN CAR STARTUP IN A CENTURY

In the early 2000s, Elon Musk invested in Tesla Motors, a small and apparently unremarkable electric car company, eventually becoming the CEO. To those who weren't studying exponential trends for opportunities, it looked like a questionable investment. Paired with his decision to build a rocket company, many assumed Elon would be just another wealthy entrepreneur who would lose his money through poor investments and chasing after space.

Elon saw something that his detractors missed. He saw that the price of batteries had been falling exponentially since the early 1990s (Figure 7). He was able to predict that the exponential decline in the price of batteries would continue for many years, since the batteries were still far from their theoretical physical limits. These data points told Elon Musk that a unique opportunity was emerging for a company to successfully commercialize electric cars. If he could get the other parts of the business model correct, he could address a Big Intractable Problem by helping move the world to electric transportation.

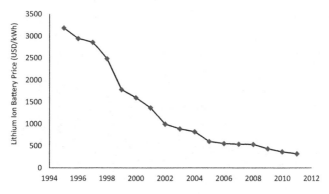

Figure 7. Price of Lithium Ion Batteries (1995-2011)[155]

In 2015, another exponential trend led Tesla to embark upon an unexpected, massive internal project. Since the company's founding, the price of batteries had continued to decrease exponentially, but demand for these batteries was also increasing exponentially thanks to the boom in consumer electronics. Tesla realized that battery production was just keeping up with demand and there would not be sufficient supply to keep up with the exponential demand growth from electric vehicles (Figure 8). So, Tesla did something unorthodox; it decided to build its own battery factory.

---

155 "Battery storage market to reach 240GW by 2030," Gas to Power Journal, February 6, 2015.

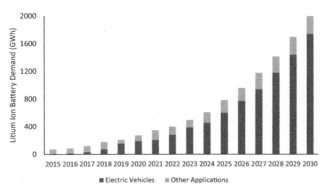

Figure 8. Projected Lithium Ion Battery Demand (2015-2030)[156]

The Gigafactory, as it has since been named, will produce enough batteries to maintain the supply Tesla requires as the company grows. While it seemed like a distraction to some public investors (especially the short-sellers), it has become clear in the time since construction began that battery supply would be a major constraint for Tesla's expansion if it had not built the Gigafactory.

Studying and understanding these exponential trends not only provided the insight that launched Tesla but helped the company's leadership set a forward-thinking strategy that will enable it to continue to pursue its mission.

SEEING THE FUTURE

We have seen that understanding exponential trends can be a powerful tool for us to identify opportunities to start Transformative Technology companies and to focus our strategy

---

156 BloombergNEF, "Electric Vehicle Outlook 2019," Bloomberg, accessed November 13, 2019.

to best address the Big Intractable Problems we set out to solve. Identifying these exponential trends is often a case of looking for them explicitly and asking ourselves if an exponential trend is emerging when data does not fit a linear or cyclical pattern.

When trying to identify exponentials that point to opportunities to solve Big Intractable Problems, start by looking at accelerating trends in industries that are needed for our survival and the continuation of modern society—food, agriculture, energy, and transportation to name a few. Ask yourself questions like, "What new problems are likely to emerge as a result of this exponential trend?" and "What problems are likely to be made worse by the trends I have seen?" Then, define what a viable solution to those problems would look like.

Seek to identify emerging Transformative Technologies that could be uniquely suited to addressing these problems in a way that was not possible until recently. By comparing these technologies with the list of problems you have generated, you can begin to develop ideas for companies that can address some of the most pressing problems of our time.

THE FUTURE OF FOOD

Let's look at how that process of exponential trend evaluation would work for the food and agriculture industry. The human population is continuing to grow exponentially and will reach nearly ten billion people by 2050. That exponential increase in people to feed will drive a need to produce proportionally more food.

Further, the number of people across the world who are moving into the middle class and adopting more Western diets is also growing exponentially. This will further increase demand for food, and animal protein in particular. These exponential trends will drive increased global consumption that will far outweigh the impacts of stabilizing or decreasing per capita consumption in late-stage economies like the US and Western Europe.

How do the trends on the production side impact our insights from the consumption trends? Our production of greenhouse gases is continuing an exponential growth trend dating back to the Industrial Revolution. Agricultural practices contribute nearly one-sixth of these total emissions.[157] To keep global warming below 2°C, we will need to reduce the carbon dioxide output of agriculture by 67 percent while increasing production to feed ten billion people.[158] Further, animal agriculture consumes several times more resources per calorie produced than plant agriculture.[159] Reducing our reliance on animals would make this exponential trend easier to manage.

When it comes to resource use, global freshwater consumption and land use for intensive agriculture are both growing rapidly. Obviously, this cannot continue indefinitely: we will eventually run out of available land and freshwater. Before

---

157 P.J. Gerber et al., *Tackling climate change through livestock* (Rome: Food and Agriculture Organization of the United Nations, 2013).

158 Tim Searchinger et al., *World Resources Report: Creating a Sustainable Food Future,* ed. Emily Matthews (World Resources Institute, 2019).

159 Janet Ranganathan, "Animal-based Foods are More Resource-Intensive than Plant-Based Foods," World Resources Institute, April 2016.

we reach that limit, however, we will move far beyond what is sustainable, consuming resources in a way that will cause a problem in the long-term if not the very short-term. Among other human activities, our agricultural practices are also driving exponential increases in the number of species at risk of extinction.[160] Collectively, these production trends indicate that successful solutions in agriculture will need to reduce the reliance on animals, reduce freshwater and land use, and reduce the impact of agriculture on biodiversity loss if they are to be successful.

So, what might a solution look like? Let's look at the exponential trends in technologies that could be applied to these problems we have identified prior. The number of demonstrated applications for targeted genetic modification and the number of easy-to-use solutions for these technologies is growing exponentially. The 3D printing sector is also growing rapidly, if not exponentially. Further, the number of companies developing commercial expertise in biotechnology and tissue engineering is also growing near-exponentially.

By evaluating the exponential trends impacting the consumer and producer, as well as the technologies that are relevant to the industry, we can identify opportunities that are not readily apparent to those who are not searching for them. Collectively, these trends indicate opportunities where these technologies intersect, like the emerging field of cellular agriculture. These intersections of exponential trends are

160 S. Díaz et al., *IPBES: Summary for policymakers of the global assessment report on biodiversity and ecosystem services of the Intergovernmental Science-Policy Platform on Biodiversity and Ecosystem Services* (Born, Germany: IPBES secretariat, 2019).

where we are likely to identify Big Intractable Problems to solve and new Transformative Technologies upon which to build our solutions.

CHAPTER 12

PRINCIPLE III: REASON FROM FIRST PRINCIPLES (NOT BY ANALOGY)

"The first principle is that you must not fool yourself and you are the easiest person to fool."

RICHARD P. FEYNMAN

As useful as exponential trends are, they merely provide a frame of reference to understand the most important shifts happening in the world around us. They help us to identify things that will soon be vastly different than they are today so we can leverage that information for our benefit and the benefit of society. To understand how to use the information and trends we discern to make good decisions—in Transformative Technology businesses and in life—we have to learn to reason from first principles.

REASONING BY ANALOGY

Typically, we rely upon a thinking approach known as **reasoning by analogy** to evaluate new information that we come across and to make decisions. In effect, our brains evolved to reason by analogy most often because it allowed us to make use of our prior experience and inherited wisdom to quickly diagnose new situations. This was valuable for our ancestors who were constantly faced with new environments where they needed to make decisions that would ensure they were not attacked by predators and were able to find food. The context in which they existed didn't change very much, even over several generations, so there was tremendous value in adapting to this way of thinking.

Reasoning by analogy is a flawed lens for viewing a rapidly changing world. It leads us to try to fit new data to prior patterns, like linear or cyclic trends we have seen before, without first questioning whether the new information we are seeing actually fits the existing models that we have. As a basis for our thinking, reasoning by analogy can yield quick answers, but they may not always be the correct ones.

Can we discern the difference between a first-principles approach and an analogy-driven one? In general, we can't definitively tell the difference, though it can often become apparent by examining the type of innovation. Reasoning by analogy yields-to-many innovations: spreading a technology across industries or geographies, turning one local business into a global chain, and creating incremental improvements. In effect, reasoning by analogy will provide the insight that a proven idea can be optimized as a separate product for use across a number of industries.

Innovating by analogy leads to inventions like the combine harvester, a farming machine that combines the three existing processes of reaping, threshing, and winnowing into one step—all done by a single machine—that dramatically increases the efficiency of harvesting grain. All three of these technologies existed, and all three were mechanized, but the combination of technologies saved additional time and labor. The combine is a perfect example of a 1-to-many innovation that further increased efficiency by bringing an improved version of existing technologies to farms around the world.

Reasoning by analogy and using it as a frame for innovation is innately constraining. We are forcing information to fit into pre-conceived patterns, ignoring potential insights that do not fit this framework and narrowing the solution space unnecessarily. Analogy-based reasoning is like wearing sunglasses that tint everything we see, creating instances in which we see new trends but do not *observe* them in a way that we can act upon. To create groundbreaking innovations with Transformative Technologies and identify the Big Intractable Problems that others miss, we must start from first principles.

THE BASIS FROM WHICH A THING IS KNOWN

We cannot rely on reasoning by analogy to develop Transformative solutions, especially when the trends are exponential. Rather than starting with a model, we should start with data and observation, interrogate what we know, and then build a model that we can use for that set of knowledge. First principles provide a basis for achieving this goal.

First principles are the basic blocks of knowledge that are not based on underlying assumptions. Scientifically speaking, they are the fundamental concepts or assumptions on which a theory, system, or method is based. The concept of reasoning from first principles came about from the earliest philosophers who studied logic and thinking in Ancient Greece.

Plato was likely the first to introduce the concept of thinking from a basis of what is known, which he called **noesis**. In *The Republic*, he said noesis is the method by which one ascends from the cave of ignorance into the light of truth.[161] His student, Aristotle, put it more plainly: "[a first principle] is the first basis from which a thing is known."[162] Since then, first-principles thinking has become a method of understanding the world without being unduly influenced by the assumptions of those who came before us.

THE SCIENTIFIC METHOD

In the modern age, reasoning by first principles is an approach informed heavily by scientific disciplines. Indeed, the scientific method itself is based upon the ability to develop a hypothesis from observations and basic principles.

The process of reasoning from first principles begins by defining observations and isolating those facts that are known. The easiest method is to discern what physical or biological principles present fundamental limits and what is limited by some other factor. Then develop a series of hypotheses,

---

161 Plato, *Republic*, 514b-515e.

162 Aristotle, *Metaphysics*, 1013a14-15.

disprovable predictive statements, based on the information you have.

Ask yourself, "How can I disprove these hypotheses?" Then pursue those actions. If after serious effort you cannot disprove the hypothesis, then you have presumably arrived at a correct premise on which you can build in the future.

This is the basis of the scientific method.

Albert Einstein himself advocated for a similar effort to understand base fundamentals on which to build a solution. He famously said, "If I had an hour to solve a problem, I'd spend fifty-five minutes thinking about the problem and five minutes thinking about solutions."

While this approach may be ideal for scientific discovery, the framework we have discussed is somewhat vague and difficult to practically implement for those interested in applying Transformative Technologies to important problems. Yet, first-principles thinking is incredibly important for innovation. It allows us to innovate in clear leaps, rather than building incrementally on existing solutions.

Thinking from first principles requires us to break down a problem into its constituent parts and to ask what is truly known versus what is assumed to be true for each component. In doing so, we gain a far deeper understanding of the elements of the system, how the components connect, and how they interact to cause the desired result. We also gain a far more fundamental understanding of the problem space. We can then use this knowledge to develop new solutions based on functions that are not anchored in the current form of existing solutions.

THE POWER OF FIRST PRINCIPLES

A number of famous inventors and successful entrepreneurs have discussed the value they find in starting from first principles, from Peter Thiel and Elon Musk to Naval Ravikant, founder of AngelList, and Shane Parish, writer of the *Farnam Street* metacognition blog. The concept of thinking from first principles has also been applied by historical inventors and discoverers of great renown including Nikola Tesla, Richard Feynman, and Thomas Edison.

Johannes Gutenberg invented the printing press by using first principles to determine how the process of printing could be made more efficient. He combined the existing technology—movable type, paper, and ink—with the screw press, used to press grapes as part of making wine, to create the printing press. Movable type was not new; it had been used for nearly four centuries prior to the invention of the printing press.[163] But by seeking to improve function without being limited by the existing form, Gutenberg was able to adapt the constituent parts of technologies from different industries to create a revolutionary product. By understanding the fundamental inefficiencies in printing, Gutenberg created a transformative innovation that enabled the mass spread of written knowledge for the first time and changed the trajectory of human society.

---

163 Steven Johnson, *Where Good Ideas Come From: The Natural History of Innovation* (London: Penguin, 2010), 151-153.

USING FIRST PRINCIPLES

As useful as examining the world from the basis of first principles can be, we cannot view the world through this lens all the time. It would be far too time consuming, and we would largely replicate the work of those who have come before us. We should not blindly ignore the value of incredible knowledge we have at our fingertips.

Much of this knowledge has been validated through multiple sets of experiments and, in most instances, the theories are well-proven enough to be relied upon. We don't individually have time to prove to ourselves from first principles that Apollo 11 landed on the moon in 1969, that Earth is actually 4.5 billion years old, or that the half-life of uranium-238 is 740 million years. We would not have time to learn anything new if we spent all our time proving from first principles of which is already known.

Instead, we rely upon proxies that we respect—whether they are scientists, "experts," or knowledgeable thought leaders—to reach these conclusions. Even in the seventeenth century, Isaac Newton recognized, "If I have seen further it is by standing on the shoulders of Giants."

But we cannot rely on the experts for everything. Sometimes the experts are wrong.

So how do you know when to rely upon proxies and when to go down to first principles yourself? The best advice would be to go deep, down to first principles, when a decision is of high personal or strategic importance. If you are making a strategic choice that could easily kill your company if it turns out wrong, going to first principles makes sense. If you are making a decision that can be changed without tremendous consequence, choosing to spend the time on a first principles analysis becomes a time versus risk trade-off in which you have to determine if the risk taken is worth losing speed of decision-making.

Jeff Bezos refers to this as the two-door method of decision making.[164] Type 1 decisions are the near-irreversible, high-impact decisions where a deep analysis is valued over speed. Type 2 decisions are easily reversible and lower-risk because of it. Bezos argues for prioritizing speed in all cases except those Type 1 decisions where it is hard to reverse course. Essentially, you should use heuristics and proxies that enable fast decision-making when the consequences of making the decision are not of critical importance.

For most people, the problem is not that they using first principles too often. Most people do not go to first principles at all. Even worse, most people rely on a very small set of proxies for the vast majority of their information, increasing the likelihood that a failure of any of those proxies can lead them astray. The key is to find a way of alerting yourself of those instances in which you are faced with a Type 1 problem when you *should* conduct a first principles analysis. In these cases, recognizing that need in hindsight is not likely to be fruitful.

---

164 Amazon, *1997 Letter to Shareholders*, (1997).

WHEN TO USE FIRST PRINCIPLES

The following recommendations can provide a useful guide for ensuring that you can identify those moments at which you should reason from first principles.

- **Always have a problem that you are reasoning through from first principles.** In our lives, we almost always have important problems to be solved, many of which cannot be addressed solely by relying on external proxies. Training the ability to make a reasoned judgment based on first principles is a valuable skill for its own sake, even more so given that you will be coming to rely upon it when you cannot trust external proxies.

- **Build a diverse set of proxies for your knowledge.** Relying upon a small set of proxies to build your worldview is dangerous. An information set lacking in diversity is easily skewed and that makes it difficult to know whether your proxies are reliable or are falling subject to groupthink.

- **Ensure that several of your proxies are in conflict at least some of the time.** Building a diverse set of proxies increases the likelihood that they will disagree with some frequency. The world is not black and white; true or false. Especially when it comes to important truths, the ones you *absolutely* want to be right about, there is often little consensus of information. When your proxies disagree, it is a good time to question your assumptions. If they never disagree, how are you to know that you should dig deeper?

Using this framework, you can build a system for gathering information that will enable you to understand when to rely on proxies and when you need to reason from first principles.

For the majority of decisions that fall into the Type 2 category and for which your proxies agree, trusting the proxies is rational and unlikely to cause significant problems. But when faced with a Type 1 decision, your proxies will likely be in conflict and signal that you should run a first-principles analysis.

In general, you will find reasoning from first principles to be most valuable when doing something challenging for the first time, when dealing with complexity, or when "common wisdom" appears flawed for a reason you cannot immediately identify.

Big Intractable Problems often present us with situations in which our proxies disagree. The information available about the scale and impact of these problems is often muddied. An agreed-upon solution that is known to be effective rarely exists. If it did, the problems would hardly be considered intractable.

The same is true for Transformative Technologies. Proxies will disagree about the maturity, cost, and viability of such technologies as solutions for these Big Intractable Problems. Those who seek to use these technologies to achieve a transformative impact on the world must be able to make decisions from first principles to develop the innovations and strategies that will enable them to succeed.

A PROCESS FOR FIRST PRINCIPLES REASONING

In truth, describing how to implement a first-principles analysis is fairly straightforward. Implementing the process successfully to develop a novel insight is where the complexity lies.

To reason from first principles to overcome an intellectual challenge, like developing Transformative Technology solutions to Big Intractable Problems, use this framework:

1. **Identify your objective.** Restructure the problem you seek to solve as an objective to be achieved. Define what a successful solution would accomplish in detail. This first step helps to reframe a problem in a way that encourages you to define specific characteristics of a solution rather than getting stuck on the various aspects of the problem.

2. **List the apparent obstacles.** Create a list of the obstacles that are preventing you from achieving your objective. Start with the most obvious obstacles, the ones that are front of mind and readily apparent to you. Then reconsider your initial concept of the ideal solution and think about what other challenges have to be overcome for that solution to exist.

3. **Question the underlying assumptions.** Review your list of obstacles and ask yourself what core assumptions you are making about the problem and its constituent obstacles. For example, why is a certain process step an obstacle to achieving your desired outcome? What is fundamentally causing the obstacle to persist? What are the underlying principles?

4. **Identify the first principles.** From your list of questions, you should start to be able to identify the first principles

that are at work in the situation you are analyzing. If you run into a roadblock, ask multiple iterations of questions to get at the core principles. Much like a young child, continuously asking "why?" until you get to the same answer works better than you might expect.

In deriving these first principles, the Socratic method is often recommended as a tool for opening the mind to things we would not normally notice. The Socratic method is a mode of argumentation that involves asking and answering questions to stimulate critical thought and reveal ideas and underlying assumptions. It relies upon asking questions to achieve one of six goals. The six modes of Socratic questions are those that are meant to:

- Clarify your thinking—*Why* do I think this is true?
- Challenge assumptions—*How* do I know this is true?
- Search for evidence—*How* can I support this assumption?
- Consider alternative perspectives—*What* is another way of thinking about this?
- Examine consequences and implications—*What* does it mean if I am wrong?
- Question the original questions—*Why* did I think that?

Asking questions from all six groups can help to identify first principles in a given situation. The Socratic method can also be used to analyze the first principles and develop your hypothesis. Once you have a hypothesis, you can use the Socratic method to think of a set of reasons your hypothesis might be wrong and to design a set of experiments to test each of those options.

That process of developing and testing a hypothesis using the Socratic method may look something like this:

1. **Develop a hypothesis.** Working from first principles, develop a hypothesis about how your system works and how you might achieve the objective. A hypothesis is essentially a predictive statement that can be disproven. The goal of the hypothesis is to come up with an idea for achieving your objective that you can directly test.

   If the hypothesis holds up to scrutiny, it presents a rational path forward. If not, you have quickly and efficiently eliminated a possible solution with minimal resources and effort. Following a course of action based on unproven conjecture will not benefit you, your team, or your supporters. Hypotheses can help maintain intellectual honesty and provide a sensible platform for testing assumptions.

2. **Ask follow-up questions.** These follow-up questions are effectively a thought experiment of how and why your hypothesis may be wrong. Think through how your hypothesis could be disproven and identify the core assumptions to be tested. Ranking them by estimated probability can help you determine which to test first.

3. **Test your hypothesis.** Based on the follow-up questions and the failure modes you identified, run tests to try to invalidate your hypothesis. If the hypothesis is disproven, question your data to understand why it failed. Then use that information to develop a new hypothesis. This is

essentially an iterative loop that repeats until the hypothesis is not disproven.

Once the hypothesis is not disproven by your set of tests, you have identified a viable path to achieving your objective. You can now repeat the process for the next challenge to be overcome.

This process of using a combination of first principles and the Socratic method to solve problems is incredibly effective. Teams can be trained to operate in this way and can then easily communicate the problems they face and what they are doing to overcome them. The first-principles framework is not just valuable when developing the initial idea for a Transformative Technology startup or identifying a Big Intractable Problem worth pursuing. It is useful for developing a strategic plan for these companies as they scale.

The development of complex technologies and scaling of companies seeking to solve big problems can be thought of as iterative exercises. For each hurdle in the path to success, break the overall challenge into its constituent parts and use the above process to solve one challenge at a time until you succeed.

We often rely upon existing conventions and use solutions and systems in their current forms without question. But once we accept these conventions, they limit our creativity and solution set. Be wary of the ideas you inherit. By working from first principles, we can identify an ever-compounding set of new solutions that increase efficiency and the likelihood of successfully achieving impact at scale.

CHAPTER 13

PRINCIPLE IV: CONSIDER SOLUTION CONCENTRATION

———

"If you only read the books that everyone else is reading, you can only think what everyone else is thinking."

HARUKI MURAKAMI

When launching a startup into an industry, it makes sense to consider the current state of that industry and to understand what other companies are working to solve your target problem. But founders must also develop a sense of the solution space—that is, the other solutions that were tried and failed and the current solutions under development.

Successfully commercializing Transformative Technologies is difficult, and the best founders recognize that they can benefit significantly from those that came before them. Founders who want to increase the odds of success have to be able to

PRINCIPLE IV: CONSIDER SOLUTION CONCENTRATION · 235

answer the questions: "Why will my solution solve this problem when so many others have failed?" and "What unique insight makes my approach better than the other solutions currently under development?"

Further, those founders who seek to maximize the impact their startup will have on their chosen problem must ensure that their solution is in fact unique in some way that makes it more likely to succeed. Otherwise, they are simply replicating effort and expending resources that could be used for higher-leverage activities. To find the answers to these questions, founders have to consider the solution concentration in their industry.

But what is solution concentration?

Broadly, **solution concentration** is a measure of how many companies are working to solve a particular problem in a similar way. At a deeper level, solution concentration is a tool that an entrepreneur can use to assess how crowded a particular market niche is based on the number of similar solutions being developed to address the specific problem and how well they are solving that problem.

How "crowded" a market segment is may not seem particularly relevant at first. After all, why should an entrepreneur worry about who else is in the market if they develop a solution that customers want to buy?

This rationale is fairly common in Silicon Valley, where it is not uncommon to see ten to fifteen startups get growth-stage investments to solve the same problem at the same time.

These companies then burn that capital in a race to achieve scale first and secure the dominant market position. After the remaining companies fizzle out, many in Silicon Valley will lament the "bubble" before looking for the next big thing.

This is not to suggest that only one or two companies should receive funding to solve a given problem. Competition in the market can be beneficial, and differences in strategy and execution may lead some companies to succeed where others fail with similar approaches. So how can we tell if a startup should target a given problem or if the crowded market will stack the odds against the startup, even if its Transformative Technology is much better than existing solutions?

MARKET CONCENTRATION AND POTENTIAL IMPACT

Almost no idea is brand new; most ideas have predecessors throughout history, often long before the technology existed to make them feasible. Further, when great, rapid advances in technology lead to the development of new Transformative Technologies, a number of companies often emerge to commercialize these technologies to solve important problems. Entrepreneurs considering how they can make the greatest impact on the world through their work must consider the solution concentration in these areas. Doing so will help to ensure that they are allocating their efforts and resources in a way that can maximize their positive impact if they are successful.

This idea of maximizing impact ties back to our earlier discussion about how the principles of Effective Altruism can be applied to entrepreneurship to maximize the expected outcome, both in terms of company success and impact on a Big Intractable Problem. In that discussion, one of the primary reasons for encouraging entrepreneurs to rationally analyze the problems most worth working on is that too many people work on problems they personally have. The result is an oversaturated market of undifferentiated solutions and an inefficient use of resources.

We often make these assessments intuitively when evaluating non-profit organizations. If we see ten soup kitchens in the same neighborhood all targeting the same group of food-insecure people, we would easily identify the duplication of effort and the inefficient allocation of resources. In fact, we would probably be able to identify complementary efforts, like organizations offering shelter or clothing, that would create a greater impact per dollar than ten soup kitchens. But for some reason, we tend to be blind to this level of duplication of effort when it comes to deciding what startup to launch and what problem to tackle.

As Transformative Technology entrepreneurs, one of our goals should be to maximize the impact we can have for the resources we expend. Startups often discuss this in terms of capital efficiency, but taking a broader view of whether we are spending time on the right problems can be even more impactful. Understanding how many others are trying to solve the same problem and why our unique approach creates a competitive advantage is critical to making this decision.

SOLUTION CONCENTRATION IN CULTURED MEAT

Consider the emerging cultured meat industry. Now, more than a dozen companies are working on cultured beef, a handful of companies are pursuing cultured chicken, and half a dozen companies are pursuing cultured seafood. New companies who think they have a novel solution for producing one of these products have to think about their unique competitive advantage to avoid a wasteful duplication of effort.

While it may seem like there are too many companies working in cellular agriculture, surely a number of unique technical approaches exist that would make good opportunities for new startups—if the startups can identify them. Compared to the plant-based foods sector, where over one hundred companies are competing to produce a better plant-based milk, cheese, or burger, the cultured meat sector is practically vacant.

THE COSTS OF CONCENTRATION

Historically, perhaps two to three companies achieve breakout success in any given sector and geography while the others either fail outright, are acquired, or remain quite small. In American poultry, those companies are Tyson and Perdue. In personal computers, Lenovo, HP, and Dell lead market share, with Apple in a close fourth. Uber and Lyft achieved market dominance in ridesharing in the US, while Ola and Grab are by far the leaders in Asia.

So the question on the mind of every entrepreneur who wants to have a massive, durable impact on the world (and to achieve the scale required to do so) should be: How will my technology or strategy enable me to be one of the top two solutions for the problem I am solving?

When solution concentration is high, more competitors will be deploying solutions that are quite similar to one another. Under such a scenario, several of the key resources a startup requires to survive can become much more difficult to acquire:

1. **People**
   For many startups, recruiting is about finding "missionaries" who believe in the mission of the company and are willing to work under more stress, for longer hours, with lower pay to help make that mission a reality. In an industry with just two or three similar competitors, the companies will likely be able to demonstrate their differentiation and competitive advantage to prospective hires. In a sector in which twelve or more companies are solving the same problem in a similar manner, attaining a recruiting advantage is much more difficult for any company.

   Building Transformative Technology companies is hard enough that recruiting the very best people to help build the company is necessary for success. When solution concentration is high, recruiting the people they need becomes much more expensive for individual companies, decreasing their chances of success.

2. Funding

As an industry experiences increasing solution concentration for particular problems, raising funding can become increasingly difficult. Particularly when several companies have similar solutions, investors are unlikely to want to invest in multiple, undifferentiated companies when they cannot identify unique advantages that make one more likely to succeed than another.

This can be especially challenging for Transformative Technology startups. As these companies grow and require larger sums of money to physically scale their operations, the number of investors who are able to provide that capital shrinks. The result is that most of these companies are approaching the same investors to secure this funding. Further, the greater the number of undifferentiated companies within a market, the lower the expected return for the investor. In these cases, predicting which companies will acquire the lion's share of the market is more difficult.

3. Customers

Early customers for Transformative Technology startups often choose the new product because it is much better at solving one problem they feel particularly strongly about, even if it underperforms in other areas initially. Now imagine those customers discovering that four or five companies make very similar products that will be equally good at solving their problem.

The lack of differentiation is likely to make the cost of acquiring these customers much higher as startups turn to large-scale marketing and sales campaigns to secure these customers before their competitors. These customers are also less likely to stay with the company long-term, as they can easily switch (barring any lock-in effects) to one of the other available options that is cheaper or that treats them better. None of these effects are good for start-ups that are already investing heavily in developing new technologies for their solutions.

Collectively, these increased challenges in markets with high solution concentration decrease the resource efficiency of the companies in the sector. Investing money and time into developing a solution that is 90 percent similar to a competitor is much less efficient than investing in a differentiated solution that can better solve the customer's problem if successful. High solution concentration inevitably means that the companies in the industry are replicating a significant amount of work. That does not benefit the company, its investors, or its customers.

Further, this duplication of effort and lower resource efficiency inevitably results in a lower **Impact Efficiency** for the company. That is, the impact created per dollar or hour is far lower than it would have been if the company had focused on a problem with lower solution concentration. Impact Efficiency is a metric borrowed from the way that we measure nonprofits: the amount of the impact metric achieved per hour or dollar expended.

Money and time are scarce resources. Prioritizing Impact Efficiency makes it possible for the same amount of money and time to be used to develop solutions to a greater number of problems and creates a better future for humanity than one in which these resources are deployed inefficiently.

THE IDEA MAZE AS A TOOL

One way to contextualize and evaluate a solution space is what Balaji Srinivasan, angel investor and former General Partner at Andreessen Horowitz, termed the Idea Maze. The **Idea Maze** is a visualization of "all the permutations of the idea and the branching of the decision tree, gaming things out to the end of each scenario."[165]

The Idea Maze is effectively a decision tree that maps the different options in a business model, technology, and philosophy that will result in different versions of solutions to the same problem. It is useful for finding good startup ideas—i.e., those that take novel approaches that are more likely to make them successful—because "anyone can point out the entrance to the maze, but few can think through all the branches."[166] In essence, those chasing "hot" problems or technologies can point to a problem they want to solve or a technology they want to use but cannot provide context to support their vision of its implementation and why those specific choices are logical.

This decision tree is described as a maze because some choices lead to dead ends that kill a company, while others lead to circuitous paths that waste time and resources before

---

165 Balaji S. Srinivasan, "Market Research, Wireframing, and Design," (Startup Engineering Lecture, Stanford University, Stanford, CA, 2013).

166 Ibid.

eventually leading back to the main path. Srinivasan says, "A good founder is capable of anticipating which turns lead to treasure and which lead to certain death. A bad founder [lacks any] sense for the history of the industry, the players in the maze, the casualties of the past, and the technologies that are likely to move walls and change assumptions."[167]

To put yourself on the path to being a great founder who develops a truly impactful solution, think about how you can "verbally and then graphically diagram a complex decision tree with many alternatives, explaining why your particular plan to navigate the maze is superior to the ten past companies that fell into pits and twenty current competitors lost in the maze."[168] If you can do that, you'll have gone a long way toward demonstrating a deep understanding of the solution concentration of an industry and that you actually have a good idea that can succeed where others have not.

MEASURING SOLUTION CONCENTRATION

How do you determine the solution concentration of a market? Unfortunately for those hoping for a prescriptive process to follow, I have not yet discovered a reliable quantitative method. Instead, I will describe a process that I have used personally and explored. Through this experimentation, I found this process helped clarify my thinking about market landscapes, competition, differentiation, and where my startup could achieve the highest leverage for the resources we have devoted to solving a Big Intractable Problem.

---

167 Ibid.

168 Ibid.

The process for defining the solution concentration of a market is as follows:

1. **Map the past and current companies developing solutions to the problem.**
   Cast a wide net. Build a list of all the companies, both past and present, that tried to solve the problem you are interested in solving. Some of these companies will be obvious and easy to find while others will have less information available. For each company, you are trying to understand what its approach was, what progress it made, and whether it still exists or not.

   As part of this information expedition, look for any clues you can gather about the specific underlying assumptions that each company made when developing and deploying their solution. Characterize the solutions, capturing information about their nature, the initial customer focus, and the costs of implementation. This is the type of information that can give you insight into whether your approach to solving the problem is actually unique or if it is based on the same flawed assumptions that led to failures in the past.

2. **Define the methods they are using to address the problem.**
   Go through the trove of information you have unearthed and classify the solutions based on commonalities. For each of these groups, explicitly define the critical assumptions they made when developing their solutions and the methods they used to produce their solutions. When we

talk about the methods used, we are evaluating how the companies specifically went about solving the problem.

For companies that are trying to minimize the climate impact of agriculture, for example, what form do their solutions take? Are they developing plant-based alternatives to animal products or trying to replicate those products through cell-based production methods? Are they using existing production technologies or developing their own methods? Do the solutions mimic current products or try to improve on them to make them healthier or allergen-free, for example?

By clearly defining the characteristics of the existing and past solutions and the methods used to produce them, you will develop a deep understanding of the existing landscape.

3. **Compare the methods you intend to use to those you have defined and identify the differences.**
   With that point of reference, your goal is now to assess how your intended solution compares to past and current attempts with regard to key characteristics and development methods. How similar is your solution to those that have been attempted before? Is your approach to development differentiated in any significant way? Do you have a unique insight that will lead you to solve the problem or implement your solution differently? These important questions will help you position your solution in the Maze and determine whether your points of differentiation are likely to provide you with a greater chance of success.

You must conduct this assessment with a clear mind and not bias your conclusions based on your desire to pursue a solution to this chosen problem. Remember that your goal is to create a massive, durable impact by solving this Big Intractable Problem. The solution that gets you there is far less important. If your initial solution does not pass this evaluation, consider how you can use what you have learned through this process to improve it.

This thorough analysis of the solution landscape, should provide you with a deep understanding of what has not worked. Perhaps it can also provide you some insight into how you can take a differentiated approach that will increase your chances of successfully solving the problem. If you are unable to find the unique differentiation you will need to succeed, your path to creating impact may lie in a totally different solution or in solving another problem.

SIMILARITY MATTERS MORE THAN QUANTITY

When considering solution concentration, recognizing the difference between a solution that is substantially different from prior efforts and one that is highly similar to those attempted in the past or currently under development is important. This is the difference between having a unique approach that avoids what others got wrong in the past and building a "me too" product.

Google was successful where a dozen prior search engines eventually failed because the founders had a unique approach to search ranking that solved a customer problem far better than prior attempts. Beyond Meat achieved far greater success than Tofurkey in large part because they recognized that customers wanted a vegetarian alternative that tasted and looked like meat, rather than a product that looked a bit like meat but tasted very different.

OmniPork's tremendous success with a plant-based pork alternative may see the company surpass both Impossible Foods and Beyond Meat on a global scale within the next few years. Where Impossible Foods and Beyond Meat first developed alternatives to commonly consumed products in the US, OmniPork set its sights on the Asian market. OmniPork recognized that the massive population and protein demand in Asia would dwarf that of the US and developed a product tailored to that market in taste profile and form factor.

These companies prove that the takeaway from a solution concentration analysis is not that the company must be the first to market or in a segment with very little competition. Rather, the founders must see something that others do not and use that unique insight to develop a differentiated solution. Using a solution concentration analysis to position yourself for success involves imagining what the ideal solution could be, determining how close other past or current attempts come to that ideal, and assessing whether your unique insight enables a differentiated approach with a greater likelihood of success.

A FOUNDATION FOR SUCCESS

Understanding the solution concentration for the problem you want to solve is a critical first step to ensuring that you have a unique insight. As we will see in the next chapter, traversing the Idea Maze enables founders to be confident in the value of their unique insights and to begin building companies based on the knowledge that their unique view of the problem presents an opportunity to solve it better than others. It validates that their ideas are, in fact, valuable.

CHAPTER 14

PRINCIPLE V: RECOGNIZE THE VALUE OF IDEAS

———

"The secret of all victory lies in the organization of the non-obvious."

MARCUS AURELIUS

One of the most widespread startup aphorisms is that ideas are not valuable. In Silicon Valley, or any startup hub around the world, this refrain is repeated almost *ad nauseum* to anyone who is discussing their startup or their aspiration to build one. This mindset has spread into the media that cover startups, as evidenced by the *Inc. Magazine* article "If You Only Have a Startup Idea, Sorry You Have Nothing"[169] or the article "Why Great Ideas Are Worthless" in *Forbes*.[170]

---

169 Hillel Fuld, "If You Only Have a Startup Idea, Sorry—You Have Nothing," *Inc Magazine*, March 14, 2018.

170 Josh Steimle, "Why Great Ideas Are Worthless," *Forbes*, September 1, 2013.

Over time, this has evolved into "ideas are worthless, execution is everything" until we have reached the point at which ideas are discounted to the point of absurdity. The suggestion is that anyone can have an idea for a solution, but those ideas have no value until they are executed upon. Common startup wisdom has evolved into telling founders to go build and test their idea without first questioning whether what they have is worth testing. Since ideas are considered worthless, no framework exists to encourage founders to vet their ideas before jumping headfirst into building and testing them.

SOFTWARE SHAPED OUR THINKING

In many ways, this perspective on the value of ideas seems to have been driven by the increasing ease of launching Internet-based startups. Starting with the dot-com boom of the 1990s, platform providers began building out much of the underlying infrastructure for Internet-based companies. In the twenty-five years since then, developing prototypes and launch products that customers will pay for has become orders of magnitude cheaper. Particularly for consumer Internet-enabled startups, the cost of launching a company is likely a hundred to a thousand times less than it was in 1990.[171]

As the cost of validating an idea decreased, people tended to ascribe less value to an idea in favor of seeing proof that the idea actually worked in practice. Given these changing circumstances for Internet-based companies, expecting some

---

171 Mark Suster, "It's Morning in Venture Capital," Both Sides of the Table, May 24, 2012.

early, low-cost proof of concept before taking a closer look at an idea for a company is reasonable. Even in such cases, however, the "only execution matters" mentality seems to serve as a filter to narrow the scope of what people choose to pay attention to.

The problem is much more significant when such advice is spread to many other sectors. This is an example of reasoning by analogy without examining the underlying first principles of a sector. In a number of the essential industries that face Big Intractable Problems, getting to an initial proof of concept can be resource intensive. Further, many Transformative Technologies do not lend themselves to the "quick and dirty" method of company building that an "execution or bust" culture uses as a proxy for evaluating the merits of a business idea.

The reason why the concept "ideas are worthless, execution is everything" became so popular in Silicon Valley and in startup circles is easy to understand. Founders and startup employees working incredibly hard to build companies likely run into others who come up to them with a "revolutionary idea" several times per week to ask for advice or funding. Often these individuals have not done any research into the problem, have not talked to any potential customers, and have no understanding of prior attempts to solve the problem. Investors may even see several of these people every day.

It is not difficult to become jaded in such circumstances and adopt proxies for serious commitment and intent to develop a solution. But are such proxies really valuable if they fail to account for the relative value of the company's underlying insight? Surely, a better method than totally discounting ideas exists.

WHAT'S IN AN IDEA?

As you can tell, I believe the notion that "ideas are worthless" and "execution is everything" is fundamentally flawed and not an accurate representation of reality. However, I do not disagree in the way that you probably think.

Rather, I think the argument has been mis-framed and, as a result, valuable intellectual capital is being disregarded to our collective detriment. To shift this conversation into a more productive frame, we need to differentiate between an "idea" and an "insight."

Traditionally, "idea" refers to a *thought* that someone had about how to solve a specific problem or a high-level business concept. The word "idea" has also been applied when a person proposes a *solution* to a problem and a strategy for deploying that solution based on a deeper understanding of the problem they are solving.

These two cases are vastly different. The first is a superficial, initial observation without any substance or data to back it up. I call these **flimsy ideas** because they aren't really concrete, just a wisp of an idea. The second type of idea is an actual solution to a well-characterized problem and a business strategy driven by a **unique insight** that demonstrates a deeper understanding of the issue.

Encouraging people in the first case to further refine their understanding of their chosen problem and to demonstrate the viability of that idea makes sense given its preliminary stage. Making the same recommendation to the person who has a unique insight is just being dismissive without acknowledging the value of that insight.

UNIQUE INSIGHTS ARE THE BASIS OF TRANSFORMATIVE COMPANIES

I find it difficult to agree with those who suggest that a unique insight into a real problem or into a Transformative Technology is worthless. Identifying and understanding problems that are either unknown, under-appreciated, or considered unapproachable is inherently valuable. Not only is this how many of the most successful, impactful startups initially began, but it is an underlying requirement to building a high-impact solution. In all cases, the solutions succeed because of the unique understanding of the problem itself.

Unique insights are the basis upon which Transformative Technology companies are built.

Consider an obvious problem: climate change. Someone with only a high-level, simplistic understanding of the problem might suggest a solution like selling electric cars or building a device to remove CO_2 from the atmosphere. But they would not have any unique approach to solving the problem and would likely fail because their solution suffers from the same pitfalls as those that came before it.

A founder with a unique insight might also suggest building an electric car company. They would have a novel approach to either the technology or the characteristics of the solution that would change their product or market strategy compared to prior attempts. Those variations in strategy are often the difference between success and failure.

Often, Big Intractable Problems are known quantities but they appear impossible to solve to many who lack a unique insight. Because these problems are well known, you can safely assume that hundreds of people are working on solutions. If Big Intractable Problems were trivial or simplistic, the group with the best execution in building and deploying the obvious solution would most likely succeed. But this is rarely the case, particularly for our most important problems.

With non-trivial problems like these, the solutions—and the unique insights behind them—are usually non-trivial. In these cases, being first to market or executing best are secondary to building upon a valuable insight. The unique insight is what creates differentiation and enables a company to leverage its durable competitive advantage to scale its operations and impact.

NAVIGATING THE IDEA MAZE

This discussion on the value of ideas is strongly related to prior discussions of solution concentration and navigating the Idea Maze. If you recall those sections, unique insights are incredibly valuable and are often the things that lead to breakthrough companies that create impact on a global scale.

Starting with an understanding of what has not worked in the past, what did work and *why*, and what approaches are currently being attempted provides a foundation for developing a unique insight and seeing what others did not. Then, applying that unique insight to develop a novel approach to solving the problem appears to be the formula for giving you an outsized chance to succeed in creating impact at scale.

Renowned venture capitalist Vinod Khosla has said that "valuable ideas are concrete in their vision but not approach."[172] In essence, a unique insight tells you broadly what the ideal outcome is and gives you a place from which to start building, but it does not provide the exact roadmap for getting there. That roadmap is developed along the way as founders learn from what does and does not work. That is where the ability to execute upon the unique insight becomes important.

HARNESSING UNIQUE INSIGHTS

If unique insights are valuable as the foundation for building solutions that have a massive, transformative potential, then finding ways to enable aspiring entrepreneurs to generate more of these unique insights should be a high priority. Instead, in a time in which humanity faces a growing number of Big Intractable Problems, we are actively incentivizing people to focus on startup ideas that solve smaller problems and thus appear less risky.

---

172 *Twenty Minute VC*, "Vinod Khosla on What Venture Assistance Really Means, Why Many VCs Are Not Qualified To Advise Founders & Why Startups Can Innovate So Much Faster Than Incumbents," hosted by Harry Stebbings, aired February 24, 2020.

But *what the most ambitious people do with their lives matters.*

If we are to solve these massive problems, we need more of the most ambitious people in the world working on them. Rather than optimizing for insights that generate short-term profits, we must optimize for our long-term future.

To do so, we have to find ways to surface a greater number of insights into these Big Intractable Problems. Exactly *how* we do that is not immediately obvious. It is, in a way, an Intractable Problem that will require a meta-insight to solve. Advocating for more ambitious people to study our most challenging problems and our history of trying to solve them is likely a good place to start.

While these insights are often portrayed as spontaneous "Eureka!" moments of the sort that Archimedes ostensibly had upon his discovery of buoyancy, many entrepreneurs have curated the development of such insights through purposeful study of problems and their Idea Mazes. Indeed, I have not seen many entrepreneurs running through the streets naked, still wet from their bath, because they were struck so strongly by their insights.

Encouraging our most ambitious people to spend time analyzing our most difficult problems may in fact be the best way to enable them to discover key insights that they can pursue through high-leverage paths like entrepreneurship.

THE FORMULA FOR SUCCESS

We should also recognize that a venture can only be as successful as its underlying premise and strategy. If our goal is to maximize the collective impact we can have on solving significant problems facing humanity, we need to ensure that the people working on these problems have the best chance at success. One way to do this is to stop discounting the value of ideas and instead talk more clearly and openly about how people can develop robust, unique insights instead of "flimsy ideas." Then, we can encourage those who have unique insights to act on them.

By reducing the dimensionality of a startup, we can simplify the definition of success to the following:

SUCCESS	=	STRATEGY	×	EXECUTION	×	OUTSIDE INFLUENCES
Impact on Chosen Problem		*Quality of Unique Insight*		*Hustle & Management*		*Luck*

Figure 9. The Impact Equation

Using this equation, demonstrating the value of a unique insight and how a poor understanding of the problem can limit a venture's upside potential may be easier.

The lens through which we view the world determines what we see and what remains obscured from us. If we have misunderstood the problem we are trying to solve, that lens is not focused correctly and will lead us astray. That blindness will lead to a poor strategy that can hinder the development and implementation of our solutions at best or kill the company at worst.

Execution is a multiplier that can change the total impact a solution has on a problem. Even if a solution resolves the targeted problem very well, it can only have a transformative impact on the world if it achieves sufficient scale. A bad strategy based on a superficial or incorrect understanding of the problem will yield a poor outcome regardless of how good the execution is because it won't scale. On the other hand, a good (but not great) strategy paired with excellent execution can still yield a good outcome. The best outcomes—and the greatest impacts—come from fantastic, insight-driven strategies upon which the team executes very well.

When tackling Big Intractable Problems, the margins for error in strategy and execution shrink substantially. Without a sound insight, the odds of a startup succeeding will be greatly diminished regardless of how well they execute. These problems are sufficiently large in scale and obdurate in nature that the founders' fundamental insight, and the strategy built on top of it, must reflect reality for their companies to succeed. The necessity of excellent execution goes without saying in these high-stakes environments, but great execution cannot save a Transformative Technology startup from a mediocre strategy or a flawed insight.

In these instances, the ideas are paramount.

ELON MUSK'S UNIQUE INSIGHT

We can see the importance of the idea in the history of electric cars in the United States. Electric cars have been around in America longer than gasoline-powered cars, but they initially faded away after the industry adopted gas cars as the vehicle for mass production. It was not until the 1990s when electric cars were reintroduced to the market in a major way.

In the mid-1990s, nearly every major car manufacturer released electric vehicle models in the US, including the Ford Ranger EV, Chevrolet S10 EV, GM EV1, Honda EV Plus, and Toyota RAV4 EV.[173] All of these cars sold poorly and were removed from the US market by 2002.[174]

These global automobile manufacturers have deep expertise in producing and marketing new cars. So why did they fail?

This failure was not due to their execution. Compared to the production challenges that Tesla has had, which CEO Elon Musk has referred to as "production hell," these companies had very smooth production scale-ups and product roll-outs. What was it that they missed that caused all of these vehicles to fail?

Every one of these traditional automobile manufacturers had a flawed understanding of the problem and what customers wanted. These companies either built replicas of the gas-powered versions of these cars or designed them to optimize for battery range. There was little consideration for whether the people most likely to buy electric cars would be motivated by those features. These cars were more expensive than their gas-powered equivalents. But cost could not have been the flaw in their understanding because Americans are paying

173 *Who Killed the Electric Car?*, directed by Chris Paine (2006; Los Angeles, CA: Sony Pictures Classics, 2006), DVD.

174 Ibid.

a premium (in upfront price if not overall operating cost) to drive Tesla's electric cars.

What these car manufacturers missed, that Elon Musk and Tesla recognized, is that people who wanted to buy electric cars wanted to *stand out*. Even the environmentally conscious consumers wanted *a reason to buy* the electric car beyond the fact that it does not burn fossil fuels.

Tesla's unique insight was that building a big enough market for electric cars would require cars that people wanted to buy, whether or not they were electric. This insight led Tesla to prioritize features that delighted users and showed off the ways in which electric motors could outperform gas cars. They gave the cars supercar-level acceleration so buyers would feel sporty driving the car. They introduced a system to keep the car cool while you shop, something that was not feasible with a combustion engine. They designed the cars to look different so they would stand out and make people proud to own the car.

All of these features and more delight Tesla customers. They all stem from the unique insight that electric cars needed a rebrand as "exciting" and "cool" rather than just being environmentally friendly if they were to gain mass market appeal.

As the Tesla case demonstrates, a company's strategy can be its competitive advantage for entering a market. Those strategies that win aren't just built from nothing though. In each case, the strategies that become lasting competitive advantages stem from the leaders' underlying unique insight into the problem or the market.

INSIGHTS INTO CULTURED MEAT

The notion that the founder's fundamental insight can create a competitive advantage for the company is also apparent in the cultured meat sector. A number of startups in this sector are taking markedly different approaches to developing solutions based on the founders' insights into the market.

One example is New Age Meats, a startup working on producing cultured pork. New Age Meats is approaching cultured meat through a lens of using automation to increase efficiency and decrease production cost. This approach is due in large part to founder Brian Spears' background in lab and industrial automation.

Blue Nalu, a cultured seafood company, is developing a platform-based approach that will enable them to produce seafood products from a number of different species using the same production system. While the majority of cultured meat companies are developing one initial product, Blue Nalu has chosen to develop its platform more broadly. This hints at the food industry experience of their CEO, Lou Cooperhouse, and a recognition of the value of being able to adapt and respond to changing consumer demand for different species based on the time of year and availability of wild catch.

A third cultured meat company, CellulaREvolution, is rethinking the design of the bioreactors the industry will need to scale its production. Today, most industrial bioreactors are suspension bioreactors, meaning the cells are suspended in a liquid media and kept in motion by an impeller to prevent them from all settling at the bottom. But many cell types, especially mammalian and muscle cells, prefer having a surface to grow on. Existing solutions are inelegant and expensive. CellulaREvolution, led by CEO Leo Groenewegen, is challenging the assumption that suspension bioreactors are optimal for cultured meat and developing a continuous cell production method that allows the cells to grow on a surface.

Without a unique insight in an emerging market like cultured meat, a company will have no real differentiation that prevents commoditization of its product as it scales. Lacking this differentiation, it will not be better equipped than any of its competitors to solve the problems it is tackling.

To achieve the scale required to solve the problems created by animal agriculture, these companies must bet on their unique insights and the strategies they build upon those insights. In an industry facing numerous technical challenges, these ideas—these insights—will determine the companies' success or failure as much as their ability to execute.

CHAPTER 15

PRINCIPLE VI: ACCOUNT FOR PATH DEPENDENCE

———

"The future influences the present as much as the past."

FRIEDRICH NIETZSCHE

For companies seeking to create impactful change on Big Intractable Problems, understanding and accounting for the path dependence of the industries in which they operate is crucial to their success.

Bringing new ideas and technologies to established industries is rarely easy. Frequently, one of the primary challenges to entering these industries is understanding how they currently operate. Learning how the industry came to its current state is just as important.

Why is it valuable for those bringing in new technologies to develop an understanding of an industry's past? Learning how an industry got to a certain point, how other technologies were adopted, and why prior decisions were made helps us to comprehend how such actions can best be approached in the present. In some industries, founders can succeed without taking these lessons to heart. But in the industries that most often contain the Big Intractable Problems, we ignore the sector's past at our peril. In these industries, path dependence plays a significant role in current thinking and in the path to adoption of new ideas and technologies.

Path dependence is the idea that the past cannot be discounted and how we arrived at the current point matters. Path dependence is effectively a way to describe how and why the status quo resists change. It helps to explain how past ideas continue to persist and can provide insight into how to displace those ideas with new ones.

Entrepreneurs and change-makers are often quick to discount this resistance to change as "legacy" behavior of "dinosaurs" that will soon be disrupted. In some cases, they are correct that the existing market leaders have grown complacent with their past successes and are too slow to adapt to changing circumstances. But in other cases, like those involving industries critical to our individual and collective survival, path dependence exists for good reason.

THE FUTURE IS BUILT ON THE PAST

Path dependence comes about for a number of reasons. In some cases, the presence of a few entrenched companies in a monopolistic market creates strong path dependence because these companies turn to rent seeking rather than continuing to innovate to maintain their position. They face few threats to their continued market position, so they are comfortable maintaining current systems and blocking changes that could threaten their market dominance.

In other cases, the reasons are far more rational. Capital equipment investments are often significant and must be recovered over the lifetime of that equipment. The equipment can be quite durable, with expected service lifetimes exceeding twenty years in some sectors. Replacing a steam turbine at a power plant with a new one can be difficult, regardless of how much better it is, when you invested in the best available model ten years ago and planned to wait ten more years before purchasing another.

Further, in complex systems, technology solutions often develop a high degree of interrelatedness. In these systems, each piece of technology relies upon a standard that ensures the different components will remain compatible into the foreseeable future. Thus, even if different technologies have very different upgrade cycles, the common elements are conserved to ensure compatibility.

Consider a railroad. Most railways in the Western hemisphere use standard gauge track, meaning the tracks are a set width apart. This is highly beneficial to everyone involved. Municipalities can build rail at a standard width without needing to know exactly which trains and rail cars they intend to buy beforehand. Locomotive manufacturers can develop entirely new designs and upgrade the internal systems as long as the train wheels are built for standard gauge. The rail operators can buy spare parts made for standard gauge rail without worrying about changes making them obsolete. Even if we learned that using a different rail gauge was *much* better, the interrelatedness of all these components would create significant friction to change.

The third rational cause of path dependence is that it yields increasing returns to adoption. For every additional user of a specific technology, continuing to use that technology becomes significantly more "sticky," and more beneficial for all parties involved. If we continue with the railway example, the standard gauge rail becomes more and more valuable to the industry as more train lines are built to standard gauge, more locomotives are standardized, and on and on. Making a universal standard increasingly ubiquitous increases its value to everyone on that standard. It also creates a coordination cost to switching, because many different parties need to agree to move to a new standard for the change to succeed.

Some proponents of technology innovation will still likely proclaim that such thinking is folly and that these industries just need to be more forward thinking and open to innovation. But consider the value that path dependence creates for a large, complex industry. Technologies that have been proven over long periods of time have well-quantified risks. Their reliability has been improved and they are now much safer than when they were initially deployed. The risk of unknown failure modes of new technologies, and the potential costs of those failures, seem unreasonable compared to these known technologies.

THE MANIFESTATIONS OF PATH DEPENDENCE

Given that many Big Intractable Problems are found in the industries that we require to survive—food, energy, health, transportation, and others—the cost of a failure in these sectors can have catastrophic consequences. A new pesticide that fails and leaves the US wheat crop vulnerable to a plague can lead to famines in parts of the world dependent on reliable, affordable access to that grain. Lives often hang in the balance when these industries fail to meet our safety and reliability requirements. In these cases, *disruption* can be sheer recklessness.

To avoid being (correctly) painted as naïve Technofideists promoting the implementation of new technology without regard for the consequences, entrepreneurs who want to solve Big Intractable Problems in critical industries must seek to understand how path dependence influences them. In particular, they must develop business plans that account for the industry's path dependence and use that insight to implement strategies that they would otherwise not have thought of.

How can we identify path dependence? Across critical industries, path dependence manifests as a set of common traits that we can develop a general plan for managing:

COMPLEX VALUE CHAINS

Due to the way these essential industries evolved, the supply chains in these industries tend to be highly complex. One company, or even a small set of companies, rarely controls the entire process of making and delivering these essential goods to the end consumers. Software companies can usually manage everything from making the product to selling directly to their customers. In essential industries, the customer that buys the product, the one that benefits from it the most, and the end user can all be different individuals served by different parts of the supply chain.

That means that companies solving Big Intractable Problems in these essential industries will need to build connections with other key contributors in the industry. These companies must understand the role of each contributor in this complex ecosystem and how the other companies create and derive value. Only then can the new entrant understand who will be willing to partner to bring their product to customers and who will try to fight or block them.

EXTENSIVE SUNK COST

The essential industries that often face Big Intractable Problems are dependent on physical infrastructure, either centralized or distributed, by their very nature. These physical assets and infrastructure generally require more significant capital investment than software and are often built to operate for twenty years or more. Further, this equipment and infrastructure often requires the operators to receive specialized training and certification to common standards. Since we live in a physical world, these infrastructure investments are essential to supplying our basic needs.

New solutions in these industries often require investing in new hardware or adopting new standards along with the considerable costs that accompany them. Though economics would tell us that the companies should view the old assets as a **sunk cost**—money already spent and cannot be recovered—that should not be factored into future decisions, the cost is usually not fully sunk. If equipment will last for thirty years, companies will seek to finance the equipment for as much of that period as possible to reduce upfront investment, and they cannot just walk away without paying off their loans and writing off considerable value on their books.

Companies who want to create meaningful change in these industries must consider how customers will view the investment required to adopt the new Transformative Technology. They must develop a go-to-market strategy that acknowledges the potential difficulties in financing the new technology, the need for feasibility demonstrations, and how to present a compelling story of the value of their solutions that will drive adoption in spite of these challenges.

VALUING SAFETY AND RELIABILITY OVER INNOVATION

In life-critical industries, the concern for the impact on human lives is often an important factor in making decisions about the adoption of new solutions. Especially in industries that relate to food, energy, and water access, the safety and reliability of essential systems is of primary importance. In these industries, "disruptive" change is viewed negatively because a disruption of these products or services can come at a cost of human lives.

If a new power plant is installed using an insufficiently validated technology, that power plant may not reliably stay online when it is needed. Imagine that this new power plant is in New Delhi, India, and fails in the summer. Daytime temperatures could easily be 45°C (113°F). Power failure in such conditions could cause hundreds to die and thousands to be hospitalized for heat stroke.

Obviously, the risk of such failures is higher than in industries that are not life-critical, and the risk tolerance is lower as a result. While some entrepreneurs would disregard this thinking as archaic, those who want to make meaningful change in these industries should recognize that the increased risk to human lives demands a commensurate degree of caution.

REGULATORY OVERSIGHT

Critical industries often have significant regulation that Transformative Technology founders have to navigate to successfully introduce their innovations. Scorning these regulatory frameworks is not usually a strategy for success, particularly because this hubris almost always results in unintended consequences the regulation was created to prevent. Successful founders understand that these regulations were often paid for in blood. That is, they were introduced because past mistakes and bad actors caused people to be harmed or killed.

Founders should consider regulation in critical industries for another reason: when introducing a new technology, the first applications can heavily influence how the technology is regulated. The regulatory bodies are likely to weigh the potential impact of a new technology against its risks when determining how it should be regulated. The application that founders choose to develop first will guide the regulators' risk/benefit assessment of the underlying Transformative Technology and thus frame their thinking about how to regulate it.

Consider two companies developing cultured meat. One company chooses to develop a novelty meat product, like saber-tooth tiger or dolphin, because it will be good for publicity. The other company launches with a cultured pork product in the midst of an outbreak that is killing many pigs and causing a pork shortage. Like most technologies, cellular agriculture is not risk-free, so the regulators are inclined to take a cautious approach to developing the regulatory framework.

Which company do you think is more likely to receive a better evaluation of potential reward versus risk and faster approval? If your first product looks like a toy rather than something that can solve a significant problem, both the regulators and the public are less likely to tolerate potential risks and more likely to react with strong caution.

For startups developing Transformative Technologies to address Big Intractable Problems, these lessons of accounting for path dependence are essential for their success.

PATH DEPENDENCE IN FOOD AND AGRICULTURE

To explore how Transformative Technology startups can achieve success by accounting for path dependence in their industry, we will examine a few relevant cases from the agriculture sector. The following are a number of ways that plant-based and cultured meat startups can account for path dependence.

PLAN TO FIT INTO THE EXISTING VALUE CHAIN

In the current meat industry, very little connects the producer to the consumer. Most meat is sold unbranded or under a consolidated brand of the processor. The farmer, rancher, or producer is invisible to the consumer.

Impossible Foods and Beyond Meat recognized that they had a unique opportunity to make their own product and expose their brand to consumers. They also knew it would be difficult to succeed in a competitive grocery store meat aisle without help. Both companies partnered with fast food chains that have incredibly strong brands to expose their products to consumers and demonstrate the consumer demand they would need to get into grocery stores.

Bruce Friedrich, founder of alternative protein nonprofit The Good Food Institute, expresses this idea of fitting into the value chain slightly differently. "Our goal is not to change anybody's metrics for food choices," he notes. "Our goal is to change the foods so that the plant-based and the cultivated alternatives have significantly lower external costs, no need for antibiotics, and a fraction of the climate impact so that consumers choose them because they are the most delicious and most affordable alternative."[175] Rather than trying to change how consumers buy meat and alter demand, he

---

175 Louisa Burwood-Taylor, "Future Food: Catching up with GFI's Bruce Friedrich to talk alt protein winners, losers, innovation whitespace," AgFunder News, December 12, 2019.

advocates for making a product that can be bought everywhere consumers buy meat and that outcompetes animal meat in those locations.

ACCOUNT FOR SUNK COSTS IN STRATEGIC PLANS

The agriculture and food industry has significant infrastructure costs across the value chain. For cultured meat startups, finding ways to use the existing infrastructure may help them to scale with much less friction than building their own production system independently. When these startups are developing strategic plans that inform their fundraising, pilot facility development, and scale-up, accounting for the different ways the industry's sunk costs could be used to their advantage would be logical.

As it turns out, cellular agriculture startups can benefit from much of the existing infrastructure in the food supply chain. Cellular agriculture startups will need to use food-grade bioreactors to grow their cells. These bioreactors are already produced for fermenting beer, and many of them may also be suitable for cellular agriculture applications. Many of these companies will also require food processing infrastructure to turn their cells into final products. Most existing food processing equipment is not especially particular about the inputs that can be used. If these companies wanted to produce a burger, they could likely use the same extrusion and forming machines whether the inputs were for bean burgers, plant-based burgers, or cultured meat.

By identifying existing sunk costs in the industry, startups can understand who stands to lose from their entrance into the market and how those same companies could fill existing capacity by working with them. In doing so, these startups will also learn that there are benefits to working with companies that have experience in the industry.

SEEK STRATEGIC PARTNERS TO BENEFIT FROM INDUSTRY KNOWLEDGE

When Transformative Technology companies seek to launch new products into these industries, partnerships can help them to avoid simple mistakes and learn from others' experiences and failures. Established industries can be complex and opaque to outsiders, and partnerships can be the difference between failing and achieving success at scale.

Recently, we have started to see cultured meat companies recognize the value of forming partnerships to strengthen the areas in which their experience is lacking. Both Blue Nalu and Mosa Meat have announced partnerships with Nutreco, one of the leading animal feed and supplements providers.[176] Though the exact nature of these partnerships is not clear, both cultured meat startups recognized that they would need help with sourcing food-grade inputs for their supply chains and that an animal feed company would have a wealth of experience with those same challenges. Perhaps these companies also recognized that creating cultured meat products shares other commonalities with formulating animal feeds, like the goal of achieving a certain nutritional balance and palatability profile. In the coming years, we will likely see a

---

176 Caoimhe Moore, "Animal nutrition and aquafeed leader Nutreco partners with cell-based protein companies," Nutreco, January 16, 2020.

number of other industry partnerships emerge as startups recognize what they can learn from existing companies in the industry.

These experienced strategic partners do not need to only be companies in the industry. They can also be investors with industry experience or background. A corporate investment arm can make introductions to other supply chain partners or help with developing a regulatory strategy. Investors with industry-relevant operating experience can help to hire talented, experienced people and enable companies to avoid mistakes that are obvious to those who have seen them before. Whether they are a corporate investment arm or a venture capital firm whose partners have industry experience, these types of strategic investors can add significant value to a startup seeking to break into a complex industry.

DEVELOP A REGULATORY STRATEGY EARLY

Because Big Intractable Problems often exist in industries that are essential for our individual survival and the continued existence of modern society, companies that seek to solve them must often contend with regulated markets. When those companies are introducing new Transformative Technology solutions, the existing regulatory schemes may not sufficiently cover their new technology. To bring these solutions to market, the startups will often need to wait for the regulators to develop a framework for regulating the new technology.

These startups have two choices: they can either wait for the regulators to develop a new framework that may be based on misconceptions of the technology and its risks or they can engage in an open dialogue with the regulatory body from the start and seek to help the regulators expeditiously develop a rational framework. Given those two options, the apparent choice seems to be that startups should develop an internal regulatory strategy and engage with regulators early on.

THE PERILS OF DISRUPTION WITHOUT FORETHOUGHT

Some entrepreneurs will seek to "outsmart" regulators or build their company strategy around ignoring regulations and daring regulators to come after them. Both Uber and Airbnb adopted this strategy. Luckily for us, the industries they were disrupting were not so essential for human survival that disruption could cause death or serious harm to millions of people.

Even so, Airbnb has had significant negative, and easily avoidable, impacts on many of the cities it operates in because the team ignored the path dependence of the real estate industry.

By turning buildings zoned for private housing into hotels, Airbnb enabled homeowners to dramatically increase the value of their properties compared to renting them for a single family to live in. Taken to its natural extreme, people realized they could make a great deal of money by purchasing homes and apartments as rental assets and renting them to different people every night on Airbnb.

Airbnb thought regulations were an obstacle to be overcome and sought to grow its business without thinking about the larger societal implications of what it was doing. This has been a major contributor to the rapid increase in rents in cities across the US, to the point that it is making these cities unaffordable for people who have lived there for years.

Some may argue that startup founders do not have a broader responsibility to society beyond creating economic value through their companies. But what is a society if not a group of people living by a shared code for the benefit of the group?

This cavalier attitude toward regulation is all too common in Silicon Valley. We should never forget how these regulations came to exist. Most regulations emerged because we collectively determined that human lives were worth protecting from unscrupulous behavior in these industries.

LOOK TO THE PAST TO UNDERSTAND THE FUTURE
Though the cellular agriculture industry is young, many of the startups are demonstrating that they have learned important lessons about working with regulators. Five of the cultured meat companies in the US formed the Alliance for Meat, Poultry, and Seafood Innovation in 2019 to collectively engage with government officials and regulators.[177] The establishment of this industry alliance is part of a larger effort to create a safe path to market for cultured meat products that is also economically viable for the startups.

---

177 Mary Allen, "5 Cell-Based Meat Startups Form Coalition to Educate and Advocate," Good Food Institute, August 29, 2019.

By forming a collective organization, these startups are ensuring they present a unified and clear message to the government officials who they will be engaging as the regulatory framework is developed. Rather than doing this work independently and likely duplicating much of their efforts, these companies have joined together to make the process far more efficient.

These companies recognized that the industry's history has led to the current regulatory environment. They understood that ignoring or attempting to circumvent the regulations would be counterproductive in the critical industry of food. More broadly, their actions demonstrate that many of the startups in the cultured meat sector understand the effects of path dependence on the current state of the protein industry.

To achieve large-scale success and to impact Big Intractable Problems, other startups will need to follow their lead in adopting strategies that account for the effects of path dependence on their industries.

CHAPTER 16

PRINCIPLE VII: START WITH SCALE IN MIND

———

"First mover advantage doesn't go to the company that starts up, it goes to the company that scales up."

REID HOFFMAN

One of the less obvious principles for succeeding with Transformative Technologies is that founders must start with scale in mind. In fact, this idea of thinking about scalability from the beginning is antithetical to traditional Silicon Valley startup wisdom.

In this case, it is not because Silicon Valley is wrong. Most of the startup wisdom that have developed in Silicon Valley in the last two decades is based entirely on experience with software businesses. The narrowness of this experience is what has created blind spots in building startups that rely upon physical infrastructure like a majority of Transformative Technology startups do.

The often-repeated wisdom when building a startup is to focus on building your minimum viable product, or MVP. The MVP is the smallest, lightest-weight version of your product that provides a customer with enough value to want to use it. Over time, you can build your MVP into a fully-featured product, and then a suite of products, as the company scales. While doing so, the company typically incurs technical debt.

TECHNICAL DEBT

Think of **technical debt** like financial debt that companies accrue when building their products because they prioritize building a solution as quickly as possible that will function just well enough for their current customers. As the company scales from one hundred to one million users, the solutions that worked for one hundred users do not scale and must often be rebuilt.

Traditional Silicon Valley startup wisdom says that this technical debt is inevitable. If you build a company that is successful enough to start scaling up, you can spend time paying the technical debt balance later on.

Reid Hoffman, founder of LinkedIn, likens this process to jumping off a cliff and assembling a plane on the way down. Your goal isn't to build a top-of-the-line plane but instead to make sure the plane flies well enough that you don't hit the ground. Nearly all the famous startups—including Slack, Microsoft, Google, and Facebook—can tell stories about the technical debt they accrued and how they tackled it as they scaled.

For software startups, this method can work quite well. The hardest thing for most software companies to do is to build the initial product and acquire customers. The cost of scaling software is (relatively) cheap, as the marginal cost of adding more users is very low.

In software, the costs of scaling are driven by the desire for rapid growth and the forward-looking hiring required to achieve it. Thus, investors are very willing to back a team building a minimally-viable product and betting that the team can overcome their technical debt as they scale by executing well. For these companies, technical debt is a problem to be overcome, but not one that usually poses an existential threat to their ability to scale.

For Transformative Technology companies, however, technical debt can prevent a small-scale solution from scaling up. Building production facilities and gaining regulatory approval are expensive tasks that these companies face early in their commercial lives. They cannot afford to carry technical debt through these milestones and hope that they can overcome that debt in the future.

(DIS)ECONOMIES OF SCALE

We know that software achieves significant economies of scale in most all known cases. Is that something we can afford to take for granted for Transformative Technology companies?

In truth, economies of scale are not guaranteed across all industries and solutions. Some businesses face diseconomies of scale, in which aspects of the business become more expensive as the operations grow. One of the most common diseconomies of scale is the **coordination problems** that arise from having to manage very large and complex operations. Most of us know these problems as "bureaucracy" or "corporate bloat" that makes large organizations move slowly and inefficiently. They can also appear in physical production.

Diseconomies of scale have appeared in the agriculture industry, particularly within aquaculture (i.e., fish farming). As aquaculture production has grown rapidly,[178] so too has the demand for fishmeal, a feed ingredient made from wild-caught fish like anchovies that is included in the feed for carnivorous farmed fish. As the demand is outpacing the supply of fishmeal, it is causing these fisheries to collapse, further reducing supply.[179]

As a result, the price of fishmeal has tripled in the last fifteen years.[180] Until aquaculture feed providers can replace their need for fishmeal, they have to buy it regardless of price. Thus, the enormous success of aquaculture has created a diseconomy of scale for inputs of fish feed.

SCALING CAPITAL—THE CLEAN ENERGY BUBBLE

A primary reason that the ability to scale is not a given for Transformative Technology businesses is the cost (and

---

178 FAO, *Aquaculture Production (Metric Tons)*, 2016, distributed by World Bank Data Catalog.

179 Allison Guy, "Overfishing and El Niño Push the World's Biggest Single-Species Fishery to a Critical Point," Oceana, February 2, 2016.

180 GEM Commodities, World Bank Group, *Fishmeal Monthly Price—US Dollars per Metric Ton, 1960-2020*, distributed by Index Mundi.

patience) of capital. One of the main reasons for the collapse of the clean tech "bubble" in late 2008 was that it rapidly became very expensive to source raw materials due to the clean energy boom. Very shortly thereafter, low-cost capital became increasingly scarce in the wake of the 2008 financial crisis.

The solar energy boom relied upon production of solar panels from polycrystalline silicon. This silicon cost about fifty dollars per kilogram in 2004.[181] Due to the sudden, rapid increase in demand from the clean energy boom, the price of polycrystalline silicon soared to nearly $475 per kilogram in 2008, nearly ten times the initial price.[182] The high price of inputs meant that these solar companies needed to raise incredible amounts of capital at a low cost if they were to be able to scale up their production to achieve sustainability.

181 Juliet Eilperin, "Why the Clean Tech Boom Went Bust," *Wired*, January 20, 2012.

182 Ibid.

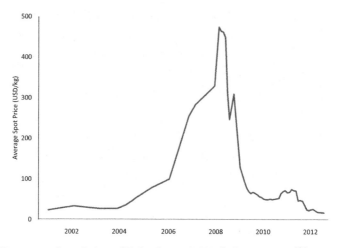

Figure 10. Spot Price of Polysilicon (USD/kg) 2001-2012[183]

But the financial crisis caused low-cost capital to vanish almost overnight, especially for businesses that needed capital for longer-term investments. These companies could not find enough capital to invest in the infrastructure and expensive consumables needed to produce at scale and were not able to reach their price targets because of it.

As a result, the industry cratered in the United States. With demand suddenly in freefall, the price of polycrystalline silicon fell precipitously below one hundred dollars per kilogram by the end of 2009.[184]

---

183 Debra Sandor, et al., "System Dynamics of Polysilicon for Solar Photovoltaics: A Framework for Investigating the Energy Security of Renewable Energy Supply Chains," *Sustainability* 10, no. 1 (2018): 160.

184 Eilperin, "Why the Clean Tech Boom Went Bust."

Today, silicon costs just seventeen dollars per kilogram.[185] The low cost has enabled production of solar panels to be feasible in countries with lower costs of manufacturing, like China. Had low-cost capital been available in the US through the 2008 financial crisis, it is quite likely that a number of these clean tech companies would have weathered the storm and emerged with sufficient scale to be price competitive in the market. however, these companies had strategic plans that relied upon the ready availability of hundreds of millions of dollars and were unable to achieve scale and profitability without them.

PHYSICAL BARRIERS TO SCALE

A number of physical challenges have been found to scaling Transformative Technology businesses that do not exist in pure-software businesses or for companies whose products have existing supply chains. These physical challenges to scaling present unique obstacles to the rapid growth that is expected of startups. They also create barriers to entry that can make new solutions incredibly "sticky" once they prove they can solve a Big Intractable Problem.

For companies like those in cellular agriculture, demonstrating the viability and reliability of a coordinated system of Transformative Technologies will be required to achieve scale. Thus, every stage of the technology validation process should be viewed as an opportunity to demonstrate that the technology was designed for scalability.

---

185 "Prices flat in polysilicon market," *Washington Post*, July 23, 2013.

Successfully demonstrating that a system based on Transformative Technologies can be deployed sustainably at scale requires understanding the traditional physical challenges to scale and showing how each can be overcome. The most common physical challenges to scale include:

1. **Process dynamics can vary with scale**
   For many processes, the dynamics of how those processes function change under different conditions. What works at a lab-scale is not likely to work at pilot-scale without some degree of re-engineering. The pilot-scale process, too, will require some degree of optimization to work at industrial scale.

   This challenge with process dynamics is most common in biotechnology but is also encountered frequently in the chemicals industry. Even for physical manufactured goods, companies will likely need to re-engineer and optimize the specific equipment, automation processes, and production systems as manufacturing moves toward full scale.

   This process engineering challenge often means redoing work the team has already done to demonstrate the technology at a smaller scale. It adds risk too, as there are no guarantees that a pilot-scale process can be successfully scaled to commercial production without substantially changing the underlying economics of the business.

   As industries become more established, a standardized process typically emerges for scaling production while reducing these risks. But for new industries, the risk is significant. Cellular agriculture, for example, can learn some things from the process scale-up experience of the beer and biopharmaceutical industries. However, the industry will need to recognize that some challenges, like tissue engineering and 3D bioprinting at scale, do not have direct parallels to provide guidance.

2. **Infrastructure development is expensive and takes time**
Once companies demonstrate their Transformative Technology at lab or pilot scale, they then have to raise financing for a commercial production facility or commercial-scale deployment. But these commercial projects require enormous capital investments, often on the order of fifty to one hundred million dollars.

These startups cannot afford to accrue technical debt during their development phase and move into a building and out of a commercial facility without overcoming that debt. They cannot build a production facility without knowing exactly what is going inside it and how the systems fit together after all. If the companies deploy their existing technology, they cannot easily upgrade it later when they overcome the technical debt and develop more robust, improved systems.

Further, financial supporters of these commercial projects will expect to see a full process model for the facility so they can understand the expected returns on their capital under nominal facility operations. At a minimum, this would require understanding every piece of equipment and process going into the facility. It would also require a demonstration of each technology and system at a smaller scale, or at least a comparable production system in which the financiers have high confidence.

The time and effort needed to scale up in a way that enables startups to procure the necessary capital is tremendous compared with scaling software. This financing process can pose a tough challenge to anyone scaling a Transformative Technology business.

3. **Regulatory approvals require demonstration**
Also, often financial outlays, long timelines, and potential hurdles need to be overcome when navigating the regulatory process for new Transformative Technologies. The proof points required to receive these approvals are often more challenging for physical products than for software. This is especially relevant in the case of Transformative Technologies that are being approved for the first time.

Startups can help to speed this process of regulatory approval by thinking through how their proof-of-concept work will look at scale, since that is what regulators primarily want to understand. That means that even in the early stages of development, it is worth considering how you will implement process controls, source key components, and prove the repeatability of the production process.

Finding ways to demonstrate the technology and prove to the regulators that you are implementing proper systems controls in the pilot-stage can smooth the approval process immensely as you move toward commercial production.

OVERCOMING BARRIERS TO SCALING
TRANSFORMATIVE TECHNOLOGIES

In general, the way to overcome the additional hurdles associated with scaling physical technologies is to find ways to "hack" the technology development cycle to move from concept to initial demonstration as quickly as possible.

Venture capital firm NFX describes the process of building a startup as climbing the Ladder of Proof by successively de-risking critical aspects of the business until you have fully demonstrated the viability and scalability of the company.[186] Transformative Technology companies should develop their own Ladders of Proof by identifying the riskiest assumptions of their business and then working to systematically validate those assumptions, starting with the highest-risk ones.

Transformative Technology entrepreneurs can think of a Physical Ladder of Proof for their businesses as well. The first step on the ladder is showing that the technology works at any scale. This usually involves a proof-of-principle, or a low-fidelity prototype to demonstrate that the engineering and physical concept actually functions.

Unfortunately, entrepreneurs can easily get stuck in the idea of demonstrating every key aspect of their technology at small scale. A viable business is not likely to be built at these small scales for Transformative Technologies. The much more impactful demonstration is that the technology

---

186 James Currier, "The Ladder of Proof: Uncovering How VC's See Your Startup," NfX, May 16, 2018.

functions reliably at production-scale and that the economics are viable at that commercial scale.

For most Transformative Technology entrepreneurs, proving viability and reliability at commercial scale is too expensive to do initially. The next best thing is pilot-scale production that resembles the commercial implementation as accurately as possible. To achieve this demonstration of scalability in the research and development phase, founders should think about how they can show that the technology will work at scale.

For a cellular agriculture startup, this could be done by growing cells in suspension culture, in a small bioreactor that has a similar design and controls as a commercial-scale reactor. While many startups are spending significant time proving they can make a product at lab-scale by growing the cells in flasks, this just shows the end product rather than demonstrating the viability of the *production process*. Proving that the process needed at scale works early on moves a startup far further up the Physical Ladder of Proof far earlier than the traditional research and development (R&D) methods.

The startups will then need to show that these production processes can be integrated into a system that will scale. At this stage, too many startups focus on just making a prototype they can showcase rather than investing effort in synthesizing the production processes early on. While a truly integrated system is difficult to demonstrate at lab-scale, it is often a critical developmental hurdle. Backloading these difficult challenges just adds risk to the later stages of development.

One method for showcasing the viability of an integrated production process earlier than could typically be done is to implement process models or simulations. These models are common for process control in the petrochemicals and biopharmaceutical industries for production management, but most of these tools can be adapted to serve as projections for future, novel production systems. Using these modeling tools can create early proof that the startup's technology can scale. Modeling can also reduce the cost and time required to validate several assumptions and refine the production system before investing capital in a pilot production facility.

Building a pilot facility is often a necessary step for physical products startups to show that they can actually run a production facility and that no hiccups arise. Too many startups rely upon pilot facilities to provide their first proof that their technology and systems can scale. They take unnecessary risk by failing to optimize their systems using modeling technology and integrated systems at lab-scale. The result is that they end up learning a number of lessons that could have been learned earlier in their development process and by focusing on production processes rather than just the end product.

Scaling startups is difficult. Scaling Transformative Technologies for the first time is especially so. Succeeding with these startups and achieving large-scale impact requires these startups to validate different aspects of their technologies and production processes along the way to commercial scale.

CHAPTER 17

PRINCIPLE VIII: HARNESS VERTICAL INTEGRATION AS THE GREAT EQUALIZER

"Vertical integration is sort of a very under explored modality of technological progress that people would do well to look at more."

PETER THIEL

Among the many challenges Transformative Technology startups face, perhaps the largest is trying to enter established industries where the existing companies may have little interest or ability to provide the necessary supply chain or support. **Vertical integration**, a strategy in which a company owns multiple stages of supply or distribution within its supply chain, can be the great equalizer that turns these startups from long shots into success stories.

The thought that vertical integration can solve more problems than it creates runs directly counter to Silicon Valley startup wisdom. Most experienced founders and investors within Silicon Valley will tell you that startups should specialize, that they should find the one thing they can do better than anyone else and deliver it to as many customers as possible. Their advice makes a lot of sense if you take into account the software-centric nature of their experience and the time in which most of them built their experience.

Starting in the mid-1990s, the infrastructure layer for software startups was rapidly established. The Mosaic browser, and later Netscape, helped to establish the early infrastructure of the Internet starting in 1994.[187] Microsoft Windows and Apple MacOS created the operating system layer that made for a unified user experience for consumers. In 2006, Amazon Web Services launched to provide a common server infrastructure experience on which companies could build and host their products.[188] These infrastructure tools dramatically lowered the cost of building software startups and significantly reduced the time investment required to build a first product.

TRANSFORMATIVE TECHNOLOGY ISN'T LIKE SOFTWARE

But in many critical industries that are faced with Big Intractable Problems, this underlying infrastructure does not exist.

---

187 Gary Wolfe, "The (Second Phase of the) Revolution Has Begun," *Wired,* October 1, 1994.

188 "About AWS," Amazon Web Services, accessed October 8, 2019.

Rather, the infrastructure is at least one technology generation old and not suitable as a platform for deploying the next-generation Transformative Technology. In many cases, this infrastructure may also be impossible or nearly impossible for startups to access. The majority of the industries in which Big Intractable Problems exist are run by established, legacy suppliers that do not work on startup timelines. The established suppliers are generally not willing to go out of their way to support startups through small-batch production of development-stage products. Even when they do, the cost is often exorbitant.

For many startups trying to launch Transformative Technologies, there is no viable option other than vertically integrating at least part of the total value chain. Hoping that another company develops the infrastructure layer for them to expand upon invites too much external risk that is entirely out of the startup's control. As we discussed in Chapter sixteen, building a company without planning for scale is setting yourself up for failure. The result is that many startups pursuing Big Intractable Problems in essential industries need to turn to vertical integration as a tool that can enable them to successfully scale their innovations.

Vertical integration is all about mitigating preventable risks in the supply chain that could stop a startup from scaling successfully.

STANDARD OIL: THE VALUE AND RISKS OF VERTICAL INTEGRATION

While using vertical integration as a tool for successfully scaling a Transformative Technology startup may be a controversial idea, a number of companies have leveraged vertical integration to build a near-unbreakable competitive advantage. One of the first companies in the United States to vertically integrate was Standard Oil, owned by John D. Rockefeller. At the time Standard Oil started to grow rapidly in the 1870s, the oil industry value chain had three levels: oil and gas exploration and production, processing and transportation to refineries, and oil refining and transportation to retail outlets.[189]

Standard Oil started in the refinery business, producing kerosene that was used in the US and Europe. Once the company established a market, it sought to improve its profit margins by reducing costs and streamlining production. First, the company bought control of the pipelines that transported the oil to its refineries.[190] This enabled Standard Oil to ensure a constant supply of oil to their refinery, something that was a challenge in those early days of the industry.

But controlling supply was not enough. Standard Oil eventually acquired its own drilling rights, providing secure production to the refineries and enabling even better negotiating rights with the railroads that transported much of the oil. This is where Standard Oil got greedy.

---

189 George L. Priest, "Rethinking the Economic Basis of the Standard Oil Refining Monopoly: Dominance Against Competing Cartels," *Yale Law & Economics Research Paper*, no. 445 (2012): 499-558.

190 Ibid.

Rather than just running a valuable and profitable business, it sought to increase profits by negotiating special rebates with the railroads that carried its oil *and* ensuring that none of its competitors could access these low rates.[191] Further, Standard Oil sought to buy out all of its refinery competition, creating a horizontal monopoly with deep vertical integration. This anti-competitive behavior, paired with their 85 percent market share, was enough reason for the US government to break up Standard Oil under the Sherman Antitrust Act.[192]

While the success of Standard Oil's vertical integration can provide useful insight for startups, its eventual downfall to anticompetitive acts should also serve as a warning. Integrating vertically to build a more sustainable and viable business is something that all Transformative Technology startups should consider (in the context of their industry). However, acting in a way that blocks or subverts competitors is unlikely to fare well for the company in the long-term and may result in legal action.

REASONS TO VERTICALLY INTEGRATE

Standard Oil's story provides a useful parallel for the industries in which Transformative Technology startups will most likely operate. Most of these industries represent large markets in the early stages of a technology transition.

Technology transitions create opportunities for integration.

---

191 Ibid.

192 Kenny Malone and Julia Simon, hosts, "Antitrust 1: Standard Oil," Planet Money (podcast), February 15, 2019, accessed October 15, 2019.

In these established industries, vertical integration presents an opportunity for these companies to carve out a competitive advantage and to build a business that can scale much more quickly. Given the importance of achieving scale for Transformative Technologies, ensuring that a startup survives to reach it, is crucial. For founders of these types of companies, there are a few specific reasons to consider vertical integration as a strategy for minimizing the barriers to achieving scale.

SPECIALIZATION IS TOUGH IN EARLY MARKETS

One of the primary reasons vertical integration is a valuable strategy is that it can be difficult to specialize in one part of the value chain. If the value chain is not well established or is missing key pieces that the new startup requires, success is impossible unless the startup works on filling in some of those gaps itself.

Solar energy provides a helpful example of this scenario. Solar panel providers ran into some business challenges because the value chain in the energy sector was developed with a large, centralized power plant in mind rather than distributed, modular power generation. One key challenge is third parties were not ready to install these panels for consumers. No financiers with loan products were ready to help consumers finance the installation of a solar system on their home either.

Though the solar companies would probably have preferred to specialize in solar panel production and distribution, they ended up having to provide the ancillary services that would get customers to actually adopt their products. If these solar companies had chosen to only act as panel suppliers, they would have been entirely at the mercy of the success or failure of solar installation and financing companies to get their panels to customers.

While Transformative Technology companies can fit nicely into the existing value chain in some cases, this may not be an option in many markets. In such instances, having a Plan B to vertically integrate to the degree required to keep the business alive can be worthwhile. Plan B protects the company from the risk that it takes longer than expected for suppliers and customers to develop.

The startups entering the cellular agriculture industry are facing this challenge now. Most of these companies aspire to have animal-free supply chains, but those largely do not exist today—at least, not at any scale. Many of the cultured meat companies intend to be manufacturers of various meat products, but they may find that the inputs required to scale their production are not being produced beyond R&D scale when they need to commercialize their product. Inevitably, some of these companies will recognize the need to produce some of these inputs internally, leading to vertical integration of critical supply chain infrastructure.

INTEGRATION ENABLES SPEED

Another reason to consider vertically integrating a Transformative Technology startup when entering an established industry is that integration lets you move faster. How can adding further development costs, time, and complexity help a company to move faster? It is best summarized by the paradoxical statement, "sometimes you must move slowly if you want to go quickly."

What integration can add in complexity, it can more than overcome in development timelines and efficiency—if implemented correctly. The key for startups considering vertical integration to accelerate their growth is to understand the context of the market into which they are launching their company.

If the startup's vendors are reliable and cost effective, the risks posed by the added complexity of vertical integration outweigh the potential reward. But in established, essential industries, these existing vendors often grow into lumbering behemoths that are unlikely to take a small, new market entrant seriously. Instead, they frequently operate on long timelines and quote high prices for their work, making vertical integration far more compelling for Transformative Technology startups.

Beyond the direct availability of key inputs and components from existing industry players, startups rarely have their product or production process fully determined from the start. Rather, startups—especially those developing Transformative Technology-based products—require a lengthy development phase to validate, optimize, and scale their production. Such development processes require rapid iteration and low-cost validation testing before moving on to more intensive, higher-fidelity tests.

But existing vendors, particularly those that may see the startup as a competitor, are not likely to go out of their way to be helpful when the startup needs a standard input to be customized. Most suppliers will choose not to offer customization, especially at the low volumes a startup would typically request. At a minimum, working with these traditional vendors relies upon their execution to deliver a critical component. This adds another layer of risk that is almost entirely out of the startup's control.

Further, startups should value time and cash above all other things during their R&D phase. Choosing to integrate vertically and develop key inputs in-house can speed the startup's pace of development. This also enables internal teams to use a rapid prototyping methodology to quickly test and adapt multiple iterations of the components to find the ones that work best for *their* requirements. Integrating input development can also enable startups to parallelize their experiments by developing and testing prototypes of different stages of their production process at the same time. This parallelization of development can be a powerful tool for accelerating the pace of development and is compounded by a company having greater ownership over its inputs.

INTEGRATION ALLOWS FOR SYSTEM-LEVEL OPTIMIZATION
Vertical integration can also enable Transformative Technology startups to significantly optimize their processes. Rather than evaluating individual components, optimizing at the process level can lead to efficiencies and cost reductions that would be impossible based on innovating only one part of the process.

SpaceX learned this from experience. Existing companies in the space industry are notorious for controlling everything from supply chains to the ability to get any government funding for development. SpaceX, a company with a relatively small budget and a lot of ground to make up, was not going to survive long enough to launch a rocket by going through existing suppliers.

Instead, it had a process for determining whether a part should be brought in-house and made in their integrated manufacturing facility. If a part was far enough from what it needed, outrageously expensive, or slow to procure, it became part of SpaceX internal development. This helped SpaceX achieve a speed and cost structure largely unheard of in the space business, overcoming old assumptions that had been built into rocket design and construction for more than half a century.

Many Transformative Technology startups can learn from SpaceX's approach. If a critical part is far from the specifications you require and getting the necessary customization is going to be challenging, evaluate whether it could be done better in-house. If you have to modify your own product or process to accommodate the existing part, ask whether the efficiency lost from the modification is important. If it is, integrate that part into your production.

Suppliers are optimizing for the requirements of their largest, most lucrative customers. In the early days of a startup, you are not that customer. You may just want a part to a minimum specification, but if the supplier's main customer wants the premium, high-performance part, that is the one that will be available.

For Transformative Technology companies in cellular agriculture, the benefits of system-level optimization will become apparent as these companies' scale. If they try to use off-the-shelf technology as much as possible, they will find themselves having to integrate food-grade bioreactor systems with tissue engineering technology designed for medical applications and using ingredients designed for biology R&D. The result would be that the companies make a number of design compromises that make their system less efficient and more unwieldy than it would have been if the primary components had been purpose-built. Though this may appear to increase the development burden for the industry, it will create significant advantage for the startups that can implement a purpose-built, integrated production system.

INTEGRATION REDUCES DEVELOPMENTAL FRICTION

Choosing to build a vertically integrated supply chain can also reduce internal development friction and help to build a seamless, cohesive ecosystem within the company. Many Transformative Technology companies require a period of significant engineering and optimization to turn their technologies into market-ready products. If the engineering teams are limited by parts that were not built for the startup's intended purpose, this creates friction, making already challenging problems more difficult for them to solve.

Further, externally developed parts can be redesigned at the whim of the supplier, potentially causing the company to have to redesign their production system at an inconvenient time. As these startups continue to improve their production systems and iterate on their products, they may find that they need to quickly make a change to components to achieve a new milestone. If those components are outsourced, the startup could see their operations stall for months waiting for suppliers to make the necessary modifications. By integrating the production of these critical parts, startups can ensure the parts are designed to fit their specific needs and that they have a reliable capability to refine these components on their own schedule.

INTEGRATION BUILDS A COMPETITIVE MOAT

The investment required to commercialize and scale a Transformative Technology is usually substantial. To attract that amount of capital, these startups must convince investors that they will build a business that can last for many years and continue to scale the deployment of its technology.

Even beyond what investors look for, achieving maximal impact requires building a business to a very large scale—and that requires the business to survive long enough to achieve that scale. Vertical integration is one tool that can enable a business to build a competitive advantage, or "moat," that keeps them ahead of new competitors and helps them scale.

Transformative Technology companies, by definition, have some proprietary technology that is at the core of their business strategy. The technology will help them have a durable competitive advantage, whether through patents or the ingenuity required to develop a better solution. Vertical integration enables these companies to develop an "innovation stack" that builds an increasingly competitive advantage over existing technologies and makes it more difficult for an improvement in any part of the chain to overcome that advantage.

Apple is a great example. When Apple first launched the iPhone in 2007, its touch screens and smartphone form factor were better than anything else on the market. But Apple knew that in only a short period, perhaps one or two years, other companies would come out with competing devices that were quite similar.

From its inception, Apple recognized the value of integrating the operating system software with the underlying hardware. Apple made a strategic choice to build out an App Store that enabled others to build for its device while still allowing Apple to maintain strong control over the unity of the ecosystem. That App Store is now one of Apple's biggest profit centers. Further, the cohesive "feel" of the ecosystem is a major factor in why people choose to purchase Apple products.

Contrast Apple's strategy with Google's strategy of building the software layer while allowing others to build the hardware. While this has enabled Google to reach a broader segment of the market, the way users experience Google's software can vary greatly based on the device they are using. This approach also creates challenges for Google's development team, who must test any updates to its software on a broad range of devices to ensure that it operates as intended.

Note that for all the pitfalls and benefits of the approaches to vertical integration that Apple and Google took, their integrations were mostly about software. The challenges without vertical integration would be substantially larger in a hardware-centric business with more significant infrastructure costs, like most Transformative Technology businesses.

WHEN TO VERTICALLY INTEGRATE

Given the reasons for Transformative Technology companies to vertically integrate parts of the supply chain, how should you choose which components to integrate? The decision comes down to the value of integrating the particular process or component versus the cost and additional risk of adding to the primary business function. You should work through the following questions and then make an assessment about whether you should vertically integrate a given part of the supply chain or not:

1. Does a commercial supplier already exist at a cost your startup can afford?
2. Do the properties of the commercially available component match your startup's needs?
3. Is there a strategic advantage that can be gained by bringing the component in-house?
4. Is the value of vertically integrating that component greater than the cost and risk of development to your startup?
5. Does your team have a unique insight, data set, and so on, that makes them think they can build the component better than another supplier could?

By answering these questions, you can identify the most valuable parts of the supply chain for your company and develop your vertical integration strategy. In doing so, you will build a more robust company with a greater likelihood of creating impact.

CHAPTER 18

PRINCIPLE IX: TRANSFORMATIVE DISRUPTION STARTS TOP-DOWN

"If you're trying to disrupt the status quo and beat bigger competitors, you're not going to do it by playing their game."

DHARMESH SHAH

One of the most difficult problems to solve when bringing a Transformative Technology solution to market is to determine the form of the first product. For Transformative Technology companies, the initial product decision is further complicated by technical, regulatory, and feasibility concerns that typical startups do not have to consider.

In particular, the cost of production at a small scale is often a driving factor of initial product selection. The cost per unit to make the initial product at a small scale may be greater, but startups often cannot raise the funds for a large-scale production facility without proof that they can execute at a smaller scale. They often must also prove that enough customers want the product to justify the investment.

Given these circumstances, most Transformative Technology companies can assume they will need to build a pilot production facility before moving to scale. In many cases, this pilot production stage is beneficial; it enables startups to test the technology in production, identify unexpected problems that may arise, and work out the kinks in production operations more cheaply than at later stages. But despite the benefits, starting with small-scale production and its higher costs leaves startups with the challenge of identifying a product strategy that they can scale.

In truth, the goal does not have to be a product that is immediately profitable per unit, though that can be beneficial. Rather, a startup's goal should be to make enough money from a product—or sustain small enough losses in the early stage—that the capital requirements commensurate with their ability to raise capital.

START SMALL TO GROW BIG

For most Transformative Technology companies, a top-down market approach addresses the majority of these product strategy challenges.

What is a top-down market approach? Essentially, it involves initially launching a high-end product at small volume, targeting customers who are willing to pay a premium price. Then, as production scales, a company releases new products at a lower cost and higher volume that target more value-conscious customers. Finally, the company reaches a mass market product that is affordable and meets the quality threshold for a majority of customers.

The benefits of launching a transformative product from the top-down are numerous.

RISK REDUCTION

The process of scaling a startup is all about reducing risk. Taking a top-down approach to entering a market provides a path to reducing market, financing, and technical risk early in the company lifecycle. Bringing a product to market earlier helps to reduce risk by enabling companies to collect user feedback faster than if they were to develop a low-cost, scalable version of the technology.

This reduction in market risk also allows companies to more easily raise funding to scale production. Combined with what the company learned from early production, an early launch of a niche, high-end product can provide startups with a significant information advantage and de-risk other parts of the business much more rapidly.

Further, launching a niche product at small volume increases the feasibility of building a company based on Transformative Technology. If these startups only focused on product development until they had a product that was ready for large-scale production at price parity with existing solutions, the vast majority would run out of money and fail before they ever reached the market.

Starting with a low-volume, higher-priced product makes scaling production more feasible by spreading the scale-up over time. It also mitigates the risk of committing to unproven production processes. As good as simulations and rendering technologies are in some fields, testing in the real world can yield some unexpected results.

Selling a low-volume, high-priced product enables startups to reduce their cash burn rate while validating these production models. The top-down market entry strategy makes the scale-up process more resource efficient and validates customer demand for the product.

BUILD A BRAND

Having a product in the market is valuable for building a brand, especially for young companies that are spending the majority of their effort on technology development. By launching a high-end product into the market, startups can build a reputation for delivering quality products and demonstrate the impact their products can have on a Big Intractable Problem. Until a product is in the market and performing, any conversation about its potential to create impact is often treated with significant skepticism.

Startups can build upon this brand awareness and impact demonstration to drive demand for their next phase of growth. Initial product reviews can build momentum for a startup and drive interest for potential customers. Companies that manage their scale-up strategically can leverage that interest to convert fans into pre-sales or even public support for the launch of their next products.

Though the initial, high-end sales are unlikely to be the work that directly meets the company's vision or drives the impact the company desires, they still help startups move toward these goals.

At this early stage, companies should convey how the initial launch is helping them to achieve their mission and their impact goals in the long-term. Telling this impact story can be a powerful tool for a Transformative Technology startup, particularly once they have an initial product on the market that validates their capabilities.

READ THE MARKET

Given these myriad benefits, a rational choice for most Transformative Technology startups would be to pursue a go-to-market strategy that involves launching products from the top-down. But startups must consider whether the market they are entering has the type of customers that this strategy requires.

Releasing a first product targeting the upper-end of a market in price necessitates a customer that is willing to be an early adopter and pay a premium for getting access to the technology before others. In consumer markets, determining whether these customers exist can be pretty straightforward: simply search for a premium segment in a market and look at the new products released specifically for those customers.

In business-to-business markets or complex industries in which a consumer may be the end user but not the direct buyer (i.e., B2B2C), validating that these customers exist can be more challenging. In these situations, studying the market and searching for cases in which new technologies were introduced can help you to understand the dynamics of that particular market. Answering the following questions will help you to understand how you can launch a top-down product into those markets:

- How were prior Transformative Technologies introduced?
- Who were the first customers?
- Did those first customers pay a premium compared to those who bought into a later version of the product?

In some markets, the customers who have the capital available to buy the high-end products are not early adopters, preferring to buy more proven technologies that are well established and fully featured. The early adopter archetype describes those who are willing to: 1) use a new product because it solves one problem much better than an existing solution *and* 2) tolerate the lack of features or performance in other aspects that are less important to them.

This combination of the early adopter archetype with the budget to purchase a high-end product can be incredibly valuable to startups. By targeting these customers, startups can launch an early version of their Transformative Technology product top-down into their selected market.

START WITH WHY

The top-down deployment strategy is not without risk. If founders are not clear about their strategy and their overall mission, their vision can be co-opted by those who are telling the company's story.

One of the most important assets a company has is the trust of its supporters and customers. Particularly for young companies that are likely to make some mistakes in the early days as they figure out how to operate efficiently, having supporters that trust the company is working toward their stated mission buys the company time to "work out the kinks." As Simon Sinek, author of *Start with Why*, frequently says, "People don't buy what you do, they buy why you do it."[193]

When startup founders and leaders do not evangelize their vision, their story often ends up being told by customers, press, and others who share their interpretations of a given action. That same startup could end up with customers wondering how they can claim to strive for large-scale impact while selling a luxury product that only the wealthiest can afford.

If founders and leaders do not tell their story, others will tell it for them—and it likely will not be the story they intended to have told.

---

193 Simon Sinek, "How Great Leaders Inspire Action," TED video, 17:58, September 2009.

TESLA'S GRAND VISION

Regardless of your views about Tesla's long-term viability, it has executed on the strategy of disrupting from the top-down better than nearly any other Transformative Technology company in the last half-century.

Early in the company's history, Elon Musk recognized that potential customers and the public could easily misconstrue the company's actions if he did not clearly lay out its strategy. For a young company that was likely to run into some challenges as they scaled up their production, losing their supporters could have been disastrous, turning potential future customers into those actively advocating against Tesla.

Instead, Musk published *The Secret Tesla Motors Master Plan (just between you and me)* on Tesla's website.[194] In this post, Musk clearly defined his vision for Tesla, the company mission, and how its initial product would help it make progress toward that overall mission.

The post begins with a clear exposition of Tesla's mission:

"As you know, the initial product of Tesla Motors is a high performance electric sports car called the Tesla Roadster. However, some readers may not be aware of the fact that our long-term plan is to build a wide range of models, including affordably priced family cars. This is because the overarching purpose of Tesla Motors (and the reason I am funding the company) is to help expedite the move from a mine-and-burn hydrocarbon

---

194 Elon Musk, "The Secret Tesla Motors Master Plan (just between you and me)," Tesla, August 2, 2006.

economy toward a solar electric economy, which I believe to be the primary, but not exclusive, sustainable solution."[195]

Following Simon Sinek's framework for compelling narratives, Musk starts with why. He puts the mission front and center before explaining how Tesla's strategy will enable it to achieve that mission. Musk's description of why Tesla started with a high-end, niche product is clear and direct: "The strategy of Tesla is to enter at the high end of the market, where customers are prepared to pay a premium, and then drive down market as fast as possible to higher unit volume and lower prices with each successive model."[196]

He does not apologize, make excuses, or pretend that the premium product will achieve the impact the company seeks. He is not trying to hoodwink customers. Instead, he explains that the cost structure of the new technology requires Tesla to start up-market and work its way down to an affordable, mass-market product that will be the primary vehicle for creating impact at scale. The post concludes with a very short recap that can be easily shared to help spread Tesla's strategy to potential customers and the public. That summary reads:

---

195 Ibid.
196 Ibid.

So, in short, the master plan is:
Build sports car
Use that money to build an affordable car
Use that money to build an even more affordable car
While doing above, also provide zero emission electric power
generation options[197]

Without presenting this coherent explanation of their mission and their strategy for achieving that mission, competitors, analysts, and the media would have been the primary voices telling Tesla's story. This coverage may or may not have been accurate and would certainly have fluctuated based on the macroeconomic environment and the company's performance. While this type of commentary will always exist to some degree, Transformative Technology companies benefit tremendously from continuing to be visible champions for their missions. Championing their mission is particularly important when the path to achieving stated impact goals are not obvious—like when Transformative Technology companies launch products into the market from the top-down.

ALTERNATIVE PROTEIN GOES UPMARKET
Plant-based meat alternative company Impossible Foods also launched its products using a top-down approach, first releasing its plant-based burgers in higher-end restaurants.

Why higher-end restaurants? Perhaps the company had data indicating the wealthier customers were more likely to be vegetarian. The primary reason for targeting high-end

---

197 Ibid.

restaurants was almost certainly the higher selling price and lower volume requirements.

In July 2016, the Impossible Burger debuted at Momofuku Nishi, a mid-scale restaurant in New York City's Chelsea neighborhood.[198] Three months later, the Impossible Burger expanded to California, making the menus at Jardinière and Cockscomb in San Francisco and Crossroads Kitchen in Los Angeles.[199] These upscale restaurants enabled Impossible Foods to release its initial product in small volumes to customers willing to pay a premium for it.

The targeted release also helped Impossible Foods with marketing. These large cities had sizable vegetarian and vegan populations that were more likely to test the Impossible Burger and generate positive press. Further, this small-scale launch enabled Impossible Foods to demonstrate its pilot-scale manufacturing capability and prove that there was sufficient customer demand to scale.

Once Impossible Foods built its first large production facility, it began to expand geographically and down market. Because of limited production volume and the prices that were still higher than traditional beef patties, Impossible Foods' strategy was to expand geographically to small, mid-market restaurant chains like Bareburger and Umami Burger.[200]

---

198 Amanda Holpuch, "Impossible burger: New York's latest food craze is a veggie burger that bleeds," *The Guardian,* July 27, 2016.

199 Sarah Buhr, "The Impossible Foods burger heads West," *Techcrunch,* October 13, 2016.

200 Hannah Goldfield, "Can White Castle Sell the Impossible—the Meatless Burger That Bleeds?" *New Yorker,* April 14, 2018.

Over the next two years, Impossible Foods continued to expand through smaller mid-market restaurant chains. Its first step into a mass-market restaurant chain came in April 2018 with a nationwide deal with fast-food chain White Castle.[201] This move was expanded with the partnership with Burger King in April 2019.[202]

Impossible Foods' example demonstrates how launching products top-down into a market can be a useful strategy for de-risking a transformative product in stages. It also highlights how the top-down market entry strategy enables companies to raise enough funding to survive until they achieve the next milestone needed to scale further. Without the ability to start with high-end, small-volume production, these Transformative Technology businesses would not likely be able to scale efficiently, if at all.

201 Ibid.

202 Jonathan Shieber, "Burger King will roll out the Impossible Burger nationwide by the end of the year," *Techcrunch*, April 30, 2019.

CHAPTER 19

PRINCIPLE X: BUILD THE MACHINE THAT MAKES THE MACHINE

"We realized that the true problem, the true difficulty, and where the greatest potential is—is building the machine that makes the machine. In other words, it's building the factory. I'm really thinking of the factory like a product."

ELON MUSK

One thing that often eludes Transformative Technology founders is how important scalability is to their ability to create impact. As we have discussed in Chapter sixteen, designing for scale early in the development process is one way to increase the probability that Transformative Technology startups can successfully scale their product and business. But these startups must also go beyond engineering products for scalability.

To prepare their businesses for success, Transformative Technology entrepreneurs also need to think about how they can make the production process and infrastructure scalable. They must consider how to refine "the machine that makes the machine."

Most entrepreneurs spend very little time thinking about the production processes required to make their products. Given that most startups are software-driven, this is understandable; the infrastructure required for those businesses was largely established ten to twenty years ago and is ubiquitous today. For hardware businesses working with existing technologies, many contract manufacturers, engineering design firms, and co-packers are willing and able to turn prototypes into production-ready products. Production feasibility, if not execution, is a solved problem for these companies.

Transformative Technologies do not benefit from these same established ecosystems. The technologies are new enough that supply chain partners who can provide the necessary inputs and manufacturing processes without significant customization rarely exist. For this reason, entrepreneurs developing Transformative Technology solutions cannot only think about the product feature set and whether it actually solves an important problem. They must also consider how they will be able to make enough of their product to meet demand and scale the business.

If these founders want to achieve impact by solving a Big Intractable Problem for many customers, they will need to invest development effort into industrializing the production system in addition to making the product.

PRODUCTION SYSTEMS ARE CRITICAL TO SCALING

Scalability appears frequently in this book because scale is the underlying assumption of creating impact. A new solution to an intractable problem is far less impactful if it reaches one thousand people than if it reaches one million people. Given that Big Intractable Problems are often felt intensely by one billion or more people, building a scalable solution and deploying it broadly are necessary to achieving impact.

Scaling can be an expensive proposition for many Transformative Technology startups. Whether it's because novel technology is often expensive or because critical industries depend upon significant physical infrastructure, deploying these types of solutions requires the investment of large amounts of capital. Because scaling is expensive, investing resources in reducing the costs of scaling is a high-leverage activity.

Now, you may be thinking the production process is far less important than the product itself when it comes to solving a problem and achieving success at scale. But this focus on the product in isolation is flawed. It is predicated on the assumption that an underlying production process exists that is both cost-efficient and scalable. While this assumption is unlikely to be challenged for most startups, it will not hold true for the majority of Transformative Technology startups.

PRODUCTION, NOT PRODUCT EXCEPTIONALISM, PUT A CAR IN EVERY DRIVEWAY

The story of how the car became widely adopted in the United States demonstrates the importance of planning for scale and investing in a cost-efficient, scalable production process.

The first car in America was invented in 1893 by J. Frank and Charles Duryea, two bicycle mechanics from Massachusetts.[203] So, why are they not hailed as the fathers of American cars? Because they never achieved real scale, and their innovation was not pervasive enough to create large-scale impact on American society.

When Henry Ford entered the market, he saw an opportunity. As with most new technologies, the challenge with cars in the early 1900s was that the high-quality vehicles were not affordable for the average person. The low-cost automobiles that did exist were poorly built and lacked the functionality that consumers wanted. Ford recognized he could rapidly scale his business if he could build a car that met the performance expectations of customers at an affordable price point.

When discussing his vision, Ford said, "I will build a car for the great multitude...It will be constructed of the best materials, by the best men to be hired, after the simplest designs that modern engineering can devise. But it will be so low in price that no man making a good salary will be unable to own one."[204] While this may seem like "marketing speak," it

---

203 *Encyclopedia Britannica Online*, s.v. "Charles E. Duryea and J. Frank Duryea," accessed January 7, 2020.

204 Henry Ford, *My Life and Work* (Fairfield, IA: 1st World Publishing, 2004), 89.

also highlights Ford's strategy of building a car at the scale needed to drive down prices and make his car affordable enough to reach the mass-market.

To achieve the necessary price point and production volumes, Ford invested in reinventing the production process. The traditional production process for cars looked a lot like a cottage industry: cars were *crafted* individually by hand. No one vehicle was exactly like the other. This production process was not scalable. It relied upon highly skilled craftsmen rather than semi-skilled or skilled workers who could be trained on a smaller range of required tasks. Making individual cars could take weeks, and an increase in demand would quickly create massive backlogs.

Ford's assembly line production method made large-scale production viable and reduced costs enough to make automobiles available to the mass-market consumer. By evaluating the flaws in the existing production process, Ford was able to identify the stages that could easily be optimized and the changes that would yield greatest improvements. Mass production enabled Ford to overtake the Duryea brothers and established Ford as the automobile company to beat. While whether Ford used a first principles lens for his analysis, is impossible to say, many of the improvements that led to the creation of the assembly line could be identified by such a line of reasoning.

THE PRODUCTION LINE: THE FIRST PRODUCTION "MACHINE"
Henry Ford's major innovation was replacing artisanal craftsmen with semi-skilled workers who were trained in

a specific subset of tasks. Separating workers into groups that performed different parts of the manufacturing process naturally led to the development of "stations" for each production stage. Organizing those stations into manufacturing lines that performed the tasks as successive steps on vehicles moving from step one to finishing was the logical conclusion of that innovation.

The investment in developing the machine that makes the machine paid off in spades. The assembly line enabled Ford to manufacture over one hundred cars per day, more than the entire US industry was producing at the time.[205] It also reduced production costs, dramatically shortening the time to make a single vehicle and improving the quality and consistency of the cars that were being made. This manufacturing process innovation enabled Ford to bring the Model T to households across America and scale production to over fifteen million units.[206]

As good as Ford's production methods were for the time, they had limitations that grew increasingly important as the car industry matured. Ford's assembly line process created an enormous efficiency gain, but his process also had a relatively high waste of material inputs and volume of re-work required to make the parts fit properly.

---

205 Agence France-Presse, "Ford Launched the Modern Assembly Line a Century Ago and Changed Society," *Industryweek*, October 7, 2013.

206 Thomas H. Klier and James M. Rubenstein, *Who Really Made Your Car?: Restructuring and Geographic Change in the Auto Industry*, (Kalamazoo, MI: W.E. Upjohn Institute for Employment Research, 2008), 98.

REIMAGINING PRODUCTION SYSTEMS FROM FIRST PRINCIPLES

When Toyota entered the car market following World War II, it sought to reengineer the automobile manufacturing process to create a sustainable advantage. Toyota noted that Ford's assembly line created expensive waste and required extensive rework. It also recognized that car manufacturers kept large inventory volumes at their factories—at significant cost—to keep production lines running at capacity. Competitors' manufacturing lines were also very inflexible, unable to easily adapt to production changes or the introduction of new vehicle models.

While their competitors accepted these constraints, Toyota saw opportunity in a flexible, capital efficient production system. The founder of Toyota, Kiichiro Toyoda, and engineer Taiichi Ohno developed a set of production principles from a fundamental insight: a just-in-time production system could minimize inefficient use of capital, space, and people.[207] The result is the Toyota Production System, which strives to eliminate inconsistency and waste due to overproduction, poor use of time, excess inventory, and unnecessary movement of people and transportation of goods.[208]

Toyota remains the most valuable car company in the world, largely because of the benefits wrought from its unique process optimization.[209]

207 Taiichi Ohno, *Toyota Production System: Beyond Large-Scale Production* (New York, NY: Productivity Press, 1988).

208 Ibid.

209 Al Root, "Tesla Is Now the Second-Most-Valuable Car Maker in the World. Look Out, Toyota," *Barron's*, January 22, 2020.

Many car manufacturers have tried to replicate the results by copying the most visible parts of the system: inventory levels. Though they reduced inventory, most of these projects failed to achieve similar results. These companies imitated without understanding the underlying insight and motivation. Toyota's initial team sought to understand the systems required for car production, defined its own specific needs, and built a system that maximized its ability to achieve its internal goals.

This was not a one-time effort at Toyota. After the global financial crisis of 2008 led to a sudden drop in car purchases, the company sought to update the Toyota Production System to make it more responsive to production volume changes demanded by shifting market dynamics. Successfully implementing this new system required Toyota to vertically integrate production of much of the production equipment for their factories; their new approach was transformative, and the existing suppliers could not make what Toyota needed.

The results of this vertical integration and investment in production system optimization speak for themselves. The new system, dubbed the Toyota New Global Architecture, will also bring Toyota closer to their initial ideal of flexible production.[210] The production lines will be able to scale capacity from fifty thousand to one hundred thousand units and will enable the sequential production of different models on the same production line.[211] Further, the new-generation of

---

210 "Toyota New Global Architecture," Toyota, September 15, 2015.

211 "TNGA explained: engineering for the future," Toyota, April 15, 2015.

Toyota factories will be 25 percent smaller, require 40 percent less investment, and produce 55 percent less CO_2.[212]

Toyota's story offers a critical insight for founders of Transformative Technology companies. Though it was entering an industry that had existed for nearly fifty years and that had advanced production methods at the time, its team did not take the production process for granted. Rather than trying to build another line of cars using existing methods, the Toyota team recognized the need to optimize the existing production methods to align with its unique goals. To make that optimization process useful, it had to be explicit about what it was optimizing for.

THE PRODUCTION PROCESS AS A PRODUCT

In determining success and impact for Transformative Technology companies, scalability often outweighs the quality of the first product. Though not a hard rule, most first products based on Transformative Technologies tend to be an order of magnitude better at addressing some part of a Big Intractable Problem that a customer deems important. These first products generally lack other features that would make them complete replacements for the existing solution.

As long as the first product meets this order of magnitude threshold in one key area, whether the company creates far-reaching societal impact will depend on its ability to scale. Reaching this scale is much more likely when these companies prioritize development of the machine that makes

---

212 Ibid.

the machine. In other words, the very best Transformative Technology companies treat the process as a product.

One of the biggest drivers of scalability and success should not be left to chance. Founders cannot afford to simply hire an engineering firm to design their production processes and facilities and consider it a job well done. Rather, founders should consider these areas of strategic importance and dedicate commensurate internal resources and attention to their development and optimization.

For these companies, the question then becomes: What is the process that is most likely to help them build the machine that makes the machine?

RATIONAL PROCESS DESIGN

Rational process design, a method of designing a process to optimize for defined functionality and performance standards, is an ideal technique for building the machine that makes the machine. As it turns out, rational process design is quite similar to the method we previously discussed for first principles reasoning in Chapter twelve. This is logical because process design involves solving a complex, multi-stage problem by reducing each process stage to the set of first principles that define it. Such a process can be defined as follows:

1. **Plan for scale early**
   Planning for scale means being aware that process development is going to be an important part of the development of your product. Once a proof of concept has

been achieved, startups developing these Transformative Technologies should strongly consider allocating budget, people, and resources to take an iterative approach to developing an optimized, scalable production process.

At this early stage, the company should also explicitly define its internal goals and how it influences what it will be optimizing for in a production process. The target criteria could be price, production speed, consistency of output product, system adaptability to multiple products, or something else. Whatever the criteria are, the company must explicitly define them early on and develop key performance indicators on which to measure its progress. Just like with a product, having a set of criteria to test against, helps to align a team toward the goal and guide the iterative process development cycles.

2. **Define the system from first principles**
Once a company knows what criteria it will be using to optimize their production system, it should outline the existing production process from beginning to end. Before trying to make improvements, the company should identify the best available process to understand what is currently done and why. With the process fully mapped out, it can consider which steps are least aligned with its criteria.

The process stages that are least aligned with the company's criteria are the low-hanging fruit for re-engineering, as they are not fit for purpose. For each stage it plans to change, the company should then define the first principles at work. The first principles provide the physical bounds—barring a Nobel Prize-worthy discovery—within which the process innovation must occur.

This is a process step Tesla is going through with its vehicle assembly process. Tesla CEO Elon Musk has been quite vocal about his thoughts on the importance of treating the production system as a product and designing it from first principles. "When you think of a manufacturing facility, for a given size of factory, the output is going to be volume times density times velocity," Musk said at Tesla's 2016 annual shareholder meeting.[213]

Though quite simplistic, this first principles analysis defines the criteria that Tesla can measure against to track their process improvement. Given the importance of manufacturing efficiency to capital-efficient scaling for a car company, the fact that Tesla is taking after Toyota and working to develop their own process innovations is not surprising.

3. **Identify the challenges to be overcome**
   Now that the company has the system and physical constraints defined, the work shifts to identifying and prioritizing the challenges that need to be overcome to achieve the defined goals. Once the full process has been mapped, a few of the challenges will likely be obvious. However, companies should not stop with the most apparent difficulties. By assessing the first principles involved during each stage of the production process, they can determine

---

213 "Tesla Motors 2016 Annual Shareholder Meeting," Youtube video, 04:31:57, posted by "Darren Bryant," May 31, 2016.

where the largest gaps exist between the current method and the theoretical limit based on the first principles. These are the process choke points in which developing an improved method should be the easiest.

Beyond the first principles analysis, consider the inputs and outputs of the current production system:

- Where is there waste in material, effort, or people?
- What undesirable consequences are currently accepted?
- Where do the current processes deviate most from our company's goals?

Just like Toyota, consider how the current process compares to company goals and identify the stages that need to be re-engineered to close the gap on production process goals.

Prioritizing these challenges based on the expected payoff and the perceived difficulty for developing improvements is rational. This prioritization can help to maximize progress with limited resources, build momentum, and provide evidence to the team that the time spent building the machine that makes the machine, is worthwhile.

4. **Determine the best way to design around choke points**
   Finally, companies are left to develop new production methods and technologies that will allow them to bypass the current choke points in the process. What are some of the tools for engineering around these choke points?

We have already discussed a few of them. In many cases, a choke point is due to a particular machine or part that is made by an external supplier. This supplier is designing for their own criteria and their product may not be the best fit for the startup's process needs. Just like Toyota did with the development of its New Global Architecture, the best solution may be to vertically integrate and produce those machines and parts internally.

Alternatively, forming a strategic partnership with another company in the industry, supply chain can help to overcome a choke point in the production system. In the case of cellular agriculture, many companies are facing significant cost and performance hurdles with traditional industrial bioreactors and cell culture media. These products were either made for the biomedical industry, where price was not significant criteria, or the beer industry, where an entirely different set of success criteria was used.

Vertically integrating these components may be viable for some companies that have the right internal expertise and adequate funding. For others, it may be faster and more efficient to partner with existing manufacturers to develop an optimized version of the product for the cellular agriculture use case.

By following a process along these lines, Transformative Technology startups can reliably and repeatably develop the process innovations they will need to build scalable businesses that have significant, long-term impact on Big Intractable

Problems. However, these companies will all be better off for investing in the machines that make their machines.

PART V

A MORE ABUNDANT FUTURE IS WITHIN OUR GRASP

CHAPTER 20

CONCLUSION

———

"The future remains uncertain and so it should, for it is the canvas upon which we paint our desires. Thus always the human condition faces a beautifully empty canvas. We possess only this moment in which to dedicate ourselves continuously to the sacred presence which we share and create."

FRANK HERBERT

To build the vanguard cohort of Transformative Technology companies that will sustainably tackle our Big Intractable Problems, we will need more people to become entrepreneurs. We will need to stoke the ambition of those who want to have a lasting, positive impact on society. Finally, we will need to demonstrate how entrepreneurship can help them achieve that goal.

In this book, we have explored the thinking that motivates this assertion and a framework that ambitious individuals can use to chart their own path into Transformative Technology entrepreneurship. One of my primary motivations for writing this book was to provide you, the reader, with the context to identify Big Intractable Problems that resonate with you and to illuminate a potential path to solving those problems. Developing the right tool kit can be one of the most significant hurdles to success with startups. The principles and tools discussed in this book should give you confidence that you can be a part of solving the extraordinary challenges we face.

For Transformative Technology entrepreneurs, those Principles for Success are:

1. Choose the Right Problem
2. Learn to See Exponentials
3. Reason from First Principles (Rather Than by Analogy)
4. Consider Solution Concentration
5. Recognize the Value of Ideas
6. Account for Path Dependence
7. Start with Scale in Mind
8. Harness Vertical Integration as the Great Equalizer
9. Enter the Market Top-down
10. Build the Machine That Makes the Machine

HINGES OF HISTORY
We appear to be at a **Hinge of History**, a historical inflection point in which our power to shape the long-term future is amplified far beyond the norm. In these Hinge moments, broader circumstances magnify the impacts of our choices and our actions. Normally, the actions of small groups of individuals do not significantly bend the arc of history. However, at Hinges of History, the actions of these small groups can substantially alter our collective trajectory.

How do we know we are currently in a Hinge of History? Our evidence comes from understanding exponential trends and how they create periods of tremendous change. The last thirty years have been a remarkable time in which a number of exponential technologies have emerged, from the computer, to genetic sequencing, to cellular agriculture. According to futurist and X-Prize founder Peter Diamandis, the convergence of these exponential technologies is amplifying their impact on our society and increasing the pace of change.

Coupled with the rise in exponential technologies, humanity has experienced a population explosion that has seen the population nearly quadrupled in the last hundred years. This exponential population growth has created or exacerbated a number of Big Intractable Problems. Though we developed solutions to a number of these problems, our prior solutions were not sustainable in the long-term. Many of them have gone on to create Big Intractable Problems of their own.

In the last half century, humanity has also found that we are able to leverage our technological inventions to slowly move beyond the natural cycles of abundance and scarcity that drive evolution. Even so, recent experiences with pandemics, famines, wildfires, hurricanes, and insect plagues have shown we still have some distance to travel before we fully master our environment.

This transitional period—in which we find ourselves with extraordinary power through our technologies but not the wisdom to always use them well—is where we face a uniquely powerful and dangerous moment in our history. With a population that is surely beyond the *natural* carrying capacity of the Earth, we face the risk of inadvertently damaging the lifeboat on which we all collectively sail through the dark expanse of space.

As we have begun to understand, our technologies have tremendous power. These technologies have enabled us to unwittingly geoengineer our planet, with possible massive, negative impacts on our planet and ourselves. Without the wisdom to use these technologies well and understand their risks, we could easily do severe, potentially catastrophic damage that makes our planet far less conducive to our continued survival.

President John F. Kennedy, perhaps due to his recognition of the power of nuclear weapons, was one of the first world leaders to recognize this threat. "The world is very different now," he noted. "For man holds in his mortal hands the power to abolish all forms of human poverty and all forms of human life."[214]

We have only really wielded this power for the last hundred years. Of the two-hundred-thousand-year history of modern humans, this is but a blink in our existence. And yet, the decisions we make in this period can bend the future, *our* future, in fantastic or terrible ways. The question we must answer is whether we will collectively work to build a more abundant future for humanity or whether we will stay on our current path and hope for the best.

---

214 US National Archives & Records Administration, "Transcript of President John F. Kennedy's Inaugural Address (1961)," Our Documents.gov, accessed November 14, 2019.

BUILDING AN ABUNDANT FUTURE

At this moment, we face a number of critical problems that we will need to overcome to build the more abundant, promising future that many of us aspire to. Some of these problems, like climate change and mass extinctions, are the result of our failure to understand our power to unintentionally change the planet at scale. Others, like plastic and toxic waste pollution, have emerged from the sheer scale of human activity and lack of long-term thinking. Sustainable food production remains one of our most prominent challenges, linked both to our population explosion and short-sightedness.

To maximize our chances of building a more equitable, abundant future for humanity, we will need to solve these problems in a way that reduces their catastrophic risk. Failing to do so may result in a far less hospitable Earth and even the eventual collapse of our civilization.

Many of the solutions we require will not likely emerge from our established institutions. This is not meant to be a rebuke of large corporations or governments, but rather an assessment of the institutional inertia that these organizations must overcome to develop the type of transformative solutions that will be needed.

Our current economic system plays a significant role in creating this inertia. Capitalism prioritizes growth from resource extraction and valorization but fails to account for anything that falls outside the market pricing scheme—an unfortunate trait it inherited from its predecessor, mercantilism. Capitalism does not account for value beyond what a customer is directly willing to pay for a product. It also fails to account for any cost beyond what it costs a business to produce that product. Today, capitalism ascribes no additional value to solutions that are better for the environment or our society and imputes no additional cost to products that negatively impact our society and our planet.

Given that mercantilism developed at a time when most humans thought it was impossible for us to affect any change on a global scale through our activities, the fact that this ideology has persisted is not surprising. The types of challenges and problems that develop from ignoring these environmental and societal impacts—those that are "external" to the market—does not pose an imminent threat in most cases. Without an urgent crisis to shift this way of thinking, it remains embedded within our model of capitalism.

Only within the last hundred years have we started to recognize that these "externalities" are not simply inconvenient side effects of our economic activity. We began to acknowledge that "externalities" is just a euphemism for a number of costs that we are ignoring, and that those costs are accumulating, unaccounted for, and outside our economic framework. Like a startup accruing technical debt, this Externality Debt will eventually have to be paid. Some of our biggest problems, like the ozone hole and biodiversity loss from pesticide use, reached a critical point that demanded a rapid response. But for the sorts of Big Intractable Problems that unfold and intensify over decades rather than years, our institutions still appear to be ill-suited to respond.

Albert Einstein famously noted, "We can't solve problems by using the same kind of thinking we used when we created them." In this case, this is clearly a literal truth. To solve the Big Intractable Problems we face, we will need an entirely new method of accounting for environmental and societal costs and benefits, one that recognizes these things to be at least as valuable as economic returns. The companies that came of age—thinking of environmental and societal harm as externalities rather than costs that must be factored into how they do business—are unlikely to be the ones to bring about this change.

"It is difficult to get a man to understand something, when his salary depends upon his not understanding it!" author Upton Sinclair, who shed light on the human cost of industrialization in *The Jungle*, poignantly stated. Solving the challenges that pose a threat to our modern civilization and our existence will require a new generation of entrepreneurs to recognize the need to account for social and environmental costs alongside their profits. These entrepreneurs will build the vanguard companies that will usher in this more sustainable, abundant era.

As we have discussed in this book, tackling incredible challenges requires increasing your leverage if you are to have any chance at success. Leverage is the meta-tool that enables individuals and small groups of people to affect significant, lasting change at a global scale. Leverage empowers us to turn science fiction into reality. Leverage brings the impossible within reach.

Building companies around Transformative Technologies is one principal method entrepreneurs can use to increase their leverage. Transformative Technologies are defined by a set of properties that makes them uniquely suited to tackling tremendous problems. Due to their exponential nature and their ability to reduce the activation energy for solving Big Intractable Problems, these technologies create possibilities. They create opportunities for entrepreneurs to take on problems that others consider impossible. They enable small groups of people to make progress when even the best-resourced groups run into challenges. Finally, they empower us to see paths that are hidden to others—paths that show us how we can bend the trajectory of humanity toward a more abundant, inspiring future.

Learning from others who have walked a similar path is the second greatest tool for creating leverage. In this book, I have laid out a set of principles for success—mental models, if you will—that I developed through studying the successes and failures of many Transformative Technology entrepreneurs who have sought to solve significant problems in their time. Far too often, we treat each decision and each startup as a unique event rather than looking to the past to learn what has and has not worked.

Entrepreneurs increase their leverage by learning from their predecessors and using the principles to improve their own odds of success. Even Isaac Newton, famous for multiple discoveries that bent the arc of history, recognized the power of learned principles. "If I have seen further, it is by standing on the shoulders of Giants," Newton observed. The principles gleaned from our predecessors do not guarantee success, but they do tip the scales in favor of those who follow them.

Throughout human history, most transformative change was wrought by the Greater Fools among us. From Martin Luther to Galileo and from Nikola Tesla to Elon Musk, these Greater Fools have taken the less rational path in pursuit of ideas that were bigger than themselves. To cultivate a brighter future for our species, we too will rely on the Greater Fools of our time.

If you choose to take up the mantle, you can be one of the Greater Fools that builds a more abundant future for humanity.

"It always seems impossible until it is done."

NELSON MANDELA

ADDITIONAL RESOURCES

For additional resources related to the ideas in *Cultivated Abundance*, including:

- further exploration of the main concepts in this book
- deep dive articles exploring Big Intractable Problems and Transformative Technologies
- worksheets for implementing the ideas in this book
- case studies of Transformative Technology companies that have implemented the Principles for Success to great effect
- interviews with Transformative Technology founders
- and more…

visit *www.mihirpershad.com/abundanceresources*.

GLOSSARY

Activation energy: the amount of energy that must be put into a system to cause a reaction to proceed to completion; influenced by addition of a **catalyst**

Big Intractable Problems: a class of the most important and compelling problems for humanity; defined by the following characteristics: 1) impact more than one billion people, 2) are encountered frequently by those affected, 3) are necessary for individual survival or the continuation of civilization, 4) are in industries that are based on physical infrastructure, and 5) are made more urgent by an approaching inflection point

Catalyst: an input into a system that reduces the **activation energy** that must be overcome for the reaction to proceed to completion

Coordination Problems: a concept from game theory that describes the challenges of getting optimal collective results (that require coordination between individuals) when certain choices may benefit individuals to the detriment of the collective; in business, often observed as office politics, bureaucracy, and "corporate bloat"

Discounting: from economics, the practice of assessing future events, earnings, or value at a reduced rate relative to current events, earnings, or value; applied based on the principle of opportunity cost and loss of optionality; applications beyond economics are a logical fallacy

Externality Debt: the concept that there is a future cost that is incurred as a result of externalities, or unaccounted for costs, that accrue outside of an economic system; the imbalance cannot be maintained or grown in perpetuity, so there is eventually a reckoning in which the deferred price of these externalities must be paid, either through a rebalancing or a collapse of the system that ignores them

Fermi's Paradox: the scale of the universe and number of independent galaxies suggest that it is (statistically) highly probable that other intelligent (read: "sapient") life exists in the Universe. Why have we detected no signs of these other species?

First Principles: the basic blocks of knowledge that are not based on underlying assumptions but which exist *a priori*; in scientific disciplines, the fundamental concepts or assumptions on which a theory, system, or method is based

Flimsy idea: a superficial, initial observation without any substance; a high-level conceptualization of a solution to a problem that does not account for any of the existing complexities (opposite: **unique insight**)

Founder-Problem Fit: a measure of how well suited a founder is to develop a solution to a given problem based on relevant prior experience (industry background or technical skill), skill set, interests, and inclination

Great Filter Hypothesis: the hypothesis that the absence of other sapient life forms indicates the presence of a highly improbable step ("The Great Filter") on the evolutionary path from abiogenesis to an interstellar civilization; initially defined by Robin Hanson

Greater Fool: someone with the perfect blend of self-delusion and ego to think that they can succeed where others have failed; a person who takes actions that are sub-optimal based solely on the risk-adjusted reward but that have transformative positive impact if successful

Hinge of History: a historical inflection point in which our power to shape the long-term future is amplified far beyond the norm, typically evidenced by greater instability and fluctuations from the norm

Idea Maze: a visualization of "all the permutations of the idea and the branching of the decision tree, gaming things out to the end of each scenario"; first described by Balaji Srinivasan

Impact Efficiency: the impact on a target problem that is produced per dollar or per hour spent; serves as a measure of the quality of the **unique insight** behind the solution being implemented and the execution of the team implementing the solution

Innovator's Bias: the belief that entrepreneurial success is based on having "big ideas" rather than solving large enough problems

Longtermism: the idea that the future is likely to be much bigger than the present and that ensuring the long-term future goes well is the best way to positively impact the greatest number of people

Noesis: the Platonic idea describing the process of thinking deductively based solely on the basis of what is known; thought to be the origin of **first-principles** thinking

Orthogonality: from the Euclidian geometry field of mathematics, orthogonality is the generalization of the concept of perpendicularity; orthogonal objects (traditionally vectors) are said to be orthogonal if they make an angle of ninety degrees; the objects do not need to intersect

Path Dependence: the notion that the path traveled to arrive at the current point is relevant to understanding why certain choices were made, why events unfolded the way they did, and what range of future paths are available from the current point

Platform: a technology or solution that enables others to solve problems by using the technology as a connector or by building on top of it

Rational Process Design: a method, most often used in engineering disciplines, of designing a process through optimization toward defined functionality and performance criteria

Reasoning by Analogy: the predominant mode of human reasoning; relies upon mental archetypes constructed from learned experience and acquired wisdom to classify new experiences and make rapid judgments; flawed in non-linear cases in which past experience does not fully represent future possibilities

Solution Concentration: a measure of how many companies there are working to solve a particular problem with similar methods; high solution concentration implies the presence of many highly-similar solutions that are built on the same technologies and using the same underlying assumptions and insights

Sunk Cost: money or other resources that have already been spent and cannot be recovered and which should not be factored into future decisions

Technical Debt: a concept in software development that reflects the future cost incurred (as additional rework or reconstruction) as a result of decisions to prioritize rapid implementation of simpler solutions instead of more robust implementations that would take longer or cost more today

Techno-optimism: the belief that technology can provide solutions to all human problems and that such technology solutions will emerge just as they are needed

Technofideism: a faith in the inherent power of technology; especially as a belief that technology will advance to solve all of humanity's most significant problems on its own, without requiring directed effort from people

Transformative Technologies: a class of technologies that have great potential to be highly impactful; defined by the following characteristics: 1) classified as an exponential or a deep technology, 2) an order of magnitude (10x) improvement over existing solutions, 3) platforms with many powerful applications, 4) catalysts that reduce the activation energy for affecting change, and 5) orthogonal to the existing solution set

Unique Insight: a solution to a problem that demonstrates a deeper understanding of the problem and its context; the holder of the insight has a well-characterized understanding of the problem and its market and technical complexities, and a strategy for implementing the solution (opposite: **flimsy idea**)

Vertical Integration: a business strategy in which a single company elects to own multiple stages of supply or distribution within its supply chain, especially when non-obvious efficiencies may exist between those stages of the supply chain (opposite: specialization)

Watershed Moment: a turning point; a specific moment in time, frequently precipitated by an event, that changes the direction of history; often only recognizable in hindsight

APPENDIX

PREFACE

Soldati, Laura, Di Renzo, Laura, Jirillo, Emillio, Ascierto, Paolo A., Marincola, Francesco M., and Antonino De Lorenzo. "The influence of diet on anti-cancer immune responsiveness." *Journal of Translational Medicine* 16, no. 1 (2018):75. *https://doi.org/10.1186/s12967-018-1448-0.*

CHAPTER 1

Aiello, Leslie C., and Peter Wheeler. "The Expensive-Tissue Hypothesis: The Brain and the Digestive System in Human and Primate Evolution." *Current Anthropology* 36, no. 2 (1995): 199-221. *www.jstor.org/stable/2744104.*

Borlaug, Norman E. "Feeding a world of 10 billion people." The TVA/IFDC Legacy Travis P. Hignett Memorial Lecture, International Fertilizer Development Center, Muscle Shoals, AL, 2003.

Easterbrook, Gregg. "Forgotten Benefactor of Humanity." *The Atlantic.* March 26, 2019. *https://www.theatlantic.com/magazine/archive/1997/01/forgotten-benefactor-of-humanity/306101/.*

Ehrlich, Paul R. *The Population Bomb.* New York, NY: Ballantine Books, 1971. *https://books.google.com.sg/books/about/The_population_bomb.html.*

Johnson, David Gale. *The Struggle against World Hunger.* New York, NY: Foreign Policy Association, 1967.

Mackenzie, Debora. "Norm Borlaug: The Man Who Fed the World." *New Scientist,* September 14, 2009. *https://www.newscientist.com/article/dn17778-norm-borlaug-the-man-who-fed-the-world/#ixzz6IAUR1AG2.*

Paarlberg, Don. "Norman Borlaug: Hunger Fighter." Foreign Economic Development Service, US Department of Agriculture, cooperating with the US Agency for International Development (PA 969). Washington, D. C.: US Government Printing Office, 1970.

Quinn, Kenneth M. "Chapter 1: Dr. Norman E. Borlaug: Twentieth Century Lessons for the Twenty-First Century World." In *ADVANCES IN AGRONOMY,* edited by Donald L. Sparks, 100:13–27. San Diego, CA: Academic Press, 2008.

Quinn, Kenneth M. "Norman Borlaug—Extended Biography." The World Food Prize Foundation, 2009. *https://www.worldfoodprize.org/en/dr_norman_e_borlaug/extended_biography/.*

Raichle, M. E., and D. A. Gusnard. "Appraising the Brain's Energy Budget." *Proceedings of the National Academy of Sciences* 99, no. 16 (2002): 10237–39. *https://doi.org/10.1073/pnas.172399499.*

Rajaram, Sanjaya. "Norman Borlaug: The Man I Worked With and Knew." *Annual Review of Phytopathology* 49, no. 1 (2011): 17–30. *https://doi.org/10.1146/annurev-phyto-072910-095308.*

Schlegel, Rolf H. J. *History of Plant Breeding.* Boca Raton, FL: CRC Press, 2018.

Standage, Tom. *An Edible History of Humanity*. London: Atlantic Books Ltd, 2012.

Tobias, Phillip V. "Homo Habilis and Homo Erectus: From the Oldowan Men to the Acheulian Practitioners" *Anthropologie* (1962-) 18, no. 2/3 (1980): 115-19. *www.jstor.org/stable/44602404*.

CHAPTER 2

Biello, David. "Fact or Fiction?: The Sixth Mass Extinction Can Be Stopped." *Scientific American*. July 25, 2014. *https://www. scientificamerican.com/article/fact-or-fiction-the-sixth-mass-extinction-can-be-stopped/*.

Bogan, Vicki. "The Greater Fool Theory: What Is It?" Cornell SC Johnson College of Business. Accessed December 27, 2019. *http://bogan.dyson.cornell.edu/doc/Hartford/Bogan-9_GreaterFools.pdf*.

Centers for Disease Control and Prevention. "E. Coli (Escherichia Coli): Questions and Answers." December 1, 2014. *https://www. cdc.gov/ecoli/general/index.html*.

Centers for Disease Control and Prevention. "Escherichia Coli (E. Coli)." September 2016. *https://www.cdc.gov/ecoli/pdfs/CDC-E.-coli-Factsheet.pdf*.

Derouin, Sarah. "Deforestation: Facts, Causes & Effects." LiveScience. November 6, 2019. *https://www.livescience. com/27692-deforestation.html*.

Dibartolomeis, Michael, Susan Kegley, Pierre Mineau, Rosemarie Radford, and Kendra Klein. "An Assessment of Acute Insecticide Toxicity Loading (AITL) of Chemical Pesticides Used on Agricultural Land in the United States." *Plos One* 14, no. 8 (2019). *https://doi.org/10.1371/journal.pone.0220029*.

Dirzo, R., H. S. Young, M. Galetti, G. Ceballos, N. J. B. Isaac, and B. Collen. "Defaunation in the Anthropocene." *Science* 345, no. 6195 (2014): 401–6. *https://doi.org/10.1126/science.1251817.*

FAO. "Animal Production." Food and Agriculture Organization of the United Nations, 2019. *http://www.fao.org/animal-production/en/.*

FAO. *World Livestock: Transforming the livestock sector through the Sustainable Development Goals.* Rome: Food and Agriculture Organization of the United Nations (FAO), 2018.

Foley, Jonathan. "It's Time to Rethink America's Corn System." *Scientific American.* March 5, 2013. *https://www.scientificamerican.com/article/time-to-rethink-corn/.*

Gerber, P. J., H. Steinfeld, B. Henderson, A. Mottet, C. Opio, J. Dijkman, A. Falcucci, and G. Tempio. *Tackling climate change through livestock—A global assessment of emissions and mitigation opportunities.* Rome: Food and Agriculture Organization of the United Nations (FAO), 2013.

Horsman, Jennifer, and Jaime Flowers. *Please Don't Eat the Animals: All the Reasons You Need to Be a Vegetarian.* Sanger, CA: Quill Driver Books/Word Dancer Press, 2007.

Jacobs, Andrew. "U.N. Issues Urgent Warning on the Growing Peril of Drug-Resistant Infections." *New York Times,* April 29, 2019.

Kissinger, G., M. Herold, V. De Sy. "Drivers of Deforestation and Forest Degradation: A Synthesis Report for REDD+ Policymakers." Vancouver, Canada: Lexeme Consulting, 2012.

Klein, Alexandra-Maria, Bernard E Vaissière, James H Cane, Ingolf Steffan-Dewenter, Saul A Cunningham, Claire Kremen, and Teja Tscharntke. "Importance of Pollinators in Changing Landscapes for World Crops." *Proceedings Biological Sciences* 274, no. 1608 (2007): 303–13. *https://doi.org/10.1098/rspb.2006.3721.*

Leahy, Stephen. "Insect 'Apocalypse' in US Driven by 50x Increase in Toxic Pesticides." *National Geographic.* August 6, 2019. *https://www.nationalgeographic.com/environment/2019/08/insect-apocalypse-under-way-toxic-pesticides-agriculture/.*

Mateo-Sagasta, Javier, Sara Marjani Zadeh, and Hugh Terral. "Water Pollution from Agriculture: a Global Review." Rome: Food and Agriculture Organization of the United Nations (FAO), 2017.

Minority Staff of the United States Senate Committee on Agriculture, Nutrition, and Forestry. *Animal Waste Pollution in America: An Emerging National Problem.* Washington, D.C.: United States Government Publishing Office, 1997.

Sagan, Carl and Ann Druyan. *Pale Blue Dot: A Vision of the Human Future in Space.* New York, NY: Random House Publishing Group, 1994. *https://books.google.com/books?id=rT-CroH6sRSoC*

Sorkin, Aaron, writer. *The Newsroom.* Season 1, Episode 10. "The Greater Fool." Directed by Greg Mottola, featuring Jeff Daniels, Emily Mortimer, and John Gallagher Jr. Aired August 26, 2012, in broadcast syndication. HBO Entertainment, *https://www.hbo.com/the-newsroom/season-01/10-the-greater-fool.*

Van Boeckel, Thomas P., João Pires, Reshma Silvester, Cheng Zhao, Julia Song, Nicola G. Criscuolo, Marius Gilbert, Sebastian Bonhoeffer, and Ramanan Laxminarayan. "Global Trends in Antimicrobial Resistance in Animals in Low- and Middle-Income Countries." *Science* 365, no. 6459 (2019). *https://doi.org/10.1126/science.aaw1944.*

Walsh, Bryan. "The Triple Whopper Environmental Impact of Global Meat Production." *TIME*. December 16, 2013. *https:// science.time.com/2013/12/16/the-triple-whopper-environmental-impact-of-global-meat-production/.*

Wilson, E. O. "My Wish: Build the Encyclopedia of Life." March 2007. TED Conference, Monterey, California. MPEG-4, 22:21. *https://www.ted.com/talks/e_o_wilson_my_wish_build_the_encyclopedia_of_life.*

CHAPTER 3

Gladwell, Malcolm. *The Tipping Point: How Little Things Can Make a Big Difference.* Boston, MA: Little, Brown, 2006. *https://books.google.com/books?id=yBDBEGBIUmgC.*

Graham, Paul. "Organic Startup Ideas." Paulgraham.com, April 2010. *http://www.paulgraham.com/organic.html.*

Hanson, Robin. "The Great Filter—Are We Almost Past It?" George Mason University. September 15, 1998. *http://mason.gmu.edu/~rhanson/greatfilter.html.*

Schombert, James. "Fermi's Paradox (I.e. Where Are They?)." Lecture, University of Oregon, December 3, 2008. *http://abyss.uoregon.edu/~js/cosmo/lectures/lec28.html.*

"The Top 20 Reasons Startups Fail." CB Insights, November 6, 2019. *https://www.cbinsights.com/research/startup-failure-reasons-top/.*

Todd, Benjamin. "A Guide to Using Your Career to Help Solve the World's Most Pressing Problems." 80,000 Hours, October 2019. *https://80000hours.org/key-ideas/.*

United Nations. "World Population Projected to Reach 9.8 Billion in 2050, and 11.2 Billion in 2100." UN Department of Economic and Social Affairs, June 21, 2017. *https://www.un.org/development/desa/en/news/population/world-population-prospects-2017.html.*

CHAPTER 4

Alexandratos, Nikos and Jelle Bruinsma. *World Agriculture Towards 2030/2050: The 2012 Revision—ESA Working Paper No. 12-03.* Rome: Food & Agriculture Organization of the United Nations, 2012. *http://www.fao.org/3/a-ap106e.pdf.*

Chaturvedi, Swati. "So What Exactly Is 'Deep Technology'?" LinkedIn, July 28, 2015. *https://www.linkedin.com/pulse/so-what-exactly-deep-technology-swati-chaturvedi/.*

Dahl, Olli, Risto Pöykiö, and Hannu Nurmesniemi. "Concentrations of Heavy Metals in Fly Ash from a Coal-Fired Power Plant with Respect to the New Finnish Limit Values." *Journal of Material Cycles and Waste Management* 10 (2008): 87–92. *https://doi.org/10.1007/s10163-007-0189-6.*

"Economics of Nuclear Power." World Nuclear Association. March 2020. *https://www.world-nuclear.org/information-library/economic-aspects/economics-of-nuclear-power.aspx.*

Encyclopedia Britannica Online. s.v. "Moore's law." Accessed November 7, 2019.

Falagas, Matthew E., Effie A. Zarkadoulia, and George Samonis. "Arab Science in the Golden Age (750–1258 C.E.) and Today." *The FASEB Journal* 20, no. 10 (2006): 1581–86. *https://doi.org/10.1096/fj.06-0803ufm.*

Gauthier, Jason. "Tabulation and Processing." History—US Census Bureau, December 17, 2019. *https://www.census.gov/history/www/innovations/technology/tabulation_and_processing.html.*

Gourville, John T. "Eager Sellers and Stony Buyers: Understanding the Psychology of New-Product Adoption." *Harvard Business Review,* June 1, 2016. *https://store.hbr.org/product/eager-sellers-and-stony-buyers-understanding-the-psychology-of-new-product-adoption.*

IER. "Electric Generating Costs: A Primer." Institute for Energy Research, August 22, 2012. *https://www.instituteforenergyresearch.org/renewable/electric-generating-costs-a-primer/.*

Markandya, Anil, and Paul Wilkinson. "Electricity Generation and Health." *The Lancet* 370, no. 9591 (2007): 979–90. *https://doi.org/10.1016/s0140-6736(07)61253-7.*

Myllyvirta, Lauri. "Quantifying the Economic Costs of Air Pollution from Fossil Fuels." Centre for Research on Energy and Clean Air, February 2020. *https://energyandcleanair.org/wp/wp-content/uploads/2020/02/Cost-of-fossil-fuels-briefing.pdf.*

Raphael, Kate. "Mongol Siege Warfare on the Banks of the Euphrates and the Question of Gunpowder (1260-1312)." *Journal of the Royal Asiatic Society,* Third Series, 19, no. 3 (2009): 355-70. *www.jstor.org/stable/27756073.*

Stromberg, Joseph. "Herman Hollerith's Tabulating Machine." *Smithsonian Magazine.* December 9, 2011. *https://www.smithsonianmag.com/smithsonian-institution/herman-holleriths-tabulating-machine-2504989/.*

Suster, Mark. "Your Product Needs to be 10x Better than the Competition to Win. Here's Why." Both Sides of the Table. March 12, 2011. *https://bothsidesofthetable.com/your-product-needs-to-be-10x-better-than-the-competition-to-win-here-s-why-6168bab60de7.*

Thiel, Peter and Blake Masters. *Zero to One: Notes on Startups, or How to Build the Future.* New York, NY: Random House, 2014. *https://books.google.com/books?id=M22fAwAAQBAJ.*

CHAPTER 5

American Chemical Society National Historic Chemical Landmarks. "Chlorofluorocarbons and Ozone Depletion." American Chemical Society, 2017. *https://www.acs.org/content/acs/en/education/whatischemistry/landmarks/cfcs-ozone.html.*

Bartlett, Allen. "Arithmetic, Population and Energy: Sustainability 101." Lecture, University of Colorado at Boulder, Boulder, CO, February 26, 2005. *https://www.albartlett.org/presentations/arithmetic_population_energy.html.*

Beaumont, Claudine. "Bill Gates' Dream: a Computer in Every Home." *Telegraph,* June 27, 2008. *https://www.telegraph.co.uk/technology/3357701/Bill-Gatess-dream-A-computer-in-every-home.html.*

Conde, Jorge, Vijay Pande, and Julie Yoo. "Biology Is Eating the World: A Manifesto." Andreessen Horowitz, October 28, 2019. *https://a16z.com/2019/10/28/biology-eating-world-a16z-manifesto/.*

Doyle, Arthur Conan. "A Scandal in Bohemia." In *The Adventures of Sherlock Holmes.* Fairfield, IA: 1st World Library—Literary Society, 2004. *https://books.google.com/books?id=GofxAKkdhDcC.*

Handwerk, Brian. "Whatever Happened to the Ozone Hole?" *National Geographic,* May 7, 2010. *https://www.nationalgeographic.com/news/2010/5/100505-science-environment-ozone-hole-25-years/.*

IEA. "Coal Information 2019." International Energy Agency, August 2019. *https://www.iea.org/reports/coal-information-2019.*

Jones, Sam. "Spain Logs Hundreds of Shipwrecks That Tell Story of Maritime Past." *The Guardian*, March 1, 2019. *https://www. theguardian.com/science/2019/mar/01/spain-logs-shipwrecks-maritime-past-weather-pirates.*

Molina, Mario, and Durwood Zaelke. "The Montreal Protocol: Triumph by Treaty." UN Environment, November 20, 2017. *https://www.unenvironment.org/news-and-stories/story/montreal-protocol-triumph-treaty.*

O'Dea, S. "Smartphone Users Worldwide from 2016 to 2021." Statista, February 28, 2020. *https://www.statista.com/statistics/330695/number-of-smartphone-users-worldwide/.*

Ritchie, Hannah, and Max Roser. "Meat and Dairy Production." Our World in Data, November 2019. *https://ourworldindata. org/meat-production#citation.*

"The Ozone Hole." British Antarctic Survey, April 2017. *https://www. bas.ac.uk/data/our-data/publication/the-ozone-layer/.*

TIME Staff. "The Greatest Survivor: Ernest Shackleton." TIME, September 12, 2003. *http://content.time.com/time/specials/packages/article/0,28804,1981290_1981354_1981610,00.html*

Wetterstrand, Kris A. "DNA Sequencing Costs: Data." National Human Genome Research Institute, October 30, 2019. *https:// www.genome.gov/about-genomics/fact-sheets/DNA-Sequencing-Costs-Data.*

CHAPTER 6

"A Quarter-Million Pounder and Fries." *The Economist*, August 10, 2013. *https://www.economist.com/science-and-technology/2013/08/10/a-quarter-million-pounder-and-fries.*

Datar, Isha, and Daan Luining. "Mark Post's Cultured Beef." New Harvest, November 3, 2015. https://www.new-harvest.org/mark_post_cultured_beef.

Fountain, Henry. "Building a $325,000 Burger." *The New York Times*, May 12, 2013. https://www.nytimes.com/2013/05/14/science/engineering-the-325000-in-vitro-burger.html.

Gray, Nathan. "Lab Grown Meat? Surely It's a Matter of Taste..." Food Navigator. William Reed Business Media Ltd., August 8, 2013. https://www.foodnavigator.com/Article/2013/08/09/Lab-grown-meat-Surely-it-s-a-matter-of-taste.

Jha, Alok. "First Lab-Grown Hamburger Gets Full Marks for 'Mouth Feel'." *The Guardian*, August 6, 2013. https://www.theguardian.com/science/2013/aug/05/world-first-synthetic-hamburger-mouth-feel.

Pitchbook, custom search of *Cellular Agriculture* and *Cultured Meat* in January 2020, Pitchbook. https://pitchbook.com/

University of Manchester. "Why Lab-Grown Meat Is a Good Thing." Phys.org, August 5, 2013. https://phys.org/news/2013-08-lab-grown-meat-good.html.

Viviano, Frank. "This Tiny Country Feeds the World." *National Geographic*, September 2017. https://www.nationalgeographic.com/magazine/2017/09/holland-agriculture-sustainable-farming/.

CHAPTER 7

Alvåsen, Karin, Ian Dohoo, Anki Roth, and Ulf Emanuelson. "Farm Characteristics and Management Routines Related to Cow Longevity: a Survey among Swedish Dairy Farmers." *Acta Veterinaria Scandinavica* 60, no. 38 (June 19, 2018). https://doi.org/10.1186/s13028-018-0390-8.

Blazek, Lukas. "FFAR Offers $6 Million for in-Ovo Sexing Solution." WATTAgNet. October 18, 2018. *https://www.wattagnet.com/articles/35884-ffar-offers-6-million-for-in-ovo-sexing-solution.*

Brulliard, Karin. "The Hidden Environmental Costs of Dog and Cat Food." *Washington Post,* August 4, 2017. *https://www.washingtonpost.com/news/animalia/wp/2017/08/04/the-hidden-environmental-costs-of-dog-and-cat-food/.*

Doganay, Mehmet, Gokhan Metan, and Emine Alp. "A Review of Cutaneous Anthrax and Its Outcome." *Journal of Infection and Public Health* 3, no. 3 (September 2010): 98–105. *https://doi.org/10.1016/j.jiph.2010.07.004.*

Food and Agriculture Organization of the United Nations. "FAOSTAT: Global Chicken Production." 2019.

Food and Agriculture Organization of the United Nations. "FAOSTAT: Global Egg Production." 2019.

Gallagher, Sean. "India: The Toxic Price of Leather." Pulitzer Center. Pulitzer Center on Crisis Reporting, May 8, 2014. *https://pulitzercenter.org/reporting/india-toxic-price-leather.*

"Global Gelatin Market Projected To Reach $2.79 Billion In 2018." Nutraceuticals World. Rodman Media, July 15, 2013. *https://www.nutraceuticalsworld.com/contents/view_breaking-news/2013-07-15/global-gelatin-market-projected-to-reach-279-billion-in-2018.*

"Introduction to Effective Altruism." Effective Altruism. June 22, 2016. *https://www.effectivealtruism.org/articles/introduction-to-effective-altruism/.*

Lamb, Catherine. "Perfect Day Launches Ice Cream Made from Cow-Free Milk, and We Tried It." The Spoon, July 11, 2019.

https://thespoon.tech/perfect-day-launches-ice-cream-made-from-cow-free-milk-and-we-tried-it/.

Levitt, Tom. "Dairy's 'Dirty Secret': It's Still Cheaper to Kill Male Calves than to Rear Them." *The Guardian*, March 26, 2018. https://www.theguardian.com/environment/2018/mar/26/dairy-dirty-secret-its-still-cheaper-to-kill-male-calves-than-to-rear-them.

Marti, Daniel, Rachel Johnson, and Kenneth Matthews. "Beef and Pork Byproducts: Enhancing the US Meat Industry's Bottom Line." United States Department of Agriculture Economic Research Service, September 1, 2011. https://www.ers.usda.gov/amber-waves/2011/september/beef-and-pork-byproducts/.

McKinnon, Mika. "This Book Is Bound in Lab-Grown Jellyfish Leather." *Smithsonian Magazine*. Smithsonian Institution, January 30, 2018. https://www.smithsonianmag.com/smart-news/book-bound-lab-grown-jellyfish-leather-180967870/.

Oliveira, Joaquim Miguel, and Rui Luís Reis. "Natural Polymers." In *Regenerative Strategies for the Treatment of Knee Joint Disabilities*, 21:100–103. Springer, 2016.

Rastogi, S K, C Kesavachandran, Farzana Mahdi, and Amit Pandey. "Occupational Cancers in Leather Tanning Industries: A Short Review." *Indian Journal of Occupational and Environmental Medicine* 11, no. 1 (2007): 3–5. https://doi.org/10.4103/0019-5278.32456.

Sclove, Richard, Madeleine L. Scammell, Breena Holland, Faranaz Alimohamed, J. S. Perry Hobson, T. Johnston, Danny R. Murphy, D H North, Ken Rapoza, Marcie A. Sclove, Tina Swift and Scott B. Waltz. "COMMUNITY-BASED RESEARCH IN THE UNITED STATES: An Introductory Reconnaissance, Including Twelve Organizational Case Studies and Comparison with the Dutch Science Shops and the Mainstream American Research System." (1998).

"Statistics: Dairy Cows." Compassion in World Farming, July 1, 2012. *https://www.ciwf.org.uk/media/5235182/Statistics-Dairy-cows.pdf.*

Windhorst, Hans-Wilhelm, Barbara Grabkowsky, and Anna Wilke. "Atlas of the Global Egg Industry." International Egg Commission, September 2013. *https://www.internationalegg.com/wp-content/uploads/2015/08/atlas_2013_web.pdf.*

CHAPTER 8

Cabello, Felipe C., Henry P. Godfrey, Alexandra Tomova, Larisa Ivanova, Humberto Dölz, Ana Millanao, and Alejandro H. Buschmann. "Antimicrobial Use in Aquaculture Re-Examined: Its Relevance to Antimicrobial Resistance and to Animal and Human Health." *Environmental Microbiology* 15, no. 7 (2013): 1917–42. *https://doi.org/10.1111/1462-2920.12134.*

Davies, R. W. D., S. J. Cripps, A. Nickson, and G. Porter. "Defining and Estimating Global Marine Fisheries Bycatch." *Marine Policy* 33, no. 4 (July 2009): 661–72. *https://doi.org/10.1016/j.marpol.2009.01.003.*

Donato, Daniel, J. Boone Kauffman, Daniel Murdiyarso, Sofyan Kurnianto, Melanie Stidham, and Markku Kanninen. "Mangroves among the most carbon-rich forests in the tropics." *Nature Geoscience* 4 (2011): 293-297. *https://doi.org/10.1038/ngeo1123.*

Done, Hansa Y., Arjun K. Venkatesan, and Rolf U. Halden. "Does the Recent Growth of Aquaculture Create Antibiotic Resistance Threats Different from Those Associated with Land Animal Production in Agriculture?" *The AAPS Journal* 17, no. 3 (2015): 513–24. *https://doi.org/10.1208/s12248-015-9722-z.*

FAO. "The State of World Fisheries and Aquaculture." Food and Agriculture Organization of the United Nations, 2016. *http://www.fao.org/3/a-i5555e.pdf.*

FAO. "The State of World Fisheries and Aquaculture." Food and Agriculture Organization of the United Nations, 2018. *http://www.fao.org/state-of-fisheries-aquaculture.*

Fisher, Emily. "Love Salmon? Listen Up." Ocean. Smithsonian Institution, December 2010. *https://ocean.si.edu/ocean-life/fish/love-salmon-listen.*

Keledjian, Amanda, Gib Brogan, Beth Lowell, Jon Warrenchuk, Ben Enticknap, Geoff Shester, Michael Hirshfield, and Dominique Cano-Stocco. "Wasted Catch: Unsolved Problems in US Fisheries." Oceana, March 2014. *https://oceana.org/sites/default/files/reports/Bycatch_Report_FINAL.pdf.*

Mancuso, Monique. "Effects of Fish Farming on Marine Environment." *Journal of Fisheries Science* 9, no. 3 (2015): 89–90. *https://www.fisheriessciences.com/fisheries-aqua/effects-of-fish-farming-on-marine-environment.php.*

Parker, Luara. "The Great Pacific Garbage Patch Isn't What You Think It Is." *National Geographic*, March 22, 2018. *https://www.nationalgeographic.com/news/2018/03/great-pacific-garbage-patch-plastics-environment/.*

Ramirez, Vanessa Bates. "Why the Future Is Arriving Faster Than You Think." Singularity Hub, August 22, 2018. *https://singularityhub.com/2018/08/22/why-the-future-is-arriving-faster-than-you-think/.*

Ritchie, Hannah, and Max Roser. "Meat and Dairy Production." Our World in Data, November 2019. *https://ourworldindata. org/meat-production#citation.*

"Seafood Handbook." SeafoodSource. Diversified Communications, 2020. *https://www.seafoodsource.com/seafood-handbook.*

Thomas, Nathan, Richard Lucas, Peter Bunting, Andrew Hardy, Ake Rosenqvist, and Marc Simard. "Distribution and Drivers of Global Mangrove Forest Change, 1996–2010." *PLOS ONE* 12, no. 6 (2017). *https://doi.org/10.1371/journal.pone.0179302.*

Watling, Les, and Elliott A Norse. "Disturbance of the Seabed by Mobile Fishing Gear: A Comparison to Forest Clearcutting." *Conservation Biology* 12, no. 6 (December 1998): 1180–97. *https:// doi.org/10.1046/j.1523-1739.1998.0120061180.x.*

World Economic Foundation, Ellen MacArthur Foundation, and McKinsey & Company. "The New Plastics Economy—Rethinking the Future of Plastics." Ellen MacArthur Foundation, 2016. *https://www.ellenmacarthurfoundation.org/publications.*

Worm, Boris, Edward B. Barbier, Nicola Beaumont, J. Emmett Duffy, Carl Folke, Benjamin S. Halpern, Jeremy B. C. Jackson, Heike K. Lotze, Fiorenza Micheli, Stephen R. Palumbi, Enric Sala, Kimberly A. Selkoe, John J. Stachowicz, and Reg Watson. "Impacts of Biodiversity Loss on Ocean Ecosystem Services." *Science* 314, no. 5800 (2006): 787–90. *https://doi.org/10.1126/ science.1132294.*

Young, Wes. "Tassal's Second Dead Zone in Macquarie Harbour." Environment Tasmania, 2019. *https://www.et.org.au/tassal_second_dead_zone.*

CHAPTER 10

Centre for Effective Altruism. "Introduction to Effective Altruism." *Effective Altruism*, June 22, 2016. *https://www.effectivealtruism. org/articles/introduction-to-effective-altruism/.*

Graham, Paul. "How to Get Startup Ideas." *Paul Graham*, November 2012. *http://www.paulgraham.com/startupideas.html.*

Hamming, Richard, 'You and Your Research' (Speech, Bell Communications Research Colloquium Seminar, 7 March 1986). *https://www.cs.virginia.edu/~robins/YouAndYourResearch.html*

Searchinger, Tim, Richard Waite, Craig Hanson, Janet Ranganathan, Patrice Dumas, and Emily Matthews. *Creating a Sustainable Food Future.* World Resources Institute, 2018. *https://www. wri.org/publication/creating-sustainable-food-future.*

CHAPTER 11

"Battery storage market to reach 240GW by 2030." Gas to Power Journal. February 6, 2015. *https://gastopowerjournal.com/ energy-storage/item/4564-battery-storage-market-to-reach-240-gw-by-2030.*

BloombergNEF. "Electric Vehicle Outlook 2019." Bloomberg. Accessed November 13, 2019. *https://bnef.turtl.co/story/evo2019/ page/1.*

Coolican, D'Arcy. "Product Zeitgeist Fit: A Cheat Code for Spotting and Building the Next Big Thing." Andreessen Horowitz. December 9, 2019. *https://a16z.com/2019/12/09/product-zeitgeist-fit/.*

Díaz, S., J. Settele, E. S. Brondízio E.S., H. T. Ngo, M. Guèze, J. Agard, A. Arneth, P. Balvanera, K. A. Brauman, S. H. M. Butchart, K. M. A. Chan, L. A. Garibaldi, K. Ichii, J. Liu, S. M. Subramanian, G. F. Midgley, P. Miloslavich, Z. Molnár, D.

Obura, A. Pfaff, S. Polasky, A. Purvis, J. Razzaque, B. Reyers, R. Roy Chowdhury, Y. J. Shin, I. J. Visseren-Hamakers, K. J. Willis, and C. N. Zayas, eds. *IPBES (2019): Summary for policymakers of the global assessment report on biodiversity and ecosystem services of the Intergovernmental Science-Policy Platform on Biodiversity and Ecosystem Services.* Born, Germany: IPBES secretariat, 2019. *https://ipbes.net/global-assessment.*

Gerber, P.J., H. Steinfeld, B. Henderson, A. Mottet, C. Opio, J. Dijkman, A. Falcucci, and G. Tempio. *Tackling climate change through livestock—A global assessment of emissions and mitigation opportunities.* Rome: Food and Agriculture Organization of the United Nations (FAO), 2013. *http://www.fao.org/3/i3437e/i3437e.pdf.*

"Graphic: The relentless rise of carbon dioxide." NASA Global Climate Change. NASA. Accessed 7 January 2020. *https://climate.nasa.gov/climate_resources/24/graphic-the-relentless-rise-of-carbon-dioxide/.*

Jones, Nicola. "How the World Passed a Carbon Threshold and Why It Matters." Yale Environment 360. Yale School of Forestry & Environmental Studies, January 26, 2017. *https://e360.yale.edu/features/how-the-world-passed-a-carbon-threshold-400ppm-and-why-it-matters.*

Ranganathan, Janet. "Animal-based Foods are More Resource-Intensive than Plant-Based Foods." World Resources Institute. April 2016. *https://www.wri.org/resources/charts-graphs/animal-based-foods-are-more-resource-intensive-plant-based-foods.*

Searchinger, Tim, Richard Waite, Craig Hanson, and Janet Ranganathan. *World Resources Report: Creating a Sustainable Food Future: A Menu of Solutions to Feed Nearly 10 Billion People by 2050.* Edited by Emily Matthews. World Resources Institute, 2019. *https://wrr-food.wri.org/sites/default/files/2019-07/WRR_Food_Full_Report_0.pdf.*

Solomon, Susan, Dahe Qin, Martin Manning, Melinda Marquis, Kristen Ayert, Melinda M.B. Tignor, Henry LeRoy Miller, Jr., and Zhenlin Chen, eds. *Climate Change 2007: Working Group I: The Physical Science Basis* New York, NY: Cambridge University Press, 2007. *https://archive.ipcc.ch/publications_and_data/ar4/wg1/en/contents.html.*

CHAPTER 12

Amazon. (1997). *1997 Letter to Shareholders.* Retrieved from *http://www.sec.gov.*

Aristotle, *Metaphysics,* 1013a14-15.

Johnson, Steven. *Where Good Ideas Come From: The Natural History of Innovation.* London: Penguin, 2010, p 151-153. *https://books.google.com/books?id=eOfUiUNby3cC.*

Plato, *Republic,* 514b-515e.

CHAPTER 13

Srinivasan, Balaji S. "Market Research, Wireframing, and Design." Startup Engineering Lecture, Stanford University, Stanford, CA, 2013. *https://spark-public.s3.amazonaws.com/startup/lecture_slides/lecture5-market-wireframing-design.pdf*

CHAPTER 14

Fuld, Hillel. "If You Only Have a Startup Idea, Sorry—You Have Nothing." *Inc* Magazine, March 14, 2018. *https://www.inc.com/hillel-fuld/if-you-only-have-a-startup-idea-sorry-you-have-nothing.html.*

Paine, Chris, dir. *Who Killed the Electric Car?* 2006; Los Angeles, CA: Sony Pictures Classics, 2006. DVD.

Stebbings, Harry, host. *Twenty Minute VC.* "Vinod Khosla on What Venture Assistance Really Means, Why Many VCs Are Not Qualified To Advise Founders & Why Startups Can Innovate So Much Faster Than Incumbents." Aired February 24, 2020. *https://thetwentyminutevc.com/vinodkhosla/.*

Steimle, Josh. "Why Great Ideas Are Worthless." *Forbes*, September 1, 2013. *https://www.forbes.com/sites/joshsteimle/2013/09/01/why-great-ideas-are-worthless/#4ba1f4178b6d.*

Suster, Mark. "It's Morning in Venture Capital." Both Sides of the Table. May 24, 2012. *https://bothsidesofthetable.com/it-s-morning-in-venture-capital-ac539cd5f0e8.*

CHAPTER 15

Allen, Mary. "5 Cell-Based Meat Startups Form Coalition to Educate and Advocate." Good Food Institute. August 29, 2019. *https://www.gfi.org/amps-innovation.*

Burwood-Taylor, Louisa. "Future Food: Catching up with GFI's Bruce Friedrich to talk alt protein winners, losers, innovation whitespace." AgFunder News. December 12, 2019. *https://agfundernews.com/future-food-catching-up-with-gfis-bruce-friedrich.html.*

Moore, Caoimhe. "Animal nutrition and aquafeed leader Nutreco partners with cell-based protein companies." Nutreco. January 16, 2020. *https://www.nutreco.com/en/News/Press-releases/animal-nutrition-and-aquafeed-leader-nutreco-partners-with-cell-based-protein/1621177.*

CHAPTER 16

Currier, James. "The Ladder of Proof: Uncovering How VC's See Your Startup." NfX. May 16, 2018. *https://www.nfx.com/post/ladder-of-proof/*.

Eilperin, Juliet. "Why the Clean Tech Boom Went Bust." *Wired*. January 20, 2012. *https://www.wired.com/2012/01/ff_solyndra*.

FAO. 2016. *Aquaculture Production (Metric Tons)*. Distributed by World Bank Data Catalog. *http://data.worldbank.org/data-catalog/world-development-indicators*.

GEM Commodities, World Bank Group. *Fishmeal Monthly Price— US Dollars per Metric Ton, 1960-2020*. Distributed by Index Mundi. *https://www.indexmundi.com/commodities/?commodity=fish-meal*.

Guy, Allison. "Overfishing and El Niño Push the World's Biggest Single-Species Fishery to a Critical Point." Oceana. February 2, 2016. *https://oceana.org/blog/overfishing-and-el-ni%C3%B1o-push-world%E2%80%99s-biggest-single-species-fishery-critical-point*.

"Prices flat in polysilicon market." *Washington Post*. July 23, 2013. *https://www.washingtonpost.com/business/economy/prices-flat-in-polysilicon-market/2013/07/23/914479d0-f3e4-11e2-9434-60440856fadf_graphic.html*.

Sandor, Debra, Sadie Fulton, Jill Engel-Cox, Corey Peck, and Steve Peterson. "System Dynamics of Polysilicon for Solar Photovoltaics: A Framework for Investigating the Energy Security of Renewable Energy Supply Chains." *Sustainability* 10, no. 1 (2018): 160. *https://doi.org/10.3390/su10010160*.

CHAPTER 17

"About AWS." Amazon Web Services. Accessed October 8, 2019. *https://aws.amazon.com/about-aws/.*

Malone, Kenny and Julia Simon, hosts. "Antitrust 1: Standard Oil." *Planet Money* (podcast). February 15, 2019. Accessed October 15, 2019. *https://www.npr.org/sections/money/2019/02/15/695131832/antitrust-1-standard-oil.*

Priest, George L. "Rethinking the Economic Basis of the Standard Oil Refining Monopoly: Dominance Against Competing Cartels." *Yale Law & Economics Research Paper,* no. 445 (2012): 499-558. *http://dx.doi.org/10.2139/ssrn.1984242.*

Wolfe, Gary. "The (Second Phase of the) Revolution Has Begun." *Wired.* October 1, 1994. *https://www.wired.com/1994/10/mosaic/.*

CHAPTER 18

Buhr, Sarah. "The Impossible Foods burger heads West." *Techcrunch,* October 13, 2016. *https://techcrunch.com/2016/10/12/the-impossible-foods-burger-heads-west/.*

Goldfield, Hannah. "Can White Castle Sell the Impossible—the Meatless Burger That Bleeds?" *New Yorker,* April 14, 2018. *https://www.newyorker.com/culture/annals-of-gastronomy/silicon-valleys-meatless-burger-that-bleedsat-white-castle.*

Holpuch, Amanda. "Impossible burger: New York's latest food craze is a veggie burger that bleeds." *The Guardian,* July 27, 2016. *https://www.theguardian.com/us-news/2016/jul/27/impossible-burger-new-york-veggie-momofuku-david-chang.*

"Impossible Foods." Crunchbase. Accessed January 10, 2020. *https://www.crunchbase.com/organization/impossible-foods.*

Musk, Elon. "The Secret Tesla Motors Master Plan (just between you and me)." Tesla. August 2, 2006. *https://www.tesla.com/blog/secret-tesla-motors-master-plan-just-between-you-and-me.*

Shieber, Jonathan. "Burger King will roll out the Impossible Burger nationwide by the end of the year." *Techcrunch,* April 30, 2019. *https://techcrunch.com/2019/04/29/burger-king-will-roll-out-the-impossible-burger-nationwide-by-the-end-of-the-year/.*

Sinek, Simon. "How Great Leaders Inspire Action." TED video, 17:58. September 2009. *https://www.ted.com/talks/simon_sinek_how_great_leaders_inspire_action.*

CHAPTER 19

Encyclopedia Britannica Online, s.v. "Charles E. Duryea and J. Frank Duryea," last modified August 08, 2019. *https://www.britannica.com/biography/Charles-E-Duryea-and-J-Frank-Duryea.*

Ford, Henry. *My Life and Work.* Fairfield, IA: 1st World Publishing, 2004. *https://books.google.com.sg/books?id=XbWEsxy-2PwC.*

France-Presse, Agence. "Ford Launched the Modern Assembly Line a Century Ago and Changed Society." *Industryweek,* October 7, 2013. *https://www.industryweek.com/innovation/process-improvement/article/21961364/ford-launched-the-modern-assembly-line-a-century-ago-and-changed-society.*

Klier, Thomas H. and James M. Rubenstein. *Who Really Made Your Car?: Restructuring and Geographic Change in the Auto Industry.* Kalamazoo, MI: W.E. Upjohn Institute for Employment Research, 2008. *https://books.google.com.sg/books?id=ERZMbFjLM2UC.*

Ohno, Taiichi. *Toyota Production System: Beyond Large-Scale Production.* New York, NY: Productivity Press, 1988. *https://books.google.com.sg/books?id=7_-67SshOy8C.*

Root, Al. "Tesla Is Now the Second-Most-Valuable Car Maker in the World. Look Out, Toyota." *Barron's*, January 22, 2020. *https://www.barrons.com/articles/tesla-stock-second-most-valuable-car-maker-toyota-volkswagen-electric-vehicle-auto-51579723791.*

"Tesla Motors 2016 Annual Shareholder Meeting." Youtube video, 04:31:57. Posted by "Darren Bryant," May 31, 2016. *https://www.youtube.com/watch?v=AKfiKvbqbQw.*

"TNGA explained: engineering for the future." Toyota. April 15, 2015. *https://blog.toyota.co.uk/tnga-explained-engineering-for-the-future.*

"Toyota New Global Architecture." Toyota. September 15, 2015. *https://newsroom.toyota.eu/toyota-new-global-architecture/*

CHAPTER 20

US National Archives & Records Administration. "Transcript of President John F. Kennedy's Inaugural Address (1961)." Our Documents.gov. Accessed November 14, 2019. *https://www.ourdocuments.gov/doc.php?doc=91&page=transcript.*

ACKNOWLEDGMENTS

As with any major endeavor, this book would not have been possible without the contributions of many people, all of whom have my deepest gratitude.

First and foremost, I'd like to thank my family. Dad, Mom, and Prayag, thank you for your love and support. You have always encouraged me to reach for the stars while reminding me to remain grounded here on Earth. Thanks for always being there to celebrate in good times and to provide support in hard times.

Thank you to all my interviewees for making time in your busy schedules to talk to me about your passions, your work, and your visions of a better future for us all.

To my friends, Nick, Dawn, Anthony, and Max: the many hours of in-depth conversations that we shared about start-ups, solving important problems, and creating structures that prioritize long-term thinking contributed substantially to the ideas in this book. Thank you for sharing your ideas, pushing me to refine mine, and encouraging me to put these ideas to paper.

Finally, thank you to New Degree Press, especially Eric Koester, Alaisha Verdeflor, and Emily Price, for helping me make this book a reality.

And to anyone else I wasn't able to recognize, thank you for your incredible support and everything you have done that made this book possible.

WITH SPECIAL THANKS TO:

———

Adam Rukin

Amy Nelson

Anastasia Soule

Andrea Wise

Andrew MacLatchie

Annie Spence

Anoop Sahgal

Ashwin Kulkarni

Braden O'Brien

Callie Brauel

Claire Pribula

Connie Bowen

Connor Moore

Daniel Bolus

David Yocom

Dawn Musil

Devin Hanaway

Donald Longcrier

Ella Simmons

Eric Hancock

Eric Koester

Ethan Summers

Gayatri Rathod

Girija Waghray

Gregory Copenhaver

Hannah Merten

Hetali Lodaya

Jack Paley

James Dolgin

Jeannie Blackwood

Jeff Biestek

John Battle

John Paul Zalaquett

Julia Wang

Kasim Ahmad

Ken Berlack

Kelli Booth
Ken Malone
Larry Han
Lawrence Taylor
Lindsay Ryan
Louis Cantolupo
Maëlle Pasquiou
Manmohan &
Susheela Barma
Mark Langley
Mary Larkin
Max Polec
Maxen Haveles
Megan Arrington
Megan Vollstedt
Michael Pallotta
Michael Iyanro
Michael Tangrea
Mirte Gosker
Nathaniel Crosser
Nick Zajciw
Paul Shapiro
Prayag Pershad

Rahul Narain
Rathi Sahgal
Sam Petrie
Saseen Najjar
Scott Brown
Sergei Revzin
Shanker & Rashmi Pershad
Shanta Sahgal
Shiv Sehgal
Shruti Sharma
Shubham Upadhyay
Simran Khadka
Spencer Keith
Suzan Shahrestani
Thomas Doochin
Tony Hunter
Trimbakeshwar &
Vaishali Pershad
Vibhore & Suneeta Prasad
Yasemin Cole
Zachary Weston
Zan Lowe-Skillern

Made in the USA
Middletown, DE
04 August 2020